⟡ RACE AND CLASS POLITICS
IN NEW YORK CITY
BEFORE THE CIVIL WAR ⟡

Northeastern University 1898–1998

RACE AND CLASS POLITICS IN NEW YORK CITY BEFORE THE CIVIL WAR

Anthony Gronowicz

NORTHEASTERN UNIVERSITY PRESS
BOSTON

Northeastern University Press

Library of Congress Cataloging-in-Publication Data

Gronowicz, Anthony.
    Race and class politics in New York City before the Civil War /
Anthony Gronowicz.
        p. cm.
    Includes bibliographical references and index.
    ISBN 1–55553–327–2 (cloth : alk. paper). — ISBN 1–55553–326–4
(pbk. : alk. paper)
        1. Democratic Party (New York, N.Y.)—History—19th century.
2. New York (N.Y.)—Politics and government—To 1898.   3. New
York (N.Y.)—Race relations.   4. Working class—New York (State)—
New York—Political activity—History—19th century.   I. Title.
JK2319.N56G85   1998
324.2736′09′034—dc21   97–10292

Designed by Lisa Diercks

Composed in Bulmer by Coghill Composition in Richmond, Virginia.
Printed and bound by Thomson-Shore, Inc., in Dexter, Michigan. The
paper is Glatfelter Supple Opaque Recycled, an acid-free stock.

MANUFACTURED IN THE UNITED STATES OF AMERICA
02   01   00   99   98   5   4   3   2   1

to my mother

and

Bill Pencak

⊰ CONTENTS ⊱

⊶ PREFACE ⊷

There is an historical circumstance, known to few, that connects the children of the Puritans with these Africans of Virginia, in a very singular way. They are our brethren, as being lineal descendants from the Mayflower, the fated womb of which, in her first voyage, sent forth a brood of Pilgrims upon Plymouth Rock, and, in a subsequent one, spawned slaves upon the Southern soil,—a monstrous birth, but with which we have an instinctive sense of kindred, and so are stirred by the irresistible impulse to attempt their rescue, even at the cost of blood and ruin. The character of our sacred ship, I fear, may suffer a little by this revelation; but we must let her white progeny offset her dark one,—and two such portents never sprang from an identical source before.

Nathaniel Hawthorne, "Chiefly About War-Matters," *Atlantic Monthly,* July 1862

THIS VOLUME GREW OUT OF A LOCAL STUDY AND A POLITICAL PARADOX. THE LOCAL STUDY COMPARED THE SOCIAL COMPOSITION and organizational structure of New York City's Democratic Party in 1844 and 1884. It yielded unexpected results. Contrary to what is commonly believed, the party was both more internally democratic in terms of class and more Irish in social composition in the earlier year. It is beyond the scope of the present work to account for these differences. I merely note that they compelled me to ponder their historical implications.[1]

The paradox is central to understanding nineteenth-century United States political history.[2] A victorious independence struggle, stirred by the declaration that "all men are created equal," led in 1861 to a ferocious civil war over slavery. By then, Americans in bondage outnumbered the entire population of the thirteen colonies at independence. In New York City, the cultural and financial capital, this civil war flamed the nation's worst riots ever, with atrocities against African Americans committed by workers who identified with the Democratic Party.

The two most recent full-length studies of the era's labor politics in

New York City, by Amy Bridges and Sean Wilentz, ignore this political paradox. They pay no attention to the critical role that the Jefferson-Jackson Democratic Party played in spreading racism among workers, and they do not acknowledge the important role workers played within the party organization.[3]

Bridges portrayed the 1840s as "more . . . a decade of political reform movements than . . . a decade of labor politics," while pinpointing 1850 as the year when New York City Democrats made "special overtures to labor in response to the upsurge in union formation. . . ." She maintained that the political wards were "rebuilt" during the 1850s to serve "as a politically meaningful place." In her last essay on New York City's antebellum politics, Bridges concludes that the Democratic Party did not "democratize its own organization."[4]

To the contrary, I found that by 1844, when Democratic-Republicans called themselves just plain Democrats, the city's political wards stood at the core of a mature party infrastructure that reflected integration of European-American male labor into the party's organizational ranks. It was upon this intact and sophisticated complex of wards that the Democrats built their dominant party machine of the 1850s, not only outside of and in response to the unskilled "famine" Irish and the skilled "forty-eighter" German, but also from within, upon an older core of Anglo-Dutch labor support. Unlike during the 1820s and 1830s, there was no "workingmen's" party in the 1840s, because the avowedly racist Democrats now played that role.

In *Chants Democratic,* Sean Wilentz does not treat the Democratic Party as New York City's labor party, even though Carl Degler had shown for the 1850s that the Democrats commanded the working class.[5] After taking to task the Progressive historical school for "looking at employers and workers primarily through the distorting lens of party politics," Wilentz offered as evidence "Counter-Progressives like [Richard] Hofstadter and [Lee] Benson demolish[ing] . . . Progressive orthodoxy by taking another look . . . at the social composition of the Democrats."[6] Yet nowhere in Benson or Hofstadter, or Wilentz for that matter, is there any systematic effort to examine actual Democratic Party social or structural composition. Rather, Wilentz colorfully assembled an array of disparate political, social, and religious groupings and made these fringe elements, such as the Washington Temperance Benevolent Society and the Skidmorites, stand in for mainstream labor politics.[7] Actually, Democratic

Party rallies were far better attended by the working class than either indoor or outdoor church services.[8]

Unraveling the paradox of slavery and democracy means analyzing the Democratic Party's role, because the party supplied the ideology—democratic republicanism—that rationalized inequality. Democratic republicanism flowered as Jacksonian Democracy and stemmed from Jeffersonian republicanism, whose ideological roots extended back to ancient Greece.

The subject here, then, is the story of how the antebellum Democratic Party employed the racist ideology of democratic republicanism to shape the political values of a majority of New York City's working class. To tell this story, I have focused on the local level. Here social relationships can be traced within the context of the forces on a national scale that determined the city's course of development. I chose New York City as my research subject because Democrats had been dominant there since the turn of the nineteenth century, and the city attracted the political insights of American literary luminaries like Washington Irving, James Fenimore Cooper, Edgar A. Poe, and Herman Melville. Their observations are included in this account. Melville, for instance, grew darkly skeptical about the potential that mass political participation and the industrial organization of society possessed to enhance the individual's virtue or morality in general.

I begin with the colonial period, in Chapter 1, because the depth of racism expressed in the antebellum period can be better understood by tracing its roots from the colonial experience. I illuminate the critical economic role slavery played in New York, the damage it inflicted on social relationships, and the significance it possessed for the emergence of the European-American democratic republican ideal that culminated in the struggle for national independence. Chapter 2 analyzes the relationship between European artisans and the African-American community, as well as the artisan shift in political party from the Hamiltonian Federalists to the Jeffersonian Republicans. The part that Irish republicans played in the democratization of the Republican Party is described. Chapter 3 considers the impact of Democratic-Republican ideology on a segmented labor force and evaluates the role that the Workingmen's movement played in shaping the resulting beliefs. Chapter 4 concentrates on the Loco Focos, an important Democratic Party movement whose radical views on banks proved less lasting than an aggressive racism that reinforced the party's commitment to the expansion of slavery. Meanwhile, the new industry gave rise to a vigorous middle class whose politics found an uneasy home in the Whig Party. Chapter 5 deals with the rise of the market culture and the mystifying impact it had on the values of men already compromised by acceptance of slavery. The crucial role that African-American New Yorkers played in shaping American cultural identity is assayed. Chapter 6 offers a detailed quantitative portrait of the New York City Democratic Party in 1844, with its significant Irish and German working-class component, and not a single female or African-American member. The party's vital ideological and organizational ties to the South are illuminated. Chapter 7 introduces "the new Republican-ism" of the Republican Party, which redefined republicanism, excluding slavery from its social vision and replacing it with a capitalist "free labor" ideology. Finally, Chapter 8 is concerned with the political defeat of dem-ocratic republicanism in New York City through the agency of civil war and the accompanying draft riots. The Civil War was a war over slavery, but also against the slaves, who were seen as merely property in the eyes of the law.

Private property was essential to the kind of democracy practiced be-fore the Civil War.[9] Because the United States Constitution was inter-preted to define slaves as property, Democrats construed an attack on slavery as an attack on democracy. Slave ownership was an indispensable right to Founding Fathers like George Washington, James Madison, and Thomas Jefferson, whose livelihoods depended on slavery. Jefferson, in particular, regarded as the father of the Democratic Party, is also the patron saint of American civil libertarians. The many Americans who admire him rarely make the association that he never freed his two hun-dred slaves, even in his last will and testament.

Jefferson's toleration of slavery stemmed from assumptions Englishmen made about political society, assumptions drawn from an agrarian-based republican tradition that extended to the English civil war of the seven-teenth century, to Renaissance Florence, and "to the glory that was Greece / And the grandeur that was Rome," of Poe's historical vision. This democracy, nourished by antebellum Democrats, was rooted in a mythical golden age of husbandry when men of middling means tilled their own soil in practical pursuit of their dreams. They formed a small but vital part of a larger social formation that required slavery and the subjugation of women to fulfill a pastoral ideal that has played an impor-tant role in shaping American social identity.[10]

The term *republican* had once possessed revolutionary potential in a land-poor seventeenth-century England. During the rule of Oliver Crom-well, English political philosopher James Harrington had provided the theory to link land distribution with social stabilization. He posited that ". . . if the whole people be landlords, or hold the lands so divided among them that no one man, or number of men, within the compass of the few or aristocracy, overbalance them, the empire (without the interposition of force) is a commonwealth."[11]

A land-rich, labor-poor United States was premised on Harrington's small-producer theory. The wars against Britain and against Mexico all resulted in more land falling into American hands. This in turn strength-ened the institution of slavery, but on an increasingly regional basis, be-cause slavery was gradually abandoned in the North for economic and demographic reasons.

The political vehicle for landed expansion became the Jeffersonian Re-publican Party, modeled after the English "country" party. During the War of 1812, sponsored by land-seeking interests in the South and West, these Republican empire builders unintentionally promoted northeastern banking and industry through an embargo of foreign manufactured goods. Industrialization provided champions of free labor with a powerful new argument to employ against slavery.[12] Instead of being coerced under slavery, men could be controlled through a wage that left to them the choice of which needs to satisfy. Consumer choice substituted for owner-ship of the means of production.

The new consumer culture was qualitatively different from the long sacrificial producer tradition. In that tradition, the classical age's accep-tance of the necessity of slavery had blended with the medieval concep-tion of serf status as a manifestation of God's will. The consumer culture encouraged salvation through material consumption.

In the United States, industrialists found a special voice in the New England branch of the Whig Party during the 1830s. Whigs sponsored national banking laws that gave the largest capitalists and financiers the competitive advantage in the marketplace. When Democratic-Republican President Andrew Jackson sought to "democratize" federal funds by ve-toing the recharter of the National Bank and dispersing its funds to state banks, his executive action was castigated as monarchical by his old Fed-eralist and National Republican opposition in Congress. They assumed the name Whigs to distinguish themselves from the Democratic-Republi-cans. The term was a historical allusion to their namesakes in the eigh-teenth-century British Parliament, who had successfully challenged the right of the king of England's supporters to tax the people without Parliament's consent.

Federalists and Republicans, Whigs and Democratic-Republicans, Republicans and Democrats all embraced John Locke's notion that the purpose of government was to protect private property.[13] Their politically adversarial relationship would intensify by the mid-nineteenth century, when railroads replaced textiles as the most important Northern industry.

Textiles had dominated American industry from the beginning of the Republic. Southern slaves grew cotton while Northern wage labor transformed it into cloth. The two labor systems were complementary until antagonism surfaced in the 1820s, as railroads were introduced in the North and free-soil farming to the West. Plantation owners resisted the demands that railroad financiers and free-soilers placed on the political system to do their bidding. Ultimately, those demands forced the Southern states to withdraw from the union, thereby precipitating civil war.

Southern planter and Northern railroad magnate shared only a belief in the Lockean values that equated the pursuit of property with happiness. Thomas Jefferson had enshrined this principle in his Declaration of Independence when he altered Locke's "lives, liberties, and estates" to "life, liberty, and the pursuit of happiness." The marriage of liberty to property spurred industrial growth in the North, as well as Southern slave expansion, a republican hybrid that Charles Dickens aptly termed "Southern Republicanism" or "Republican Slavery."[14] Nature supplied a bounty of resources which, when combined with labor and capital, provided the necessary ingredients for capitalist production.

The American national state smoothed the way for this economic journey, as three party systems evolved in just three generations to reflect the northeastern states' paradigmatic shift from garden to machine.[15] The stage had been set for a fratricidal conflict between North and South led by parties that held different visions of an American future,[16] while sharing a belief in the redemptive power of violence.[17]

When he dueled with Federalist Alexander Hamilton, Republican Aaron Burr drew first American blood in this contest between agrarian and industrialist. Thirty years later, Federalists became Whigs. They sponsored manufactories as an integral part of an "American system" that competed for national identity with slave-based agriculture. The latter's sponsorship of wars against Native Americans and Mexicans became essential to replenish Southern territory.

This second party system was inherently unstable because it simultaneously promoted the mutually exclusive labor systems of slave and wage in one country. It was replaced in 1854 by a third party system of Democrats and Republicans. The latter reformulated the concept of republicanism with an expanded notion of the federal government's power to exclude slaves from new states. This third party system is responsible for the most popularly confusing aspect of American political history, namely that Jefferson's Republican Party mutated into today's Democrats, while their political counterparts, the Hamiltonian Federalists, became the modern Republican Party.

The term *republican* was central to the self-conception of both parties, but each held a different meaning of the concept. These ultimately opposing meanings are essential to understanding American history. The new Republican Party was united against the expansion of slavery,[18] while the Democrats were most united when opposing any rights for African Americans.

To the common man swept up in the social maelstrom of an expanding industrializing America,[19] and traumatized by psychosocial displacement provoked by wide swings in business cycles, the compulsion to associate freedom with property proved irresistible.[20] While many nineteenth-century Americans succumbed to the new mass consumer culture that mystified and glorified property, America's literary giants—Irving, Cooper, Poe, Thoreau, Hawthorne, and Melville—protested this trend through their writings.[21] Its painters, Thomas Cole, for example, created landscapes that foretold the same dire consequences of materialism that had befallen those empires that historically possessed, then rejected, their republican roots.

The deep social divisions fostered by radical changes in political economy were reflected in a labor segmentation that in New York City first discriminated against native peoples forced from the Dutch New Amsterdam colony in the early seventeenth century. The Dutch then engaged the English interloper, while both simultaneously profited from African labor.

The toleration of slavery gravely weakened the American labor movement. It cheapened the value of labor, undermined a worker's self-esteem, and led most whites to hold a low opinion of most blacks. Freed European and chained African reflected a splintered labor force whose condition helps to explain why the United States produced no mass-based labor party. The United States comprised an uprooted people tied to the currents of world trade and acculturated through political parties that served the economy and actively promoted racism.

In New York City, the closest organizational model to a labor party was the globally unique Democrats. In the decade of the 1840s, they actively enrolled European-American workingmen as officials of the party in proportionally greater numbers than in any subsequent period of U.S. history. This political development lent substance to one contemporary's boast that American democracy had "done more in fifty years, to elevate the moral and political condition of man, than has been achieved by any other civil institutions since the Christian era. [It was] perhaps the greatest achievement of modern times."[22] Another observer, a character drawn by Dickens, yet no less genuine in his observations, described the American continent as "the palladium of rational Liberty at home . . . and the dread of foreign oppression abroad . . . the Envy of the world . . . and the leaders of Human Civilization."[23]

By the 1840s, advances in industrial production were being legislatively fostered throughout the North. A significant shift in the industrial center of gravity had taken place. A Northern textile industry dependent on Southern cotton was joined to a network of railroads, built mainly by recent immigrants. The railroad provided the key that opened the prairies.[24] It promoted a new kind of farmer, one who used machines rather than slaves to till the soil and harvest the crop. The West aided the North in confronting the issue of slavery in the South. But for too long, New York City had profited from the trade in slaves and the commodities they produced. Any amelioration in the condition of African Americans met strong resistance, and this resistance culminated in the 1863 draft riots.

Artisans played a reactionary political role in the context of a New York City undergoing massive immigration. The fragmented nature of American labor, caused by its acquiescence to slavery and consequent racism, does not lend itself to epic treatment;[25] the popular heroes generated are outlaws like Billy the Kid, a New York City native. The labor movement was brutally racist and fought, more often than not, to uphold slavery.[26]

Political movements that arose in the colonial and revolutionary eras did not pose serious challenges to the authorities. On the contrary, political identification often cut across class lines to concern itself with how much power ought to be relinquished to a national state whose service to international trade was in keeping with the objectives of the Founding Fathers.[27] Class antagonisms expressed after the ratification of the Constitution were absorbed into the binary party system, with the assistance of short-lived third parties like the Workingmen's and Liberty Parties. These third parties, which reflected the strains caused by capitalism's need for wage labor in the second and third party systems, acted as catalytic agents to dominant-party reformation. As on the theatrical stage, where protagonist and antagonist alternate, each change of major party occurred whenever a third party emerged strongly enough to act as a crucial player that catalyzed the system and drove the historical process forward. (See Appendix 1 for a schematic of party evolution.) These major changes in political parties were reflected in changes over time in the meaning of *democrat* and *republican*.

In this study, *Democratic* and *Republican,* with initial capitals, refer to the party organizations; lowercase designates the ideology. Since the term *republican* was adopted in different eras by both dominant parties, it is essential to define what each manifestation meant to potential voters.

The antagonistic Federalists believed the Republic ought to foster the power of the national state through modernization, which became associated with factory labor that undermined the economic and social independence of yeomen and artisans. Mercantilists, capitalists, and financiers regarded national power as a positive good, and soon Federalists styled themselves National Republicans, then Whigs, and finally Republicans in 1854. They pioneered in the acceptance of wage labor over slave labor.

The Jeffersonian Republican Party nostalgically harked back to the traditional values of small-producer farmers and artisans who allegedly constituted the repository of civic virtue necessary to the maintenance of an agrarian republic, and who demanded slavery of African Americans. Since the Jeffersonian Republicans claimed to represent the majority, they called themselves Democratic-Republicans.

I employ the term *democratic republican* throughout, as it was implicitly used in antebellum America, to stand for this ideology of the small-producer citizenry who sanctioned slavery. In contrast, those who favored wage or free labor during the 1850s looked to the Republican Party of Lincoln as the guarantor of the kind of industrial progress that had no need for slaves. It was a minority view that only captured the support of the majority through the agency of civil war.

In this study, the changes are traced by examining the interaction between local political rhetoric and party morphology, defined as the social composition and infrastructure of the political party viewed in the context of development of the social formation that is the city of New York.[28] I focus on the Democratic Party, for it was the party that set the city's political agenda, especially on issues of race.

Although we lack reliable census data on occupations and wages,[29] we do have a scrupulous listing of party personnel in contemporary newspapers. When this information is matched with occupational data derived from city directories and other primary sources, we can construct a portrait of the party and compare it with the larger society. This is done in Chapter 6. The results demonstrate that before the Civil War, laboring men did not develop a political identity divorced from control of the dominant classes. The majority of politically active workers were absorbed into Democratic Party ranks in such numbers by 1844 that independent political action became an impractical pursuit. Their political consciousness was perverted by the racism of a party possessing an organizational structure that was occupationally, but not racially or sexually, democratic.

It is precisely because this ideology of democratic republicanism rested on the acceptance of slave labor that it posed a threat to the capitalist insurgency. This ideology contributed to the ferocity of the 1863 draft riots, which revealed deep and fatal developmental divisions within the working class, for which the bloodletting was a cathartic outlet.[30] As a consequence, no heroic figures emerged from among workers during the antebellum period.

Earlier this century, progressive scholars Charles Beard, Carl Becker, and Vernon Parrington sought to synthesize politics, economics, and culture. They ignored slavery and the important role that African Americans played in shaping political discourse and an American national identity.[31] My study is meant to extend the scope of their quest by integrating this racial dimension into an understanding of our political culture.

❧ ACKNOWLEDGMENTS ❧

I would like to thank Michael Bernstein, Alan Brinkley, Eric Foner, Robert L. Harris, Jr., James Oakes, Bill Pencak, William Shade, Richard Stott, Michael Wallace, and Harry Watson for their insightful readings of the manuscript; and Walter Licht for massaging the data in Chapter 6.

Thanks also to the staffs of the New York Historical Society, the American Irish Historical Society, the Schomburg Collection, the Columbia University Rare Book Division, the Municipal Archives, the New York Public Library, the Library of Congress, and the New York Society Library—most especially librarian Mark Piel, whose congenial stewardship of that venerable repository made my research and writing life easier.

I also appreciate the readings of my colleagues at the Penn State Hazleton campus—Jim Concannon, Bill Ellis, Monica Gregory, Mary Murray, and the late Vince Gutendorf who together with his mother provided the most delightful dinners, at which we discussed each other's work.

To those members of the Penn State History Department who awarded me the Kent Foster Teaching and Research Award, which provided me with a semester's leave to expand and revise the manuscript, I am very grateful.

RACE AND CLASS POLITICS
IN NEW YORK CITY
BEFORE THE CIVIL WAR

❦ 1 ❧

DEMOCRATIC
REPUBLICAN ROOTS

From the First Settlers to the First Party System,
1626–1794

When virtue is gone, liberty soon follows.
New-York Journal and Patriotic Register, May 18, 1791

The captain inquiring what were the pretensions of these men to be elected; he was told that they all had stock in the funds, and lived in brick buildings; and some of them entertained fifty people at a time, and ate and drank abundantly . . . living an easy life, and pampering their appetites.
Hugh Henry Brackenbridge, *Modern Chivalry* (1792)

. . . America.—where more than in any other region upon the face of the globe to be poor is to be despised.
Edgar A. Poe to Charles Anthon, October ?, 1844

———

NEW YORK CITY WAS FOUNDED "BY TRADE AND FOR TRADE, AND FOR NOTHING ELSE," WROTE HENRY CABOT LODGE.[1] THE PROFITS skimmed from the natural port at the mouth of the deep and wide Hudson River made this settlement an important colony of the Dutch West India Company. The first building erected in 1626 was the company's headquarters, which also served as countinghouse. It was constructed of stone, whereas the other buildings on the island were made of wood. Animal skins and lumber were the stock-in-trade, and Christian worship was practiced. The Bible was used to justify slave labor and to reinforce the social hierarchy and sense of place in the great chain of being that began with worms and ended with God.[2]

At the bottom of the human chain were the slaves, whose economic importance is depicted in the earliest existing print of Manhattan's inhab-

Earliest print of New York City, from I. P. N. Stokes, The Iconography of Manhattan Island 1498–1909 *(New York: Dodd, 1915–1928).*

itants (see above). Above a harbor choked with sailing vessels, a tradesman displays his recent material acquisitions to a lady. His possessions include, directly behind and below the two figures, the four brawny black porters who convey the goods of which the Dutchman is so proud. Within one generation, this primitive outpost became home to thirteen hundred persons, including more than one hundred Africans whose enforced exertions ensured labor stability and handsome profits.

It is hard for us to imagine, but for most of human history slavery was a normal condition for labor. From ancient to medieval times, labor had little value because slavery was so widespread. Medieval Christianity at least promised the individual the prospect of a better fate in the afterlife. Even though men were still bound to the land under serfdom, they had rights and were equal before God; all men possessed souls. Thus did labor gain value and produce the surplus value that in medieval Europe provided the basis for capitalism, which in turn freed labor from its attachment to the land and transformed it into a commodity that industrialists conspired to price as low as possible. New York City's colonial experience reflects the growing contradiction in labor practice between slave and free labor systems that was mediated through republican doctrines. At the same time, Dutch republicans were less oppressive toward New Amsterdam slaves than were their English counterparts.

Dutch masters treated their slaves little differently from their white indentured servants, whose labor contracts sold for a term of up to seven years to a sponsoring master. Freed blacks possessed all the rights enjoyed by whites, including ownership of slaves and indentured servants and the right to intermarry with whites.[3] In 1641, Paul d'Angola and Domingo Anthony became the first freed slaves to receive land from the city corporation. The same year, New York City's first execution took place when the tallest of six Africans caught fighting was hung as an example to the others.

The Dutch West India Company did not have to contend with organized dissent from the colonists—just with general demoralization bred of the constant warfare with the Indians that left much of the colony a smoldering ruin by 1643.[4] The main threat to Dutch control came from an England whose ruling circles coveted Dutch possessions[5] and demonstrated the capacity to adapt to changing economic circumstances through creative social engineering. When, in sixteenth-century England, prices rose, wages fell, and men were driven from the land to be replaced by sheep and cattle, yeomen reverted to gathering rather than growing as they wandered the countryside in search of food. It became incumbent upon the authorities to export vagrants, paupers, and the underemployed. The dispossessed made their way as indentured servants to places like New York, expecting to partake of a Garden of Eden and ill-suited to the strenuous tasks of agriculture in the New World.[6] Though many of them were trained as artisans and anticipated earning a living in nonagricultural occupations once they completed their indentured obligations, most became inefficient small farmers.[7]

Agricultural work was associated in men's minds with slave labor, an association that became more common by the late seventeenth century as African slavery replaced rural servitude and the English demand for slaves increased their economic value. The Dutch West India Company complained that the colonies incurred great expense to transport agricultural laborers who sooner or later went into trade and neglected agriculture altogether.[8] To combat this practice and foster agricultural incentive, the corporation in 1647 relinquished its monopoly over the merchandising of slaves and allowed citizens to trade in that commodity with Brazil.

A year later, the corporation council restricted trade within the municipality to residents of at least three consecutive years who built "a decent citizen dwelling."[9]

New Amsterdam inhabitants were encouraged to identify socially and politically with the Dutch West India Company. On February 2, 1653, the company board joined with the director-general, Peter Stuyvesant, to delegate authority to nine officials: two burgomasters, five *schepens* (aldermen), a *schout* (sheriff), and a clerk. These men were chosen from a list of eighteen nominated by the settler-employees,[10] a process of involvement that gave the inhabitants a sense of political control. Even then, the goal of most New Amsterdam common corporations, chartered municipalities, and church parishes was to foster profitable pursuits, leading to the widely held belief "that any laborious honest man may in a shorte time become ritche in this Country."[11]

In 1657, the Dutch government formally created the Corporation of the City of New Amsterdam. The municipal corporation granted "freedom of the city," that is the right to ply one's trade within the city's walls,[12] to all men who paid a fee, fulfilled a seven-year apprenticeship, or were honorifically granted the right of "freemanship" by the authorities. The freemanship, equivalent in rank to that of the Dutch burgher, consisted of a formal contract with the municipal corporation certifying the right to work and vote in the city regardless of how much property or freehold a man owned. Its granting, however, did not guarantee employment or just treatment. At the same time, the Dutch restricted municipal office to the minority of the populace who could afford to pay a steep "great" burgher fee.

Meanwhile, in 1664 the English, who had carved out settlements to the north in Westchester and to the east on Long Island, decided under the leadership of the Duke of York to conquer Manhattan. Burgomaster, *schepen,* and *schout* became mayor, alderman, and sheriff. The Duke of York immediately granted more religious freedom to whites. He disestablished the Dutch Reformed Church and permitted any Protestant religion to practice openly. But when too many Africans tried to convert to Christianity in order to obtain promised freedom, the Duke amended the law that "no Christians could become slaves" to stipulate that African Christians would remain slaves. Under the Laws of 1665, blacks' terms of indentured servitude were extended for life. One historian has aptly concluded, "Unlike the Dutch West India Company, which had used slavery to implement colonial policy, the Royal African Company used the colony to implement slavery." After 1697, even if they were Christians, blacks were forbidden burial at Trinity Church.[13]

New York's Charter of 1683, granted by Governor Thomas Dongan and generally known as Dongan's Charter, marked the first instance of a city's incorporation into the British Empire. It created six political wards—each represented by an alderman elected by the freemen— together with a mayor and a sheriff appointed by the governor. This structure replaced the old form of government consisting of seven magistrates and a *schout* or constable. English authorities were determined to prevent a repetition of the brief fifteen-month Dutch reconquest of the city, begun on August 12, 1673, that had revealed how shallow the depth of support for English administration had been among the Dutch inhabitants.[14]

The reorganization of city government made New York City more of an autonomous corporate entity by extending the powers of municipal officials. It also reinforced residential segregation along racial and ethnic lines. In 1677, a growing municipal debt had prodded the Common Council, the city's legislative body, into taxing the city's 290 families. City ordinances became a means of organizing private action, even into the sea, for the municipal corporation was given title to all land and water rights extending two hundred feet beyond the low-tide mark, except four hundred feet around Manhattan's southern tip.[15]

The wards became the electoral communities that provided a political identity for small-scale production oriented toward a global market. They consisted of the five wards in the extreme southern section of the island and one "out" ward that included all other settlements on the island of Manhattan, like Harlem. From the perspective of New York City's laboring class, Dongan's Charter held promise because it permitted the mayor and several other political appointees to confer freemanship upon white newcomers. The artisan majority hoped that cautious granting of this privilege would restrict unlicensed competition and preserve their local control over output and the setting of prices.[16]

However, artisan success depended on the scale of enterprise remaining small, technologically backward, and geared to a local market. Mechanics and tradesmen could then continue to work for common goals in European-style craft-based guilds. Unfortunately for artisanal social integrity, the colonial American market was from the outset tied to price fluctuations wrought by global trade, in labor as well as commodities. When the price of slaves fell to new lows in the West Indies during the 1680s, traders brought large numbers to the Chesapeake area. The descendants of these blacks were trained in skilled crafts, and they undercut artisan status.[17]

Slavery ensured economic stability for the colony, because whites steeped in the notions of "the rights of free-born Englishmen" would rebel if forced to work under slave-like conditions. Contemporary Malachy Postlethwayt echoed that argument when he noted that no free white man could be had as cheaply as a black slave.[18]

While artisans supported the employment of blacks as their helpers and as field hands, they were opposed to Africans advancing in the trades. In 1686, New York City's licensed porters lobbied successfully for the first formal regulation of the apprenticeship system undertaken by municipal authorities, one that effectively excluded African Americans. Five years later, English authorities barred the city's African Americans from carting and portering, depriving them of any role in the vital transportation network. In 1730, slaves were even forbidden the right to peddle merchandise on city streets. It is not surprising, therefore, that there were never more than one hundred free African Americans at any one time in colonial New York City, even though the slave population ranged from a few hundred in 1640 to two thousand in 1770. The city corporation also excluded the only twelve Dutch carters from plying their trade and for the next century awarded the freemanship to fifty-five English-American cartmen as against only six Dutch Americans.[19]

The Dongan Charter of 1683 had created precedents by establishing New York City's first elected government at the time of the city's formal integration into the British Empire. The city was granted more rights than any other British "plantation."

A year later, Charles II rescinded most of the inhabitants' rights to self-government. James II followed this up in 1686 with the abolition of the elective state assembly. He also required Governor Dongan to seek approval from the royal Committee on Plantations for the removal of judges, sheriffs, and other officials.[20] In 1688, taking advantage of the political turmoil in England caused by the overthrow of the Stuart monarchy and its replacement by the House of Orange, an integrated force of Dutch, English, and other European New Yorkers staged their own rebellion. Its leader, Jacob Leisler, became New York City's only popularly elected mayor before 1834. He manipulated the elections for local officials to ensure that political opponents would not come to power. Leisler's Protestant zeal in seeking to conquer French Canada alienated the local populace, who offered the English little resistance when they reconquered New York City. The anti-Leislerians then restored the reforms of 1683, which Leisler had suspended, while Leisler himself was suspended from a gallows.[21]

To bolster local initiative, the English allowed the assembly to become a countervailing political force to the royal governor and his council. The latter appointed New York City's mayor, recorder, town clerk, sheriff, and clerk of the market. The assembly was authorized to enforce city laws enacted by the city's Common Council, which consisted of the mayor, recorder, and elected aldermen and assistant aldermen who sat as one body. Thus was inaugurated the contest between city and state governments that persists to the present. A permanent political division arose between those men "attached to the governor's interests and the men who made use of the assembly to thwart that interest."[22] At the same time, an intimate correspondence between politics and production allowed for a "participatory" or quasi-democratic adult white male republican politics to develop on the local level, so that in the city election of 1701 60 percent of the eligible electorate cast ballots.[23]

Soon the Dutch were collectively outnumbered by the English, a scattering of Jews and French Protestants, and the 14 percent of the population who were African. Robert Livingston of New York's prominent eighteenth-century political family noted, "We have a poor dispirited people . . . they are not unanimous, and do not stick to one another."[24]

New York City had become the principal depot for the North American market in slaves, at the apex of the triangular trade between North America, the Caribbean, and Great Britain. Its European-American citizenry took advantage of this bounty; in 1703, 43 percent owned one or two slaves. To meet growing demand, a slave market was established at the foot of 9 Wall Street at the East River in 1709. The most prominent New York families, like the Livingstons, established their fortunes as slave traders. The most profitable wharves—those of Crommelin, Schuyler, Van Zandt, and Walton—provided space for slave auctions, conducted almost immediately after the unfortunate victims disembarked onto American soil. Except for Charleston, South Carolina, no other North American locality was more economically dependent on slavery than New York City, a circumstance encouraged by the fact that English authorities exempted slave property from the tax rolls.[25]

In 1712, New York City authorities cruelly crushed a slave rebellion that had been joined by white indentured servants, retrying acquitted slaves until guilty verdicts were reached. Once they acquired the desired verdict, authorities meted out capital punishment in as horrible a manner as the technology of the time permitted. One of the Roosevelt family's slaves was roasted to death over a ten-hour period, while others were burned more quickly or slowly stretched to pieces on specially constructed racks, which the English governor considered "the most exemplary [punishments] that could be possibly thought of." In the aftermath of this state-sanctioned cruelty, the city prohibited newly freed slaves from owning land or other property and forbade more than four Africans or Native Americans to assemble in one place in their free time. Free black contact with slaves became a punishable offense. Slaves discovered to be planning escape to freedom in Canada were summarily executed.[26]

In 1713, the Common Council passed a law that forbade any African or Indian slave from venturing onto the streets at night without a lantern. This act prevented slaves from attending the only school designed to provide them with an education. Violation resulted in any citizen having the right to escort the slave to jail, where the master was summoned to pay a fine and, if he so desired, could have thirty-nine lashes administered to the offender at no charge. In 1717 and again in 1730, the few remaining rights of African and Native Americans were curtailed. In 1735, a master whipped his slave to death for being sighted on the streets by the watch. The coroner's jury ruled that "correction given by the Master was not the Cause of his Death, but that it was by the visitation of God." Ethical justification was fueled by Anglican or Presbyterian religious fervor, the repressive behavioral strictures of which sanctioned "good works" like productive plantations while providing grace and little else for those who labored.[27]

Philosophical sanction for slavery was provided by England's most renowned political theorist, John Locke, who viewed slave ownership as "just," animals as "beasts," and forests as "waste." To Locke, an investor in the slave trade through his holdings in the Royal African Company, slaves were

> captives taken in a just war . . . of nature subject to the absolute dominion and power of their masters. These men . . . forfeited their lives and with it their liberties, and lost their estates, and being in the state of slavery not capable of any property, cannot in that state be considered as any part of civil society, the chief end whereof is the preservation of property.

What is more, Locke believed that the legitimate recourse for the individual slave was suicide, not escape, and certainly not rebellion. For Locke, protection of slaveholders was the duty of the state.[28]

Locke's views on slavery marked no advance over classical Athenian democracy, which excluded slaves, as well as women, from participation in civil society. Taken together, Lockean and Athenian democracy provide us with the perspective necessary to understand the kind of democracy that arose in antebellum New York City. Anti-black animosity contributed to a collective sense of superiority that bound whites together in a cross-class coalition that in turn most benefited the economic elite but also gave white workers better jobs than blacks.[29]

This sense of superiority was encouraged by the climate of racial repression fostered by the English. In 1741, a series of fires in New York City led to the arrests of almost half the male slaves over the age of sixteen, along with a number of whites. Over a five-month period, after a bitterly cold winter, thirty-four men and women were either burned alive or hung for conspiracy and theft. A politically opportunistic, unscrupulous judge, Daniel Horsmanden, was in charge. Four of those executed were white, including a mother and daughter and one John Ury, falsely accused of being a Catholic priest. This charge allowed Ury's Protestant prosecutors to indulge their most sadistic anti-papist fantasies. In a rare exception to a hideous policy, African Americans were permitted to testify against whites earmarked for execution.[30]

English aristocratic biases shaped the trial proceedings and the brutal verdicts. One African American was lashed in chains over a lamppost on a street corner where his children watched his death agonies. Two other men, one black, the other white, were hung in chains. Both were soon "black and blackening" in the summer sun, in full view of New York City's tranquil harbor and its fishermen. For days they dangled, until a rumor arose that the white man had turned black and the black man white. Finally, the ballooning body of one victim burst, spraying the air with a nauseating odor that forced fishermen to go far from shore.

Then, almost as unexpectedly as it had begun, the inquisition groaned to a halt as the star prosecution witness, an indentured servant girl named Mary Burton—falsely promised freedom for her perjured testimony—widened her accusatory dragnet to include whites who were more socially respected. The trial dramatized the struggle between "haves and have-nots,"[31] between rich whites and mostly poor blacks and whites in a city now at the hub of global trafficking in human beings, where the prevalent form of production was the master-controlled artisanal workshop employing between one and four apprentices and journeymen, and one or two slaves.

In 1730, the Montgomerie Charter superseded Dongan's. It clarified legal ambiguities that had arisen subsequent to Dongan's Charter. It granted the right to sue on behalf of the city to the mayor, aldermen, and commonalty (freemen and freeholders), who collectively stood for New York City; the city itself was legally defined as an individual entitled to buy, sell, or lease property. Since most Africans were already defined as property, why not define a city as a person? Such was the power of English law to alter social reality.

City land became the private property of the corporation, whose business was the management and disposal of the real estate it owned.[32] At least four aldermen and assistant aldermen, plus the mayor and recorder, were charged with passing laws, and civil and criminal courts were established. The wider society's sense of participation extended to the debate over home rule, which took place in a colonial assembly made up of white men whose concerns revolved around such local matters as the regulation of highways and the killing of wolves, wildcats, and foxes.[33]

New York City merchants dominated political affairs and until 1763 enjoyed a majority voice on the Common Council. Their participation would soon be eclipsed by a rise in the number of lawyers engaged in politics, as colonial leaders couched their arguments against British rule in legal language. This development was not popular, but it generated no active protest.[34]

New York's gentry were secure in their belief that no class-based opposition would challenge a rule solidified by frequent intermarriage. They were confident enough to sanction public meetings to ratify private selection of candidates to the assembly, because artisans and mechanics had only the two-party choice of being governed by Livingston or Delancey family stalwarts.[35] A small number of powerful individuals enjoyed extensive public support through a franchise that was more widely available for popular use than the desire to use it. Even in 1776, voting was not an issue in New York City, because most European-American adult males could vote.[36]

As the voter base expanded, it became less feasible for political candidates to be on personal terms with every potential voter. Since self-nomination by notables was also no longer tolerated, the formal public mass meeting came into being in 1769, during the last elections held prior to the War of Independence. Candidates accustomed to one-on-one appeals quickly learned to stage nominating rallies orchestrated to demonstrate the intensity of popular feeling. They developed sophisticated electoral techniques, as republicanism came to be equated in men's minds with vote-getting. The candidates understood that a measure of political participation by the transplanted European masses would assist in strengthening a social formation based on the trade in slaves and other commodities.[37]

The large numbers of slaves in colonial New York City helped to expand democratic rights for European men. The slaves provided the economic foundation on which European Americans prospered; or as Edmund Morgan so aptly put it, "The rights of Englishmen were preserved by destroying the rights of Africans."[38] The absence of slaves would have placed the common immigrant at the bottom of the human chain. Their presence provided a social cushion. In spite of harsh treatment, poorer Europeans fancied themselves as being somewhere in the middle of society, even before there was any conscious sense of a middle class.

When considering the question of formal rank, American revolutionary democrats believed there was "no rank above that of freeman." Europe, meanwhile, was condemned for permitting inherited rank to formally divide men. Whereas a hierarchy of feudal "ranks" persisted within British and French political culture, it never took root in America, except vis-à-vis the slaves.[39]

Hierarchy in America was associated with prior right, which in turn was equated with property rights. Thus, a man who owned waterfront land in New York City customarily had first choice in acquiring from the city corporation those waterlots that fronted his property. Hendrik Hartog has found that Harrington-Lockean values prevailed, with "the concerns of a property owner best defin[ing] the business of the corporation of the city of New York."[40]

By the time of the American War of Independence, European men steeped in commonwealth values that sanctified property and rationalized slavery had uprooted Native American cultures and replaced them with an invasive transatlantic mercantilism. Nowhere was "the national love of trade" more evident than in New York City, where nearly everyone depended on the harbor for their livelihood.[41] British and Dutch investors tied the city's destiny to an international mercantile system that provided matchless political rights for New York City's European-American males.

The franchise was an issue never raised during the War of Independence. Rather, the question of independence was framed in legal language upholding the right of an individual to act freely in the marketplace, thereby favoring those who already possessed the material resources to act independently.[42] Verbal attacks against the "aristocracy" only served to strengthen the mercantile class's control of capital generated by commercial ventures.

While democratic rhetoric accelerated, so did the concentration of wealth. The percentage of assets owned by the wealthiest 10 percent of New Yorkers increased from 46 percent of the city's landed property in 1701 to 54 percent in 1789 and 61 percent in 1796.[43] Charles Beard concluded that

> It was discontent with economic restrictions, not with their fundamental political institutions, which nerved the Revolutionists to . . . driving out [England]. . . . The American Revolution, therefore, was not the destruction of an old regime . . . it was not motivated by levelling doctrines with which the French middle class undermined . . . feudalism.[44]

The *New-York Journal* editorialized that if Britain prevailed, the colonies "must dwindle down into 'common corporations,' " for taxes "enforced dependence" and undermined a man's virtue.[45] Opposition to taxes imposed from overseas united mechanic and merchant, planter and yeoman in a struggle whose outcome was ultimately determined in favor of the colonists by the French navy.

Still, if elections are any measure of popular strength, it was clear in New York City that the majority desired continued ties to Great Britain. Only a minority of all classes in the city, including a fraction of the working classes, actively opposed the British. In the 1768 local New York City election, carpenter Amos Dodge received 12 percent of the workingmen's vote—the worst showing among a slate otherwise made up of merchants and lawyers. A year later, in the last assembly elections held prior to the Declaration of Independence, mechanics allied with the Delancey faction supported popular Whig merchants and lawyers over Livingston men by an almost two-to-one margin.

When the Sons of Liberty burned effigies of British officials, broke hundreds of windows, and looted official residences to gain repeal of the Stamp Act, artisans were led by the merchants John Lamb, Isaac Sears, and John Morin Scott, who were identified with James Delancey's "popular Whig" faction. Yet Delancey's ties to England were more extensive than those of any other native-born New Yorker of the eighteenth century. They were even stronger than those of the royal governor he opposed. It was with political ease that the Delancey-Anglican faction transformed itself from the "popular Whigs" of 1768 into the core of royalism by 1775.[46]

There was no recorded instance of spontaneous resistance to the British occupation of New York City, which lasted from 1776 until 1783, but then there were no taxes either. The absence of trial by jury did not distress the populace. Common Council duties were routinely conducted by nineteen British appointees. The assessment of Arthur Schlesinger, Sr., that "the radical cause lacked . . . an opposition divorced from the control of the merchant class" is substantiated by the political evidence.[47]

Occupational divisions within the labor force in New York City during the Revolution were greater than divisions between employers and employees.[48] The mechanic "radicalism" that did surface was confined to a republican egalitarianism that denied women, non-Europeans, and the dependent poor any voice in formal political affairs.

Unlike their French counterparts, the radical republican *sans-culottes,* American mechanics or skilled artisans did not insist that democratic principles be extended to all persons. While the French Revolution produced the revolutionary communist "Gracchus" Babeuf, New York City radicals behaved more like eighteenth-century English radicals. They were, in Bernard Bailyn's words, "preoccupied not with the need to recast the social order nor . . . economic inequality . . . but with the need to purify a corrupt constitution and fight off the apparent growth of prerogative power." These radicals fought British rule by organizing extralegal committees composed of mechanics but led by merchants. Common laborers or the unskilled were not politically engaged. For Stuart Blumin, "it is the strength of the culture of rank, not its weakness that stands out . . ." in the American Revolution.[49]

What accounts for New York artisan conservatism? For one thing, as preindustrial manufacturer-producers who subscribed to the master-journeyman-apprentice hierarchy and code, artisan mechanics had traditionally employed most of the indentured servants and slaves, a circumstance that invited abuse.[50] The psychological corruption borne of having others do work for which one claimed both material and personal credit contributed to the incipient "middle-class" stance of the artisan.[51] The power that master artisans exercised over all others in the workplace was internalized by those who labored in this mode of production. Journeymen and apprentices alike expected to one day become master artisans. They were resigned to laboring subserviently, confident in their belief and historical experience that some day they too would be able, on the basis of craft proficiency, to lord it over younger practitioners. As Iowerth Prothero has pointed out with respect to the English workshop, artisans were not "particularly egalitarian but rather hierarchical, differentiated in tasks, status, authority, age and gender, with particular ruthless exploitation of juveniles."[52]

Alexander Hamilton shrewdly offered additional reasons for the artisans' spirit of dependence:

> Mechanics and manufacturers will always be inclined, with few exceptions, to give their votes to merchants, in preference to persons of their own professions or trades. . . . They know that the merchant is their patron and friend; and they are aware, that however great the confidence they may justly feel in their own good sense, their interests can be most effectively promoted by the merchant than by themselves. They are sensible that their habits in life have not been such as to give them those acquired endowments, without which, in a deliberative assembly, the greatest natural abilities are for the most part useless.[53]

Hamilton's characterization of mechanic motivation helps explain why, when the First Continental Congress adopted a trade embargo in 1774, opposition to British rule did not conform to class lines. A Loyalist cross-class coalition arose among merchants and artisans fearful of losing British business. "Humble" carters displayed significant support for the British cause.[54] Those cartmen who fought for the stars and stripes accepted merchant leadership, while African-American carters supported the Loyalists who, in turn, favored licensing them.

On balance, the British occupation of New York City benefited the African-American population.[55] Unlike the Americans who terrorized blacks with minutemen patrols and a judicial system that meted out swift executions for petty crimes, the British provided a powerful incentive for blacks to join their side by allowing them the right to work in occupations of their own choosing. Many blacks were able to flee the region, in what Graham Hodges regarded as the largest slave revolt in New York and

New Jersey during the eighteenth century. Those who remained assisted the British as army laborers or worked for the first time as carpenters, wagon drivers, and cartmen. They established their own churches, schools, and political organizations.[56]

While the British actively recruited African Americans, the Continental army only reluctantly enrolled its first African Americans on St. Patrick's Day 1781 in a fifty-nine-man company. Their service was accelerated by a provision that allowed European Americans to be exempted from military service if they could find African-American substitutes. Given that a minority of Americans were actively engaged in the movement for independence, the revolutionaries needed to broaden their base of support, especially when the British freed all slaves who served in their ranks, an offer of which three thousand African Americans took advantage.[57] Only in 1781 did the New York legislature belatedly grant freedom to slaves who had served as soldiers in the Continental army.

Once the war was over, the number of New York City slaves increased, with all classes sharing in this awful bounty. In fact, slaveholding was considerably more evenly distributed than wealth. During the 1790s, New York City's near-record decadal increase in slaves of 23 percent was exceeded by a 33 percent rise in the number of slaveholders. Artisans now owned more slaves than merchants and retailers combined.[58]

Soon, though, Irish immigrants increasingly competed for jobs with Africans. The city's African population declined relatively until 1840, when it reached a pre–Civil War high of about 16,500. It declined absolutely until the end of the Civil War, when New York City's black population numbered less than 10,000, the lowest in numbers since the War of 1812 (see Table 1), and the lowest in percentage terms since the founding of the city.[59]

The most popular pamphleteer of the Revolution, Thomas Paine, stood alone in New York City in his public opposition to slavery. His rank ordering of "classes"—which placed farmers at the top of an ideal society, followed by mechanics and then merchants—endeared him to artisan activists.[60] They toasted "Public Virtue" through "Loom, Hammer and Plough," while tailors applauded "the rights of man," coopers pledged to "support agriculture and commerce," hatters vowed to "cover heads without foreign products," and masons meant to ensure that the Constitution be "built of free stone." At no time did these craftsmen take note of Paine's opposition to slavery, which he placed on the same level as "murder, robbery, lewdness, and barbarity."[61]

Artisans justified their denial of rights to Africans on grounds of a racial superiority that helped justify and ensure the franchise for white males.[62] European-American immigrants did not favor equal rights for African Americans, even though the majority of immigrants before 1800 were legally indentured for several years; rather, they viewed blacks as unfair competition working for lower wages.

African New Yorkers were acutely aware of the adverse feelings of the average citizen, who in 1800 was likely to be a native-born artisan. It is no accident that free black households tended to cluster for protection around the homes of prominent New Yorkers, prosperous Federalists who favored a more restrictive franchise[63] and were more evenhanded in their treatment of black and white labor. These Federalists differentiated people according to social rank, assigning more value to those who counted among their ancestors some of the earliest settlers. They drew political strength from English or Dutch skilled workers, who like the freed slave profited from the imposition of rigorous entry-level employment requirements for Irish immigrants, of whom only a small percentage were of artisan status. In this respect, New York City was little different from other American seaboard cities of the time, where skill differentials within the working class were reflected in ethnicity and time of arrival.[64]

In America, the few craftsmen who became employers above the rank of ordinary master formed the social nucleus for a new middle class. Many more craftsmen never advanced to journeyman status. Even as journeymen, they were relegated to the carrying trades, with commodities for these trades in New York City normally ranging from slaves in the eighteenth century to cotton in the nineteenth.[65] Economic dependence on the South reinforced artisan political support for slavery.

Although the number of New York City slaves declined after 1810, the importance of Southern plantation cotton to the city's foreign commerce grew until the Civil War, by which time the city enjoyed "a virtual monopoly."[66] Cotton fueled America's industrial revolution, begun in the wake of Jefferson's disastrous embargo on British and French goods followed by the War of 1812. From having hardly a factory on its soil before the war, the United States swiftly rose to third in global industrial production by 1860, behind Great Britain and France.

Plantation owner and New York City merchant were natural political allies because many of the city's Democratic merchants subsisted off the profits of slave labor.[67] These Democrats supported the extension of slavery. They followed the precepts of James Madison's *Federalist Paper*

No. 10 in that they emphasized geographic expansion as the key to social stability while they stressed preserving distinctions in property and power.[68]

Party leaders were primarily lawyers who, once freed from royal restrictions, served as political brokers between entrepreneurs and the public. Lawyers reentered politics in greater numbers than before the War of Independence. In December 1783, in the city's first postwar local and ward elections, they captured eight of the fourteen aldermen and assistant aldermen seats and, a month later, all nine state senate seats in a New York undergoing explosive growth.[69]

The Revolution did not alter the social composition of the local elite. Voters elected the same class of men to office who had held office before the conflict began. "All classes" were found "sedulously employed in the business of ELECTION," unlike in England, where no matter how hard an Englishman worked, he could not vote if he did not own substantial property.[70] On March 9, 1784, one month after the Common Council resumed its duties, a law was passed charging every handicraft tradesman a fee of twenty shillings for "use of the Corporation" and freeman status, the legal prerequisite to being allowed to practice his occupation within city limits.

Twenty shillings was a lot to men who resented the power of the elite to run roughshod over their sense of honor and tradition, as well as pick their purses. Despite elections that seemed to suggest unchallenged elite rule, workers expressed their indignation at unpredictable moments. An example is the 1788 Doctor's Riot over privileges accorded the medical profession. Interns had routinely hired laborers to dig up deceased African Americans and unclaimed bodies for use as teaching aids. But in this episode, a surgeon provoked popular wrath by jokingly telling a boy that an arm he had just severed was that of the boy's mother, who had recently died. The boy's hysteria led an angry mob to attack Doctor's Hospital. The governor, mayor, and other rich men were pressed into service to defend the hospital, and John Jay and Baron von Steuben were injured in the ensuing fray. Finally, soldiers fired into the crowd, killing and wounding several persons. Exhumations and dissections resumed shortly thereafter.[71]

Such outbursts, however, did not threaten a conservative social order. Imaginative writers of the time stressed elite domination. Novelist Hugh Henry Brackenbridge had his protagonist captain observe the following regarding New York City politics:

"It is a strange thing . . . that in the country . . . they would elect no one but a weaver or a whiskey-distiller; and here none but fat squabs, that guzzle wine, and smoke segar." . . . "No, faith" (said his friend), "there is na danger of Teague here, unless he had his scores o'shares in the bank, and was in league with the brokers, and had a brick house at his hurdies, or a ship or twa on the stocks . . . all is now lost in substantial interest, and the funds command everything."[72]

The greatest American writer of the first quarter of the nineteenth century, Washington Irving, ridiculed public illusions about party politics. As a critic of the democracy of appearance, Irving targeted the staged campaigns of candidates for office. He mocked republican support of the French Revolution: "I have seen liberty; I have seen equality; I have seen fraternity! I have seen that great political puppet-show—*an election.*"[73]

Both Brackenbridge and Irving recalled Tory satirist Samuel Peters, who a generation earlier in his history of Connecticut had remarked,

The people of New-England are rightly stiled republicans: but a distinction should be made between the learned and unlearned, the rich and poor. The latter form a great majority; the minority, therefore, are obliged to wear the livery of the majority, in order to secure their election into office.[74]

Upper-class figures who dressed like the masses projected the widely held belief that an undifferentiated republicanism of the people would arise from the struggle for independence. It did not.[75] New York City did not "in Process of Time . . . fill with a Race of Artisans and Mechanics . . . educated in the Principles of Virtue."[76] President John Adams observed that no sooner had the war ended than America "rushed headlong into a greater degree of luxury than ought to have crept in for a hundred years," being "more Avaricious than any other Nation that ever existed."[77]

This rush to wealth was fed by a generation of unparalleled prosperity based on the re-export trade that began with the Treaty of Paris in 1783 and was fed by war between Great Britain and France. From 1792 until 1807, the value of New York City's exports increased from $2.5 million to $26.3 million. This prosperity was unevenly distributed, primarily flowing to merchants and skilled adult European-American males. Even the most militant journeymen sanctioned a "moral economy" that excluded women, Native Americans, slaves, the dependent poor, and the unskilled.[78]

In the score of years succeeding the War of Independence, sexual harassment intensified against laboring women. Their access to both property and skills declined. A married woman's legal status was that of domestic chattel, with the principle of coverture granting whatever property she owned to her husband. According to Christine Stansell, it was "the republican beliefs of the Revolution, broadly disseminated among New York laboring men," that "amplified and strengthened assumptions of female subservience and male authority."[79]

This decline in the rights of women found a parallel in the treatment of African Americans. Only Federalists Alexander Hamilton and John Jay and Republican Aaron Burr made an effort to implement a constructive social policy toward blacks. In 1786, Burr sponsored a bill in the New York State legislature to abolish slavery in New York. It was rejected by a vote of thirty-three to thirteen. The same year Hamilton and Jay helped establish the African Free School, the organizational precedent for New York City's public school system. Hamilton had observed that African-American "natural faculties are probably as good as ours," but "the contempt we have been taught to entertain for the blacks, makes us fancy many things that are founded neither in reason or experience." He and Jay founded the New York City Manumission Society, half of whose members owned slaves.[80] The Manumission Society only aided freed slaves, and it could provide no assistance to the slave poet Jupiter Hammon, whose sale of six editions of his 1787 *Address to the Negroes in the State of New York* proved insufficient to buy his freedom.

The existence of black slavery lent social standing to most men who were not of African descent; if they did not actually own slaves, they could still enjoy a sense of social superiority. In addition to ensuring a labor force segmented along racial lines, black slavery raised the level of intraclass violence. It should therefore come as no surprise that African Americans first sought protection from the British Crown, and not from the fathers of the American Revolution.[81]

Slavery's decline in New York can be attributed to slaveowners profitably selling their slaves to Southern planters rather than emancipating them. No public official, including Hamilton and Burr, dared speak up about integrating the ex-slave into the social or economic mainstream. In fact, it was during Jefferson's presidency that racial segregation first appeared in New York City's prisons. Other than permanent slavery, removal to Africa received the most public support from whites, and the least from blacks.[82]

The two processes of black slavery and white freedom were intertwined.[83] The democratization of New York City politics reinforced racial patriarchy in accordance with democratic republican principles. While male whites benefited from reduced property qualifications for voting, African Americans found their voting rights curtailed.

◅ 2 ▻

BANKS, FARMERS,
AND MECHANICS
1781–1812

No Republic can exist without virtue, nor can virtue exist unless fostered
and cultivated by the people.
Public Advertiser, March 16, 1811

In our country, wealth has more power than in any other.
"Thoughts on the Times," *United States Magazine and Democratic Review,*
December 1839

The present political struggle, in this country, appears to be a contest
between men and dollars . . .
James Fenimore Cooper to Bedford Brown, March 24, 1838

———

THE ESTABLISHMENT OF BANKS IN NEW YORK CITY DURING THE
1780S SIGNIFIED THE NEED TO FUND DEBT AND FINANCE PRIVATE EN-
terprise like the "manufacturing society" of Alexander Hamilton that
became the city of Paterson, New Jersey. The proliferation of banks
placed farmers and mechanics at a growing disadvantage in the marketplace, but it represented a crucial step on the road to world power for
the United States.

Early American bankers survived through the welfare of the state. They
did not possess the capital resources of their European counterparts who
began private banks in mature societies. In America, public banking came
first. After expending public monies, these public banks, such as the
Bank of North America, were then privatized without repaying the initial
public investment. The free loan to bankers was rationalized by claiming
that the public interest was being served. Is it any wonder the belief was
widespread that banks were mere tools to advance the interests of a new
aristocracy? In 1786 the political risk attached to the support of banks

loomed so large that George Washington sold his Bank of England stock; and if the Constitution had made any mention of banking, it would never have been ratified.[1]

It was left to Alexander Hamilton in 1781 to put his political capital in jeopardy by drawing up the blueprint for the continent's first bank, the Bank of North America. This institution positioned private bankers to set national economic policy, given that state currencies like New York's were undergoing alarming depreciation. Hamilton ingeniously transformed the dictum of the most popular pamphleteer of the American Revolution, the radical republican democrat Thomas Paine, from "No nation ought to be without a debt" to "A national debt . . . is . . . a national blessing . . . a powerful cement to our union."[2]

Jeffersonian Republicans opposed funding a national debt, for it threatened, as in England, to surrender control of the government to "an inflationary conspiracy of politicians, investors, officers and contractors." Bank lobbying for currency and credit regulations riled the "Republican Farmer," who complained that "politicians must be egregiously ignorant or studious to deceive who pretend to doubt or deny the influence of Banks in controuling the elections of the people."[3]

As a political counterweight to the growing power of banks, New York City democratic republicans stressed the importance of land as a source of wealth that would guarantee an expanding electoral base, even though most New Yorkers were now engaged in the various mechanic trades. Democratic republicans accused Federalists of trying to bring on a "National Debt, Standing Army, and National Church." Their leader, Jefferson, opposed a national bank because a corporation that owned land would soon undermine agricultural independence.[4]

New York City mechanics split over the bank issue, supporting banks when mechanics, not merchants, were in charge. Their trade societies, like the General Society of Mechanics and Tradesmen, became mutual loan associations to prevent merchant entrepreneurs from undermining artisan control over wages and prices. Some manufactories, like the New-York Manufacturing Society, even minted their own paper currency redeemable in gold and silver.[5]

By issuing bonds, the National Bank fostered the growth of ever larger manufactories. It also permitted foreign interests to invest and own part of America, in keeping with the founding mission of the colonies to further international trade. Later, this objective would be facilitated by increasing the amount of paper currency in circulation.[6] The influx of foreign capital helped banks to wrest control from artisans of decisions governing production and price. Federalist leaders personally encouraged this trend. They were not alone.

Artisans with residential real estate holdings also subsidized banks, if only regional ones. Their political influence was considerable since half the mechanics elected to New York City public office in the early republic were landlords. They demonstrated the affinity of artisan republican values with property. This "middling order" branded banks as "large associations of overgrown monied importance and ambition"[7] but tolerated regional banks because they served local interests like Anglo-Dutch artisan mechanic workshops subsisting in symbiotic harmony with Southern plantation agriculture.

The most successful regional bank was the first: the Bank of New York, still in operation, which was established by Hamilton, in 1784, and was the only bank in the city for seven years. But it was the Bank of the United States, which Hamilton sponsored in 1791, that provoked a storm of protest. Hamilton's banking and tax proposals influenced artisan mechanics in the affected trades to switch their support by 1797 to the Jeffersonian Republican Party.[8]

Jeffersonians favored expansion of the franchise to European Americans in Northern cities like New York that were financially dependent on Southern trade and were undergoing massive immigration. These "Republicans" contrasted their belief that "sovereignty resides in the great mass of the people" with that of "Federalist Tories" who desired "a government of war and taxes on the corrupt principles of the English government." Only farmers and mechanics, Jeffersonian Republicans declared, were sufficiently virtuous to guarantee a "republican" government based on "democratic principles," one that prized merit over riches.[9]

That a dramatic change in party allegiance occurred in the 1790s demonstrated the capacity of a two-party system to channel political discontent and ensured that artisans would not form their own political party, especially since they remained divided in allegiance between the two dominant parties. Republicans quickly absorbed the Democratic Society created in 1794 when artisan mechanic members cited the French Revolution to defend their rights to equal opportunity in the marketplace. This democratic ethnic-craft coalition recruited "mechanics in general . . . Taylors, Coopers, Hatters, Masons and Shipwrights." It appealed to newcomer Germans and Irish, while Federalists mobilized the skilled and those, like the cartmen, who possessed a tiny amount of capital and were likely to be of older English and Dutch immigrant stock.[10]

Republicans pursued a sound short-term political strategy in publicly pressing for an alliance of small-scale manufacturing and large-scale trade to service agriculture. Many republicans opposed any increase in the number of workshops, which they felt should be consigned to Europe in what amounted to a global division of labor.[11]

Support for Jefferson came from the Clinton family, who championed the "middling classes" against Federalist estate holders. This new two-party politics replaced the Delancey-Livingston rivalry of earlier years. Clinton's organizational base was Tammany Hall, founded in 1786 as a secret fraternal order for "the benevolent purpose of affording relief to the indigent and distressed."[12] Its founders looked to Europe for guidance and found European custom dictated that a nation have a patron saint. These Republicans sensibly settled upon Tammany, an American Indian from Germantown, then a short distance from Philadelphia. After all, who was more American than a Native American?

Several Tammany men immediately became city officials, including Episcopalian William Mooney, New York Tammany's principal founder. Mooney qualified for Revolutionary War veteran status, even though he resigned from the army, before it was clear the colonials would win, to set up an upholstery business. Political connections presented him with the opportunity to become involved in the repaving of city streets and then to take the post of superintendent of the almshouse. As the man in charge of care for the city's poor, Mooney was able to legally satisfy the charity clause of Tammany's charter, while most of the money collected went to those who oversaw the assistance. Under Mooney's stewardship between 1808 and 1809, almshouse expenditures, ostensibly to keep the poor warm, included disbursements for rum, brandy, and gin that doubled, quintupled, and sextupled, respectively. An entry in his account book, "Trifles for Mrs. Mooney," became part of the public folklore of political corruption. On September 18, 1809, he was dismissed as superintendent.[13] A year later, Mooney had amassed sufficient capital to buy real estate, but not enough to pay arrears on his city taxes. Naturally, both the almshouse and his real estate speculations brought him into close contact with immigrants, who increasingly provided his party with votes. As a reward for his services to Tammany, Mooney was chosen grand sachem again in 1811. The practice of rewarding corruption in politics had exploded with the growth of the economy.

The first of several ornate Tammany headquarters was erected in 1810, just as Manhattan north of Houston Street was laid out in a grid and the city formally recognized its residential neighborhoods. Over the years, Tammany headquarters became identified in the public mind with the Democratic Party because the party's executive branch met there and several members belonged to the Tammany Society. The steering committee for the Tammany Society, the Council of Sachems, used legal title to the building to designate the party faction permitted to use its facilities. Occupational analysis of the 112 new members who joined the society between 1797 and 1801 reveals that over half of them were artisans.[14]

From the outset, artisan activists within what became the Democratic Party were divided over the merit of Common Council decisions that gradually transferred corporation trading rights to wealthy private individuals. A number of these artisans believed they would benefit from the trickle-down beneficence of the rich. As Eric Foner has pointed out respecting artisan culture, it was "pervaded by ambiguities and tensions, beginning with the inherent dualism of the artisan's role . . . as a small entrepreneur and employer and . . . as a laborer and craftsman." Artisans had difficulty successfully defining their role in a changing society because the success some enjoyed in expanding their small firms spelled failure for the many who were unable to do so.[15]

Typically, artisans earned ten dollars a week, exclusive of meals, for six twelve-hour days. One anonymous shoemaker, *Crispin*, lamented, "Of course, I have but little time to appreciate to domestic affairs, the education of my children, and the improvement of my own mind." There was no vacation allowance, only the three holidays of Christmas, New Year's, and July 4th. Twelve days were allotted to illness, and two for military duty. Rent averaged one hundred dollars a year. Wood cost about forty dollars. With a wife and four children, board amounted to five and a half dollars per week. *Crispin* apologized, "We cannot partake of many dainties, nor . . . drink much grog, which it is often said mechanics use so frequently." Annual clothing costs were thirty-four dollars for six people. Finally, there was education for the two eldest children and payment to the doctor:

> If any of the family are sick, I dare not call the Doctor; for the most moderate Doctor's bill . . . is great for a person in my situation. . . . My wife, in most cases of sickness, performs . . . nurse and doctor, assisted by myself & Dr. Buchan. And, as for the education of my

children . . . nor can I, for the want of time and talents, aid them much myself.

Still, most employers complained about the cost of labor.[16]

Lack of minimum standards for all workers was reflected in the decentralization of political control on the ward level, which was blamed for a "spirit of electioneering . . . the man who wears a brown coat in one company, and a blue in another, cannot be *known*."[17] While the Republicans opted for a political coat of many colors, except black, Federalists chose to retain property qualifications for citizenship, white as well as black. They attacked Republicans for politically exploiting "immigrants in a manner calculated to make the blood of every American boil in his veins."[18]

Republicans seized hold of an important political issue, one that identified them with the First Amendment to the Constitution. On January 6, 1806, the congregation of St. Peter's Church on Barclay Street, spiritual home to the only Catholic parish in New York City, petitioned the state legislature for removal of the Test Oath, which excluded Catholics from public office. Over vigorous Federalist opposition, state senator and mayor De Witt Clinton successfully steered a bill accomplishing this objective through the state legislature.

That Christmas Eve, Protestant fanatics attacked St. Peter's Church. Christmas Day, Irish Catholics confronted a Protestant mob intent upon demolishing their homes. A watchman was killed trying to intercede. The following spring, an American ticket, listing the same candidates for office as the Federalist electoral slate, lost on an anti-Irish platform.[19]

These "American" tickets against Irish "strangers" drew their strength from Federalists. According to Washington Irving, "Americans insist[ed] that *their* party is composed of the true sovereign people, and that the others are all jacobins, frenchmen, and *irish rebels* . . . a term of great reproach here."[20]

Federalists viewed the Irish as the source of urban crime. In 1808, they charged that in sixth-ward municipal elections nearly six hundred Irishmen "drove every American Federalist from the neighborhood," shouting as they did, " 'Kill the federalist scoundrel!' This is freedom of suffrage; this is the way we support freedom and independence."[21]

Federalists did not appreciate the depth of Irish hostility to any party that favored British foreign policy. While victorious Americans expelled the English military from the colonies, the defeated Irish were forced out of their own country by "the most iniquitous government that ever insulted Heaven and oppressed mankind." During the celebrations marking Evacuation Day—November 25, 1783, the day English troops finally left New York City—the Irish republican cause was linked to the struggles of the English people for their political rights. Glasses were raised to toast "the oppressed British and Irish" and their movement for "a complete representative system of pure republican principles."[22]

Bittersweet memories of their homeland were seared into the consciousness of succeeding generations of Irish immigrants, who believed that the United States was the earth's hope for salvation. As pauperized victims of English industrial policies, the Irish were grateful to come to a "money-making country," though they resented their treatment by local authorities. In 1795, and again in 1796, Irish republicans staged protests against Federalist Mayor Richard Varick's abortive cover-up of the prison floggings of two Irish prisoners, one of whom died as a result of his injuries. They also held the mayor responsible for permitting thirty Irish convicts to be pressed into service on board the British man-of-war *Thetis* as it lay berthed in New York harbor.[23]

After the Irish Rebellion of 1798, the city became a haven for Irish republicans who reinforced "the spirit of '76." From the end of the Napoleonic Wars until the Great Famine, almost one million Irish, twice the previous two centuries' total, sailed to North America.[24] Many brought their political experience in the Irish Catholic Association, the 1823 brainchild of Daniel O'Connell.

From the time of Emmett's Conspiracy of 1803, attempting to establish a free Irish state, until the Great Famine of 1845, O'Connell was more identified with the cause of Catholic Irish national liberation than any other nineteenth-century figure. He inspired the common people of Ireland to feel they were taking an active part in political society by creating a mass organization to act as a countervailing nonviolent force to England's brutal dictatorship.

The Catholic Association had three categories of membership. The largest and most unique was the one that made Ireland's seven million Catholics eligible to join at a shilling a year. The dues would be collected by the parish priests at the doors to their churches. The response was overwhelming. After the first year, more than a million people had joined an organization that strenuously lobbied for a democratic republic.[25] The Catholic Association paralleled the rise of Jacksonian Democracy in the United States.

Even before the War of 1812, it was apparent to many that Irish republican fervor was contributing to the development of Democratic Party ideology.[26] New York City newspapers commented on how the United Irishmen acted as the "democratic party" in city politics.[27] I find no evidence to substantiate Gustavus Myers's assertion that "the Irish were bitter opponents of Tammany Hall" during the early republic; unfortunately, even the most recent mammoth work on the pre–Great Famine Irish accepts the standard account asserting the lack of meaningful Irish participation in Democratic politics until the alleged rise of the Tammany boss in the 1860s.[28]

New York City's Irish were, however, divided between wealthier Federalist Protestants who were said to control the Hibernian Provident Society and the more Republican recent poorer immigrants who tended to be Catholic. Republican newspapers attributed these divisions within Irish ranks to imported British attitudes. Their hostility to the English was counterbalanced by Federalist support for British rule over Ireland. The Irish embargo of English-made goods, meant to encourage manufacturing in Ireland, reinforced the Jefferson-led embargo against all imported goods. Both embargoes failed, but joint efforts such as these helped fuse the Irish to the Democratic-Republican Party.[29]

This political fusion had its drawbacks for social progress. As Irish immigrants were forced to compete with African-American labor, they were soon taught in Tammany's school of democratic republicanism to publicly shun the African American if they wished to climb the ladder of material success. Daniel O'Connell had no obligation or need to do so. In the first issue of abolitionist William Lloyd Garrison's *Liberator,* he proclaimed, "Look at the stain on your star-spangled banner. . . . I turn from the Declaration of American Independence, and I tell him that he had declared to God and man a lie."[30] His frank assessment provoked a serious split in Irish-American ranks, with only a minority sanctioning O'Connell's statement.

Generally, New York Republicans exploited racial tensions in an urban environment that offered freed blacks more opportunities than in any other American city to enter the skilled trades, although not the professions. For 1800, Shane White has calculated that 37.8 percent of black male household heads were artisans. A decade later this figure had declined by one-fourth.[31] In response, New York City's first legally recognized black organization, the New York African Society for Mutual Relief, was established on June 6, 1808. The African Relief Society provided assistance to indigent artisans. It also sought to prevent freed blacks from being kidnapped off city streets to be sold into slavery in the South. Although the 1799 Gradual Manumission Act freed all slave children born after July 4th of that year, and mandated freedom for their parents twenty-eight years later, by then a number had been spirited to Southern states.[32]

American fears concerning the terrible consequences of freeing the slaves were heightened by the 1791 Haitian slave rebellion led by Toussaint L'Ouverture, in which more than thirty thousand persons were killed in what amounted to a genuinely democratic revolution. In its aftermath, any gathering of black Americans anywhere in America provoked alarm.[33] For example, "A Friend to Order" published an indignant letter in which he reported the following:

> Returning last Sunday from divine worship, contiguous to the Fresh Water Pond . . . I saw at a moderate calculation, near two hundred Negroes, Boys & *Gentlemen* (I mean those who have the appearance of Gentlemen) skating. I was struck with amazement at the scene, and drew the conclusion that certainly this must be unknown to our Magistrates—But ignorance of this flagrant violation could not have been the case, for I am informed, two or three of them live within pistol shot of the place.[34]

In 1800, city blacks did manage to stage a parade on July 5 in honor of "Black Independence Day." Although its organizers would have liked to participate in the previous day's national celebrations, they had been denied the right to do so by Tammany Hall. A year later, the city's first black riot erupted when a few hundred African-American New Yorkers tried to prevent a slaveowner from shipping her slaves to Virginia. Other slaves attempted or succeeded in committing suicide to avoid transport back to the South, or in general despair over their plight.[35]

It was more profitable for Southern plantation owners to have their agents kidnap freed blacks off New York City streets for transport to Southern plantations than to pay auction-block prices. As soon as the War of Independence concluded and the British were no longer in a position to interfere, kidnapping increased. Constitutional abolition of the slave trade only intensified the need to circumvent the law to ensure a stable labor supply. In 1808, the state legislature passed a law against this practice, to little avail.[36]

No day was sacred to the slaveholder. On July 4th, 1821, the *Commercial Advertiser* reported, a poor Negro was seized near the [City Hall] Park, by one from another state, who claimed him as a slave. He protested that he was free; but to no purpose. A cord was produced, and he was pinioned, and dragged away without opposition from those around, who would doubtless instantly have joined any one who should have uttered a word against *Liberty and Equality.*[37]

Republican newspapers stirred the racist pot by publishing ugly parodies like "Zambo," in which a black degraded himself by pandering to his racial stereotype:

> Missa, dey say dat our black skin
> Be ugly, ugly to de sight;
> But surely if de look vidin,
> Missa, de Negro's heart be vite.
>
> You coca nut no smooth as silk,
> But rough & ugly is de rind;
> Ope it, sweet meat & sweeter milk
> Vidin that ugly coat ve find.
>
> Ah Missa! smiling in your tear,
> I see you know vat I'd impart;
> De cocoa husk de skin I vear,
> De milk vidin be Zambo's heart.[38]

Jeffersonian Republicans promoted interethnic rivalry by contrasting Federalist detestation of the Irish with Federalist enthusiasm for "the black ones of Santo Domingo."[39] They deemed factory labor worse than plantation slavery. The *Public Advertiser* noted in this vein, "England . . . has abolished slavery among the blacks, but a more intolerable slavery still exists, the slavery of the *whites.*"[40]

Democratic Republicans rhetorically lashed Federalists for letting slaves vote, saying Federalists had the city corporation appoint Federalist inspectors who failed to check voter eligibility. Federalists were also accused of receiving "nineteenth-twentieths of the black votes. In the seventh ward they brought up negro and negress two and two in federal coaches, which were labelled *American ticket*—filled with 'American lads and lasses!'"[41] In retaliation, Federalists identified the Democratic Republicans with slavery. "If, there is a SLAVE in the United States, it is the fault of the DEMOCRATS," proclaimed the Federalist *Evening Post.*[42]

Harlem, at the time a separate village, was already a black ghetto. Although slaves made up only 3.4 percent of New York City's population in 1790, they were 22.7 percent of Harlem's population, the highest percentage of slaves for any of the eight wards. In 1807, Republicans felt besieged by "Federalists, Tories, Burrites, Lewisites and Negroes." The latter were concentrated in the first, third, and ninth wards. In 1813, Republicans blamed their loss in the assembly elections solely on Federalist appeals to "people of color," even though African-American freedmen had by 1810 been effectively stripped of the franchise by the state legislature. Yet the democratic republicans continued their campaign to deny African Americans any form of official political expression.[43]

Republican mechanics were not only hostile toward African Americans. They also opposed "public workshops," which would "degrade" mechanic "dignity" by employing discharged inmates from the state prison. Rumors circulated that two-thirds of the shoes worn in the city would soon be made by convicts. The penitentiary, the largest "State-Workshop," possessed "immense capital," which "under the direction of an incorporated body of directors, [would] soon reduce the profits of the tradesman, and form a rival that it would be in vain to contend with. . . ." In Republican literature, these "gentlemen monopolisers" became stock whipping boys, said to possess the valued leisure to indulge in the finer things in life because they had at their command other men who depended on them for daily bread. Such exploiters were capable of any activity that would buy them the financial clout to ensure their status, even prostitution. So we can find a Livingston, Delaplaine, Lorillard, and Fisher gaining security and social standing for their families by surreptitiously selling the bodies of poor women.[44]

Republicans, in contrast, pictured themselves as men of simplicity and honest effort, working so hard for a living they had no time for cultural refinement, but upon whom "divolves the fate of almost every description of persons; in particular, the comfortable situation of the *poor*." This self-inflated sense of social responsibility was starkly conveyed in a tract on the future course of American society, published in 1801 by the Republican-affiliated Mechanics Society. It forecast the "critical situation *Mechanics* will be driven to, in the spirit of *combination* and *monopoly* of *Mechanic* branches, by *monied capitalists,* if not timely checked by our Legislature." The example cited was New York City's "bread company," which introduced "speculations into a number of other mechanic branches," employing the argument that *"Public good"* would be served since monopoly provides leverage for international trade. More immediately, "the connection which *monied* men have with Banks . . . will induce *them* to make it a common *concern,* to enter into the scheme of *rivalship* with mechanics in the line of their professions."[45]

As a class, mechanics were doomed when the legislature began chartering banks, for banking conducted on a national scale, by promoting mass production, undermined the independence and livelihood of the small producer. It robbed the little man of control of his product in exchange for tempting him to acquire goods that he did not really need, but that might serve to console his wounded pride.

His self-esteem might be periodically redeemed through personal identification with military expansion westward, for the delusion was widespread that "the return of PEACE will set *monied* and overgrown *capitalists,* in schemes to employ their money to advantage." Certainly, as president, Madison sought to give teeth to the expansionist solution put forth in *Federalist* No. 10 by involving the United States in the War of 1812. Banks benefited from military largesse, which has led Bray Hammond to conclude that "the evolution of banking in the United States has received from war some of its most powerful impulses."[46] Yet at the time, the democratic republican *American Citizen* stood opposed to this institutionalized militarization:

> The two great political parties by which our country has for several years been agitated, have . . . favoured every measure of our government which has had for its object the augmentations of the public burthens. They have acceded to the principle of a standing military force—they have voted away large sums of the public money for the equipment of a small useless navy.[47]

During the first quarter of the nineteenth century, bank opponents could find little solace in the domination of national politics by the Jeffersonian Republicans. Even though the Bank of the United States expired in 1811, a new national bank was chartered in 1816 at the height of Republican power. In these five years, the number of banks increased from 90 to 250. By 1821, they exceeded 300. Again, Hammond: "It is hard to imagine how banking could have been propagated more under its sponsors than it was under its enemies."[48] Until the devastating 1808 Embargo Act, the United States had been tied to the export and re-export trade. Within a generation, the economy reflected a diversity of enterprises funded by a multitude of "republican" banks.

The pipedream of accumulating vast wealth was accompanied by a general rise in the standard of living that placed New York City's bank opponents on the defensive. Three hundred mechanics and tradesmen, fearful of an inflationary paper currency that reflected the need to encourage international trade, formed "one great Association" to petition the legislature "not to incorporate monopoly." This was no radical collectivist anti-clerical grouping. Rather, it was an association in which the Typographical Society conceived of God as the "Great Compositor," and it venerated Benjamin Franklin as one "from whom small capital, acquired capital reputation." With the embrace of such entrepreneurial values, it is not surprising to find unabated consolidation in publishing, while printing-shop employees averaged seven dollars per week in wages.[49]

The Republican Party responded to the increasing scale of enterprises by supporting lower minimal property qualifications for voting, since the "right of property to a controuling influence in elections . . . leads to aristocracy."[50] In the vigorous election campaign of 1800, at a time when assemblymen were elected at large, not by ward, clusters of propertyless New York City men banded together to buy jointly held property. To many, it seemed that

> the Corporation has become a *close,* if not a *rotten* borough, the *property* of a few individuals . . . purchasing freeholds. . . . The refusal of the Corporation to confer the freedom of the city upon any mechanic or retailer of goods . . . renders it necessary . . . that he should become a proprieter of freehold property.[51]

In January 1801, amid Federalist charges that "mob" rule would ensue, Republicans presented a list of proposals to democratize election procedure, including employing the secret ballot for local municipal elections, limiting a person's franchise to the ward of residence, and allowing non-freeholders to vote for members of the Common Council. A ballot could be cast only by a male citizen who had resided in the city for six months prior to the election, rented a tenement for at least twenty-five dollars, and paid some tax. Meeting all these qualifications, he was then legally judged a "free man" eligible to vote in any election. Still, election inspectors continued to be plagued by men who spent one night in a ward in order to vote there the next day.[52]

In 1801, the votes of a few dozen poor Republicans in fourth- and fifth-ward contests afforded Tammany a Common Council majority. Two years later, electors chose one alderman, one assistant alderman, two assessors, one collector, and two constables for each ward; and a Common Council quorum consisted of mayor, recorder, at least five of the nine aldermen, and an equal number of assistant aldermen.[53] After a vociferous campaign conducted by both parties, the state legislature passed a law giving the vote to freeholders who were not freemen, thereby circumventing the city charter.

Politics in the early national period had not yet broken with the chief political legacy of the landed gentry—the rule of families whose ties were frequently augmented through banking connections. The important role that banks played is revealed in the political gyrations of Aaron Burr, De Witt Clinton, and Alexander Hamilton. In November 1803, Burr supporters were accused of secretly aligning themselves with Federalists. That year, Governor George Clinton, who enjoyed Irish support because he called for a reduction in the nationalization requirement from fourteen to five years, appointed his nephew De Witt as mayor of New York City. De Witt, ex-scribe to Tammany, sought to extend his powers at Tammany's expense. But when he attempted to ally politically with Burr so as to counteract Livingston-family influence over newly elected Governor Morgan Lewis, the mayor's popularity plummeted.[54]

Clinton had permitted ambition to overwhelm political sense. He had been made a director of, and exercised effective control over, the city's second bank, the Manhattan Company.[55] The city's first local bank, the Bank of New York established by Hamilton in 1784, had been granted monopoly control by the state over the city's banking needs. The Manhattan Company quietly arose fifteen years later, under the guise of a waterworks, when Republican leader Burr sponsored a charter bill in the New York State legislature. On December 3, 1804, with the state legislature offering a legal guarantee against competition, Clinton as mayor ordered city tax receipts transferred from the Bank of New York to the newer bank.

The Manhattan Company is a classic case of the common marriage between private enterprise and politics. Its public purpose was ostensibly to provide fresh water to the city to prevent yellow fever epidemics, which periodically forced a retreat of more prosperous inhabitants from lower Manhattan to what was then the separate bucolic village of Greenwich. Concealed in the text of the charter bill was a single clause investing this corporation with banking powers. According to Gregory Hunter, the supply of water was a secondary activity, while "the *real* focus of the company's efforts was banking. . . ." The Common Council debated whether it should "tax the citizens . . . to the amount of two or *three hundred thousand dollars* for the benefit" of the bank's stockholders so that the city could purchase the waterworks from the bank. This was not done; still, the Manhattan Company had become the city's second largest financial institution by 1840, and an important source of campaign funds for Democratic-Republican officials.[56]

The Bank of New York and the Manhattan Bank competed via the two parties and intensified the rivalry between Hamilton and Burr that resulted, in 1804, in Hamilton's death at Burr's hand. Two Tammany potentates acted as Burr's seconds. In a pistol duel the following year, Mayor Clinton wounded John Swarthout, the Manhattan Bank director. In 1806, the Federalists obtained a charter for another rival, the Merchant's Bank, by bribing state assemblymen. The only ensuing punishment was the removal of Teunis Wortman as city clerk for disclosing the scandal.[57]

Prior to the 1804 mayoral election, Tammany publicly announced the formation of a General Committee, made up of three delegates from each of the wards, to manage the Republican campaign. Each ward also sent seven delegates to an open convention at Martling's Tavern, Tammany headquarters, to choose candidates for municipal office. "Great popular meetings" were then arranged in each of the wards to "ratify the nominations." Ward associations, rooted as they were in the city's neighborhoods, struggled to act independently of a General Committee that employed "caucuses of the select few" against the will of the majority.[58]

As mayor of a city that had grown to more than one hundred thousand inhabitants, Clinton called the council into session, made all appointments in trades that provided municipal services like police and sanitation, and monitored liquor sales. In addition, together with the deputy mayor, recorder, and aldermen, he acted as ex-officio justice of the peace. He also lobbied on behalf of the Franklin Bank, whose president was subsequently charged with defrauding the public in 1826.[59] The jurisdictional wrangles among mayor, wards, and the state government at Albany generated considerable political heat, especially since governor and mayor belonged to the same family.

Mechanic altercations were more narrowly focused on other issues:

the increasing population . . . and the easy access [the city] affords to strangers . . . burthened . . . with . . . Paupers also with a numerous class . . . who, during a very considerable period of the year, are thrown off employment . . . and . . . are drawn by poverty and idleness, into . . . vice, or . . . crimes. This class is swelled too by a number of persons discharged from the State Prison.[60]

On New Year's Day 1803, the mayor submitted to the Mechanics Society a proposal to use one hundred thousand dollars in city corporation funds to erect, under the society's supervision, a manufactory that would employ a total of two hundred drawn from immigrant "strangers," the unemployed, widows and orphans able to work, and former state prison convicts. The society immediately rejected the proposal, even though it was similar to the one drawn up for London by Thomas Paine in his *Rights of Man.* The only assent came from Tammany's Grand Sachem, Matthew L. Davis.

The objections to the plan were many. One argument revolved around the mistaken belief that New York City's "lowest orders" were better fed and clothed than the English middle class. Another complaint, encouraged by the fact that Matthew L. Davis was also a brothel owner, was that this immigrant factory would become a breeding ground for vice; and it would pose severe competition for mechanic workshops because "the capital will be immense compared with that of the greatest manufacturer in this city." Although this project never materialized as a formal state enterprise, factories employing immigrants dominated by the end of the nineteenth century.[61]

Clinton's workhouse scheme was one more sign that the old republican order was breaking up owing to the growth of banking and manufacturing. The city had grown to a size that no longer bred familiarity of face and a civic republican sense of common purpose. Centralization of authority was occurring on both economic and political fronts, as masters achieved greater control over their journeymen and Tammany Hall extended its powers over the individual ward committees. The party required more personnel engaged in a greater variety of tasks that would address the growing complexity of economic and social life.

Democratic-Republicans created nominating, correspondence, ward, and vigilance committees to generate candidates and shepherd voters to the polls, and assigned the General Committee to oversee all these committee activities. As the party put down more roots in the social infrastructure, the political establishment, especially Mayor Clinton, became less tolerant of extra-legal behavior by mobs. The "appeal to the people," successfully applied during the War of Independence and the passage of the Constitution, could now be used to promote party unity. Complaints arose that the people must overcome faction or else "faction will enslave the party."[62]

Tammany Hall republicanized its appeals while the conflict sharpened with the British over commerce and westward expansion. Their racial character was expressed in the resolution of April 9, 1811. African Americans would now be compelled to submit proof of their freedom in order to vote in New York City, because as Tammany explained, white voters were becoming "the abject slaves of *family autocracy* or the victims of *federal tyranny.*"[63]

Tammany favored war more than any other party or faction and labeled its opposition as the "British tory peace ticket."[64] After armed skirmishes erupted on America's western frontiers, Clinton's softness on the issue of British impressment of American sailors allowed Tammany to strengthen its hold on the Republican organization. In 1812, just before war broke out, Clinton switched from the Republican to the Federalist American ticket to run for president. Tammany suspended display of Native American costumes at its ceremonial functions, since Native Americans occupied western lands and were allied with Great Britain. Still, the December local elections gave the Federalists control of the first, second, third, fourth, sixth, seventh, and ninth wards because the Jefferson-Madison embargo had crippled the premier port city.[65]

The power of agriculture as a tool in foreign policy had failed with the embargo. Only a nation that emphasized large-scale manufacturing could hope to challenge England or France for global domination. With war fast approaching, banking and manufacturing were assured a pivotal role. The bellicose farmer of the western frontier would play into the hands of the wily financier and crass capitalist, while the stubborn mechanic would reluctantly acquiesce to their lead. Neither farmer nor mechanic possessed a viable political alternative.

◅ 3 ▻

DEMOCRATIC REPUBLICANISM
UNLEASHED
1812–1833

Little by little, the aggressions of power steal unperceived upon the body
politic, like the debility of age upon the human frame. Twenty years ago
. . . a proposition to tax the present by a multiplication of monopolies, and
the future by a hopeless accumulation of debt, would have been repelled
either by moral or physical force. . . . The power of man to do mischief to
his species, is infinitely superior to that of doing good.
Colonel Samuel Young (1836)

In America, "the democrat is the conservative."
James Fenimore Cooper, *A Letter to his Countrymen* (1839)

It is a very difficult thing to be a democrat, and to be a member of what is
called the democratic party; for the first insists on his independence and
an entire freedom of opinion, while the last is incompatible with either.
James Fenimore Cooper, *The American Democrat* (1838)

———

With the political triumph of Jeffersonian republican
principles in the 1800 election, expectations again rose that virtue in common men could be enhanced by extending "The Empire
of Freedom." Washington Irving satirized such expansive talk when he
depicted a "Grand Procession . . . a grand Democratic Pantomimic Fete"
in which a horse disguised as an ostrich bore a standard "on which was
painted the words, 'Extension of the Empire of Freedom.' "[1] It was believed that the shedding of American blood in imperial adventure would
serve, in Stephen Watt's words, "as an exercise in self-sacrifice and an
antidote to luxury," and would bind together the divisions caused by
party. Instead, the War of 1812 became "an exercise in frustration, inept-
ness and survival."[2] As in the War of Independence, when France tipped

the military balance in the patriots' favor, the move of a stronger European power saved the United States from defeat. After burning the White House and beating Napoleon, British forces were content to withdraw from United States soil.

Once again, a united republican people had failed to arise. But there was hope. War against Native Americans yielded the land to fulfill republican dreams, although it also encouraged domestic manufactures accompanied by tariff protection that many regarded as "anti-republican."[3] Yet another effort on behalf of democratic republican virtue would be mounted in the 1840s to secure the freedom of slaveholding Texas.

Westward expansion and the extension of banking credit led only to agricultural growth, not to overall farm prosperity. The country was inundated with propaganda extolling the virtues of the plantation system, while no public attention was paid to the plight of the Northern farmer.[4] In acquiring the vast Louisiana land tract that doubled the size of the United States, not only did Jefferson stray from his publicly stated policy of narrowly interpreting the Constitution, but he also did more to guarantee slavery's growth than any other president. Five years later, Jefferson's embargo against British and French goods betrayed a naivete in agriculture's political power that crippled New York City's economy and led to the War of 1812.

This war did not enhance the status of the small producer as democratic republican dreamers had hoped. New York City's poor continued to grow poorer, particularly its African-American poor. City newspapers began to carry widespread reports of local poverty and prostitution, especially among children. The Society for the Prevention of Pauperism in the City of New York was established in 1817 to look into "the causes of the poorest want and misery among the poor" and to establish committees in each of the wards. On just one cold February day, it was charged with feeding 5,279 people. Four years later, it was estimated that there were 13,000 paupers out of a total population of 124,000 inhabitants.[5]

Nor did the War of 1812 bring political unity to New York City. In the 1813 elections, Democrats carried the fifth, sixth, seventh, eighth, and tenth wards, with the Federalists taking the rest—the second ward without any opposition. A year later at the Hartford Convention, the Federalists surrendered their national identity as a party when the New England section stood accused of plotting withdrawal from the United States to end the war. The New Englanders lamely defended their move, in retrospect, as one against "republican party . . . *policy*, not the *justice* of the war with England." In 1815, Tammany secured control of New York State's government, and in 1816, absolute control of the city's political offices. The Federalists then changed their name to National Republicans,[6] in an effort to project a more respectable image by appealing for a strong union in the face of the social anarchy allegedly fostered by Democratic-Republicans.

This theme of federal order versus democratic disorder would become the political leitmotiv for the Hamilton-Clay-Lincoln party, until civil war restored bloody order to millions of American households. But in the wake of the War of 1812, the party of federal law and order had reached its popular nadir in New York City. National Republicans survived only as the political vehicle of the Anglo-Dutch community and had to contend with the formidable political threat posed by General Andrew Jackson.

If for no other reason, another party had to exist to keep a check on the corruption of its rival. In 1817 and 1818, two former Tammany sachems, one grand sachem, and one future sachem—in their respective roles as sheriff of New York County, county clerk, U.S. surveyor of the Port of New York, and lottery keeper—were removed from office for stealing public funds and either were arrested or fled the city. Grand sachem and real estate mogul William Mooney sought to divert public attention by inviting the "Scourge of British insolence, Spanish perfidy and Indian cruelty"—Jackson—to a Tammany banquet held on February 23, 1819.[7] But instead of paying court to Tammany, Jackson praised Governor De Witt Clinton.

Clinton had fashioned his own political organization, the "People's ticket." He manipulated the concept of republicanism to personal political advantage, in part by cultivating the practice of referring to opponents as Tammanymen, Mooneyites, Martlingmen, Madisonians—while reserving the sobriquet *republican* for himself. Clinton succeeded in defeating most Tammany-backed assembly candidates and three congressmen, all Jackson supporters.[8]

The immorality bred of war, the Panic of 1819, and industrialization, accelerated the disparity between rich and poor. In the year of the panic, as if to signal the onslaught of the new industrial order, a New York City court with the mayor presiding as judge ruled that pigs could no longer roam the streets at will. Letting their pigs forage was a right artisans had enjoyed since the city's founding. Hendrik Hartog has concluded that "the mayor made the equal citizenship of all in the city a justification for an attack by wealthier citizens on the practices of poorer ones."[9]

Until the War of 1812, murders were rare in the city and merchants could leave their produce in the streets without fear of theft. While the population rose 63 percent between 1814 and 1834, the number of criminal complaints increased by more than 400 percent. Numerous personal bankruptcies resulted in appeals to abolish imprisonment for debt, while public executions did not deter crime. In fact, they were associated with a rise in the rate of capital crimes.[10]

A spirit of "reform" led to popular calls to abolish the state Council of Appointment, whose duties included selecting New York City's mayor. Sectional tensions sharpened party differences. In 1820, the Missouri Compromise congressionally guaranteed slavery's expansion for the first time, and city Republicans swept all eleven assembly seats. A year later, the Common Council was given the right to choose the city's mayor. Local control had been strengthened. With a state constitutional convention set for the same year, Democratic Republicans pleaded that "WE MUST ERADICATE FROM THE CONSTITUTION, ALL SEEDS OF DISCORD BETWEEN THE RICH AND POOR." The *National Advocate* questioned "whether the extension of the state suffrage . . . will be . . . sufficient to counter-balance the growing influence of wealth?"[11]

The issue of race prevented this growing economic inequality from generating a class-based party, especially since the men who raised the issue of rich versus poor were in the forefront of moves to disenfranchise African Americans. Democratic-Republican Colonel Samuel Young led this effort by attributing to "custom" the African Americans' "degraded" status, which rendered it "unsafe" to grant them the franchise. He would reconsider his position if in the future their condition should be "elevated to an equality with the whites." In the end, the delegates hammered out a racist compromise. While no restrictions were placed on European-American voters, African Americans had to own 250 dollars in property, a sum that excluded all but one hundred potential black voters. Contemporary Jabez Hammond found it to be

> somewhat curious that . . . Colonel Young, [and] Mr. Livingston . . . who were most anxious to abolish the property qualification and extend the right of suffrage to all white men, were equally zealous to exclude black citizens from the right to exercise the elective franchise; while those who most strenuously contended for retaining the freehold qualification as respected white citizens, were very solicitous to prevent an exclusion of the blacks from an equal participation with the whites.[12]

Hammond's analysis points to the importance advocates of democratic republicanism attached to the social exclusion of African Americans as cotton production and the demand for slaves accelerated. Phyllis Field has noted that "anti-suffrage forces showed little caution in their tactics and simply employed the common stereotype of the black to condemn equal suffrage." In contrast, pro-suffrage forces had to struggle against public opinion, and therefore were "guarded in their attacks on discrimination, relying primarily upon 'reason' to persuade people to change their racial views."[13] They were also more likely to emphasize suffrage restrictions on European immigrants, because they generally identified with an older federal elite who did not care about the color of its labor, so long as its labor behaved subserviently. To the left of both Democratic Republicans and National Republican Whigs were African Americans, who were more inclusive in their concept of democracy. They favored immediate abolition of slavery and no voting restrictions.

Whatever European-American support existed for the education of blacks came from the Federalist community. The *Commercial Advertiser,* alone among city newspapers, gave prominent coverage to the success that the Free School of New York had demonstrated in educating black youth during the first quarter of the nineteenth century. It had begun in 1806 with fifty pupils. Nine years later, a new school for black girls was built on William Street for $2250. Four years after that, $6800 went toward the construction of a boys' school on Mulberry Street. In 1823, 866 African-American children were educated at a cost of $1420; expenditures for 4,089 whites were $6706. It was claimed that no city white school was as well run, and that Southerners might learn something positive about blacks from this project. The *Commercial Advertiser* observed that the contrast could not have been greater between these African-American students and

> those idle ones who are suffered to grow up uncultivated, unpolished, and heathenish in our streets; and who for the want of care and instruction, are daily plunging in scenes of sloth, idleness, dissipation and crime, until they pass from step to step, into the state prison, and at last up to the gallows.

The reporter went on to point out that only three out of the thousands of blacks educated by the African Free School had ever been convicted of a crime, while "at every turn of the court of sessions . . . many blacks, generally from twelve to twenty, are convicted of crimes. . . ."[14]

Such sporadic favorable journalistic coverage could not outweigh the pro-slavery interests of the cotton merchants and clothing manufacturers who were at the heart of New York City's commerce. Their advertising provided an increasing source of revenue for the city's newspapers, a circumstance reflected in statistics for the cotton trade. In 1810, two-thirds of all clothing had been sewn at home, but during the 1820s, the South became the first market to fall to the nation's earliest mass-produced commodity—ready-made clothing, with its industry centered in New York City. A decade later, the city's clothing market had become national, with half the port's business.[15]

The national free trade in slaves was assumed and rarely mentioned in print, and then only in passing. Working conditions of European Americans received somewhat more coverage. The progressive economist Matthew Carey maintained that Northern workers were treated "far worse" than Southern slaves.[16] In one instance, a reporter portrayed journeyman carpenters as being forced "into a combination to raise their wages" against a coalition of builders and those master carpenters who recruited journeymen from other localities and states. Journeyman carpenters were following an organizational path already trod by masons, painters, glaziers, and other such skilled tradesmen. Masters secretly combined to deprive craftsmen of control over "*measure* and *value*," and received assistance from the city corporation, whose move to license butchers was characterized as "a lamentable comment on republicanism and equal rights." These feeble attempts at worker organization occurred in response to the expansion of markets that resulted in the reorganization of artisanal production and a worsening quality of life for African Americans after the Panic of 1819.[17]

The maturing banking system placed small individual producers—western farmers and eastern mechanics—at a competitive disadvantage in pursuing loans. They vainly rallied behind Andrew Jackson, whose rise to power in the 1820s became a catalyst for the second party system as the South moved to expand slavery and industry and agriculture raced westward into the Great Lakes region.

The greatest single spur to industrialization was the Erie Canal, the pet project of Governor Clinton that provided New York City with a direct link to the West through the Mohawk Valley. Democrats jeopardized their Irish support when, in their zeal to defeat Clinton, they attacked the canal as the "political project . . . of *one man*," while ten thousand people massed to acclaim him.[18] The immigrant Irish desperately needed the wages earned from digging a canal that gave New York City manufactures cheap transport to western markets and provided the most important new transportation link for industrial growth.

The Erie Canal exemplified the state-sponsored corporation that "nationalized" production and helped destroy the insular world of the artisan that prevailed in New York City prior to 1825. Capitalizing on the republican belief that "there can be no *Equality,* unless Property is in some way represented,"[19] such large, Democrat-sponsored projects generated more jobs for semiskilled immigrants than for skilled native artisans.

In the wake of the collapse of war-fueled land speculation that provoked the 1819 panic, industry surged forward in the 1820s as a seemingly more stable guarantor of America's independence and progress. It threatened, for the first time since the Middle Ages, to usurp the control artisans had traditionally maintained over manufacturing. The competition for jobs in this changing economy spilled over into conflicts between native Protestant artisans and immigrant Irish unskilled or semiskilled labor,[20] and also between Irish factions.

Symptomatic of the artisanal political dislocation created by industrialization was the Anti-Masonic movement, which served as the third-party catalyst for the second party system.[21] In 1826, an apostate Mason, William Morgan, disappeared in upstate New York and was presumed murdered by Masons upset over his revelations of their rituals. The ensuing political backlash swiftly coalesced into the Anti-Masonic Party. This first national opposition third party in U.S. history directed attention to the consolidating monopolistic course of the American political economy. It drew into its ranks a socially mixed group of men who saw a Masonic conspiracy behind the social dislocation caused by the growth of banking and industry. Its national prominence rested on keeping before the public eye the notion that a conspiratorial freemasonry was behind an anti-republican secret caucus dedicated to denying Jackson the presidency in 1824.

By enhancing Jackson's power, Democrats sought to mute some of the Anti-Masons' appeal. They supported the president's efforts to foster westward expansion by state land speculators not tied to the federal establishment. By 1832, though, Anti-Masons had become disenchanted with Jackson over his capitulation on the tariff issue. They fielded their own candidate, William Wirt, a Mason who for twelve years had been attorney general under Presidents James Monroe and John Quincy Adams. Thereafter, Anti-Masons declined in numbers, but not without having irreparably damaged Whig standard-bearer Henry Clay's chance of becoming president. Clay had thrown his electoral votes to John Quincy Adams in 1824, even though Jackson won a plurality of the popular vote. Many voters never forgave Clay for the anti-democratic move that made Adams president.

During the fractious 1824 presidential contest, New York City's ten Democratic-Republican ward organizations divided over Adams and Jackson. In October of the preceding year, Tammany Democratic-Republicans had held a political rally billed as the largest in the history of the city, while other republicans, who wanted to give "to the PEOPLE the choice of Presidential Electors," conducted a counterdemonstration. The wards had become so large and dense with inhabitants that subdistricts were created. The relative success of the Adams slate in the city can be attributed to Clinton's People's Party, whose coalition of "High-Minded" Federalists and anti-Crawfordites on behalf of Adams resulted in their choice for both governor and president being elected. Their orderly nomination process, which included the first delegated party convention in New York history, provided a model for political organization, not only for the Anti-Masons but also for the dominant parties.[22]

Democrats jealously criticized the People's Party for its emphasis on mere appearance of public input into decision making:

> A public meeting is called in the wards, and three persons are chosen from each to form a general committee . . . *from* the *people* . . . this committee issues a public notice, calling upon the people to meet and select from among themselves, *seven persons* from each ward, to constitute a nominating committee, to draft an assembly ticket. These seventy persons, the immediate representatives of the whole city . . . designate an assembly ticket . . . a general meeting of the people is called . . . the people are called upon to vote it . . . the *ticket of the people*. Now mark the contrast. . . . [Various officeholders] meet in conclave, and designate candidates from each ward—they call meetings—a friend is prepared to nominate a chairman and a secretary, and another friend draws from his pocket a ticket, prepared at the Marble House, which is adopted, and this abortion is called the *people's ticket*.[23]

The Democratic hierarchy was concerned about the threat that the anti-caucus faction of the People's ticket, together with the Anti-Masons, posed to their control of the nomination process.

Key to Tammany electoral successes was the staged "regularity" of Democratic-Republican nominations. Tammany stalwart Teunis Wortman had warned, "The nominating power is an omnipotent one. Though it approaches us in the humble attitude of the *recommendation,* its influence is irresistible. Every year's recommendations are commands. That instead of presenting a choice it deprives us of all option."[24] In reaction to this authoritarian trend, anti-caucus men "refused" to attend the 1820 state constitutional convention.[25]

Four years later, Adams won with People's Party's support, even though Jackson received a plurality of the popular vote. The popular outcry against this presidential outcome was the greatest until Lincoln's victory in 1860. In both the 1824 Adams and 1860 Lincoln contests, most Democrats felt cheated by the electoral college. The watershed election of 1824 represented a betrayal by Clay of "republicans beyond the mountains.[26]" With Jackson denied the presidency, Democrats co-opted the one significant Anti-Masonic organizational innovation, a national nominating convention designed to eliminate "King Caucus." This innovation added to Jackson's victory margin in 1832 and assisted Democratic-Republicans in becoming just plain Democrats twelve years later.

In 1828, dissatisfaction with the corruption fed by the traditional two-party system had led in New York, among other cities, to the founding of the Workingmen's Party. According to Fitzwilliam Byrdsall, one of its founders as well as its official historian, it was "the progenitor, to some extent, of the Equal Rights [Loco Foco] Party."[27] The Workingmen and their Loco Foco successors strove for a coalition of yeomen and artisans to preserve a pristine democratic republicanism that relegated blacks to slavery.[28]

These minor parties did not constitute a premature manifestation of proletarian consciousness, as one might categorize the United States labor movement of the 1870s and 1880s that arose from a qualitatively different southern and eastern European tradition.[29] While in England the massacre of the unemployed and their families at Peterloo furthered class consciousness, in the United States massacres of Native Americans by Democrat Jackson and Whig Harrison galvanized Northern workers and western farmers in support of politicians who advanced capitalism.[30]

In land-poor Great Britain, social conflicts were articulated in class terms, while in a land-rich America, they were directed westward. Bipartisan attacks on Indians by republican settlers eager to fence in Native American land promoted political cohesion between classes. The defeat of the powerful Indian chieftain Tecumseh in 1812 by future president William Henry Harrison and Jackson's 1818 attacks on the Seminoles and his barbaric uprooting of the Cherokee held immense political appeal for the European-American lower classes, even among those who favored a third party.

The Workingmen's Party reaffirmed Jeffersonian principles in an economic environment that appeared to vindicate the values of Alexander Hamilton. It constituted a reaction to the new economic order that concentrated capital and resources in the hands of financiers and capitalists. Workingmen were not the unskilled or semiskilled, but artisanal small manufacturers and tradesmen with the same mercenary values as the larger capitalists, and they were eager to curtail the latter's appetite for self-aggrandizement in order to advance their own interests. With the exception of Thomas Skidmore, every one of the Workingmen's leaders condoned slavery. Their political program focused on land reform—more muddy, stumpy turf for the "republican pig," as Dickens put it.[31]

At its inception, the Workingmen's Party attracted visionary figures like Frances Wright, America's first publicly recognized women's rights advocate. Wright employed polemics similar to Paine's in attacking the right to inherited property.

Soon, however, the Workingmen's key demand became the return of unused speculative property to the public domain. Undeveloped land, as well as the National Bank's increase of the money supply from 12 million dollars at the beginning of 1829 to 21 million two years later, were blamed for the inflation that eroded the fortunes of average men.[32]

Workingmen feared banks because banks fostered monopoly, and they opposed "labor saving machines by which drones are enabled to grow rich without honest industry."[33] They sought to preserve a preindustrial production that existed in harmony with slavery. When a Workingman was criticized for being a "radical," he was being cast as "an old Republican of the Jefferson school. His object is a radical reformation of all the responses, abuses and extravagances which have found their way into our government since the year 1800."[34]

In Sean Wilentz's forty-five-page account of the Workingmen in *Chants Democratic*, of which twenty-four pages is devoted to Thomas Skidmore, he ignores the slavery issue, except to note that Skidmore was against it.[35] The impression is conveyed that Workingmen opposed slavery. But Skidmore's faction never received more than one-half of 1 percent of the popular vote. The other 99½ percent accommodated slave interests.

Thirty-seven years ago, Walter Hugins summed up New York City's Workingmen as "expressing, not a proletarian animosity to the existing order, but the desire for equal opportunity to become capitalist themselves."[36] Yet Wilentz slights Hugins's conclusions, which were based on solid quantitative evidence. If indeed, as Wilentz claims, "ordinary artisans rallied to the Working Men,"[37] then they did so imbued by a desire to maintain or achieve petty master status. Samuel Savetsky and Lee Benson have argued that the Workingmen's roots were in Tammany Hall, while Wilentz has countered that they developed independently of the Democrats. Either way, one is hard-pressed to disagree with Hugins's assessment that "as representatives of this working class, the Workingmen were struggling against law-created privilege, rather than attacking the business community of which they considered themselves actual or potential members."[38] In fact, as Susan Hirsch has observed, "Industrialization was not alien to, but often emanated from, the preindustrial American artisan class, and the inventiveness, entrepreneurship, and capital of small producers was a vital force in early nineteenth-century industrialization."[39]

Both Hugins and Wilentz used voting returns to demonstrate the success Workingmen had in drawing votes from the National Republican Party.[40] In 1829, the Workingmen had their best showing at the polls in New York City, receiving six thousand votes and one assemblyman to Tammany's eleven thousand votes and eight assembly seats, while the National Republicans took two seats. In the 1830 campaign, by an allegedly bribed one-vote margin, Tammany reelected banker Walter Bowne to the mayoralty; he then returned as grand sachem of the party. The Workingmen then split into three factions and, less than a year later, dissolved. Abetting this process was a Democratic-Republican Party, reinvigorated by the Jackson presidency, with a sophisticated organizational structure and ideological flexibility that allowed it to outmobilize the opposition.

More than any other man, Andrew Jackson served as the catalyst for the dissolution of the Workingmen's Party and its reabsorption into the Democratic Party through the agency of the Loco Focos, a process that took over a decade to complete. And more than any other man, Martin Van Buren was instrumental in securing citywide ward support for Jackson's presidential candidacy.

Van Buren's superior organizational skills overwhelmed Adams's political supporters. He led a newly systematized Democratic-Republican

Party in capturing the fourth through fourteenth wards in 1828, while the older, richer wards voted for Adams. For the first time in the history of New York City journalism, the day-to-day electoral activities of a political organization were routinely reported. Election fraud ultimately increased Jackson's margin to five thousand votes out of twenty-five thousand cast, the largest percentage margin separating the two major parties to that date in New York City history.[41] When De Witt Clinton died before Jackson's inauguration, the president became the undisputed figurehead of the Democratic-Republican Party in New York State.

Jackson's political stature grew in a New York more prosperous than any major city in Europe, despite the severe winter of 1828–29 and the acute suffering it caused among the poor. Even though rents were high, boardinghouses were more numerous and tenements roomier than the hovels immigrants had left behind. For the artisan, indoor plumbing became the norm; gas lighting and central heating were common for an emerging middle class whose standard of living increased relative to the working class. Dickens marveled, as Irving had done forty years earlier, at the colorful clothing seen on Broadway.[42]

The city's expansion astounded contemporary observers. Poe, having paddled up the East River to a spot off what is now Manhattan's fabulously rich Sutton Place, lamented the inevitable:

> I could not look on the magnificent cliffs, and stately trees, which at every moment met my view, without a sigh for their inevitable doom—inevitable and swift. In twenty years, or thirty, at farthest, we shall see here nothing more romantic than shipping, warehouses, and wharves.[43]

Before 1820, the business district had been centered below Maiden Lane, while city inhabitants were concentrated below Broome Street.

The *National Advocate* declared that New York "now contains more freemen and more wealth than any of the Republics of the Grecian peninsula." But the wealth was unevenly distributed. Prosperous as the nation's most populous city had become, ward committees to assist the poor indicated that poverty had become institutionalized. Extreme poverty was now a permanent feature of the American urban landscape. After Jackson's first presidential bid in 1824, riots occurred with greater frequency. The normative standard by which artisans evaluated a larger society had been strategically weakened by capitalist competition and state support for entrepreneurs. Legislation—An Act to Create a Fund for the Benefit of Creditors of Certain Monied Corporations—created a safety-fund banking system that guaranteed note redemption for insolvent banks. Insolvent artisans had to rely on their own devices.[44]

The second party system meant more than new parties; it meant the legislature's surrender of traditional artisan enterprise to the new order of banking and finance. This is why New York City Democratic-Republicans attached the greatest significance to the reelection of Andrew Jackson. They recognized that voter discontent was high given the sea change taking place in the economy. They characterized the contest as "the second great political era in the history of our constitution . . . the second struggle between the two great parties."[45]

Contemporary diarist Philip Hone judged Jackson to be "certainly the most popular man we have ever known. Washington was not so much so . . . he was superior to the homage of the populace . . . men could not approach him with familiarity. Here is a man who suits them exactly. He has a kind expression for each . . . but each thinks it intended for himself. . . ." As if to usher in this earthy brand of politics, Charles Carroll, the last signer of the Declaration of Independence, died in 1832.[46]

Jackson's supporters claimed that big government blocked the mobility of the average man, whether frontiersman or eastern laborer. The Democracy, as they now called themselves, sought to promote America as a republican confederacy of small independent producers in harmony with plantation slavery. They extolled equality of opportunity in the marketplace, which included the right of men to traffic in slaves. Jackson men were at odds with the older eastern mercantile establishment, exemplified by influential Whig merchants like Hone and George Templeton Strong, whose diaries provide insight into elite values. Jackson's frontier image displeased them, until they recognized that his substance was less threatening to their interests than his style was offensive to their traditions.

To minimize the threat Jackson's democracy could pose to propertied interests, the New York City charter was amended in 1830 to separate the mayor, still not yet popularly elected, from the city council, now divided into two distinct legislative bodies—the board of aldermen and the board of assistant aldermen. Each had veto power over the other, but the mayor had the final say. According to Alexander Saxton, Whigs believed that "without the continuity of upper-class culture, without the refinements of education and moral sensibility that flowed from it, a nation . . . would find itself . . . defenseless against ignorant leaders or vicious pretenders."[47]

The second party system emerged as New York City began to require services for which there was no organizational precedent, such as aqueduct-supplied water and a professional police department. The new charter therefore provided for the creation of regular departments under Common Council supervision. The potential for graft increased exponentially. Private entrepreneurs received city contracts to build rail lines, pave streets, and cart wastes, all at inflated cost to the public. Tied to downturns in the business cycle for which scapegoats had to be found, greedy politicians periodically found themselves censured as public object lessons for demanding too much material incentive during the economic growth that modernized the political system in a manner helpful to private interests.

The aldermen's sale of city land to private developers for a handsome and secret profit merely whetted the appetites of party officials. The relegation of workers to older housing added to a growing sense of inequality among the general public.[48] A construction boom scarcely kept pace with the rapid growth in population. Hone reported as follows:

> The city is now undergoing its usual annual metamorphosis; many stores and houses are being pulled down, and others altered, to make every inch of ground productive to the utmost extent. Pearl Street and Broadway in particular are rendered almost impassable by the quantity of rubbish with which they are obstructed, and by the dust which is blown about by a keen northwest wind.[49]

Led by Martin Van Buren, New York City Democrats stood to benefit from the capital released by dismantling the Second Bank of the United States, the cornerstone of Whig policy. They opposed in principle the use of the federal tariff to accumulate capital for mercantile corporations like the National Bank, preferring instead to have Tammany lobby the state legislature into granting charters to banks on whose executive board Tammany citizen-warriors might serve. To the public, however, Tammany proclaimed its opposition to any "manufacturing party," boasting that in its "stronghold of Democracy would be found no 'Swiss' Federalism, no British partizans, no opponents of the late war, no bribers or bribed for bank charters, no trimming politicians, no lobby members of legislative brokers."[50]

Bribing or lobbying the New York State legislature ensured bigger profits for bigger businesses through the nineteenth century. In the early days of the Republic, Tammany attributed corruption to Tories and their wealthy associates. Over the course of a generation, Whigs were successful in passing the public stigma of corruption onto foreigners, mainly the poorer Irish, even though the available evidence suggests that immigrant involvement in corruption was proportionate to their numbers in the general population.[51]

The offering of a bribe had once been considered as serious as taking one. The balance of this moral equation changed when New York City lost its corporate autonomy in 1824. Private entrepreneurs were now free to develop the city as they saw fit, and through the new corporate charters, they gained official state protection as well as largesse,[52] creating, in Poe's words, "aristocracies of dollars."

Newly created corporations played a prominent role in New York State economic development from Jefferson through Jackson. Before 1800, the city had only 28 business corporations. In the next ten years, 179 businesses were incorporated, while in the 1830s the figure was 573. Their number multiplied thanks to a general incorporation act, which replaced specific incorporation acts. The proliferation of charters of incorporation led the rich to withdraw from politics, leaving their political surrogates, the politicians, to legislate on their behalf. Meanwhile, they continued to reap major benefits through insider trading information and other practices designed to circumvent the law.[53]

The level of scandal reached a new peak in 1826. Tammany sachem Jacob Barker, the most important bankroller of Madison's War of 1812, and members of the board of directors of his Exchange Bank had invested the life savings of mechanics and laborers in failed companies. The two most powerful politicians involved, Barker and Matthew L. Davis, although convicted, did not go to prison; the less powerful did, but for no more than two years. This case illustrates the inverse relationship between proximity to control of the means of production and likelihood of prison sentence that characterizes the American criminal justice system.[54]

Barker, Davis, and their cohorts had hastened the demise of the artisan in favor of the larger banking and manufacturing interests, concentrated in the southernmost wards, that were transforming New York City and forcing its less fortunate inhabitants northward. By Jackson's second term, the commercial district ran along the East River to Catherine Slip, while residents lived as far north as Fourteenth Street. Only about 10 percent of the inhabitants now lived south of city hall, and only a third resided south of Canal and Chatham Streets.[55] To all practical intent, New York had ceased to be a walking city.

It was during the second quarter of the nineteenth century that a new middle class asserted itself in the political arena.[56] To be sure, it did not define itself as being in the middle until the 1850s, when the corporate form of enterprise generated significant numbers of clerical and retail service workers who distinguished themselves from blue-collar workers, skilled or unskilled. The middle class arose from an industrialized republicanism that bolstered the standing of a middling interest between rich and poor, as class divisions replaced the rank ordering of earlier times. Unlike artisan republicans, this middle class depended on and supported the new industrial order. Yet like the working class, this middle class fractured along ethnic lines according to time of arrival and skills. The newer immigrants favored those policies that emphasized economic development over regulation, roughly dividing the older, mainly Protestant immigrants from the more recently arrived Catholics. In the half-century beginning in the 1830s, Germans took a disproportionate share of the skilled jobs, while the Irish filled the ranks of the unskilled.[57]

Acting to further divide the older crafts from newer industry was the tariff. Artisans complained that "the tariff strikes directly at the interests of our chair makers, carriage makers, merchant tailors, jewellers, cabinet makers, hatters and shoemakers." Immigrants supported the tariff if they worked in factories to produce goods not protected from European competition. In addition to foreign competition, shoddy, "defective and smuggled" goods sold through public auction undermined standards of workmanship.[58] Jackson's banking deregulation policies, the creation of New York's Governor Martin Van Buren, contributed to a deterioration in the quality of life for the average New York City resident.

Space was at a premium. The desire to build on every plot of green intensified. The "development" of City Hall Park brought the following lament:

> The sole good of a community does not consist in making every inch of ground produce some pecuniary profit. . . . It will be a bold enterprise of the Common Council if they undertake to barter the health and commerce of New York, to sell the air we breathe and the light of heaven over our heads for a few paltry thousands.[59]

Poe predicted the "prevalent shanties of the Irish squatters" would "thirty years hence . . . be densely desecrated by builders of brick, with portentious *facades* of brown-stone or brown-*stonn,* as the Gothamites have it."[60]

Property rights were more important than human rights. The watch received a bounty for recovering stolen property, but not for capturing murderers. This anti-human set of values led to a rise in the number of unsolved homicides, so in 1833 the city offered a 250 dollar reward for information leading to conviction.[61] Eight years later, a Common Council committee determined that the watchmen's "leisure is devoted to studying the ways of criminals, to learning their language, discovering their crimes, and thus accumulating knowledge, not for the purpose of preventing crimes, but for the purpose of getting rewards." The watchmen were also accused of encouraging crime in order to collect the fees.

In 1845, when a regular salaried police force was established, fees and rewards were officially disallowed, but corruption continued unabated. Ten years later, a number of police justices were indicted, including one who allowed persons arrested for assault and battery to be released on their own recognizance. Another justice sentenced an Irishman to the state penitentiary for forty years for stealing six cents, while releasing another man guilty of a felony.[62]

Prosperity continued to be unevenly distributed, even though New York City was now "the mighty metropolis" and claims were made that the years of the early 1830s were "the most prosperous period the country ever saw. . . ."[63] In the decade ending at mid-century, the cellar-dwelling population increased threefold, to 29,000 persons. The most optimistic forecast placed the city's population at 540,000 by 1855 but added, "it can hardly be expected that this rate of increase will continue." Actually, that figure was surpassed by 90,000.[64]

New York City's African-American population did not share in the city's economic bounty, nor did it obtain any greater social or political acceptance. Instead, led mainly by their Protestant ministers, African Americans became more involved in the abolition movement, an opportunity unavailable to their Southern brethren laboring under the legal barbarisms of slavery. Since the American Revolution, freed blacks, especially in urban centers like New York, had been in the forefront of both the struggle against slavery and the opposition to the American Colonization Society's efforts to transport blacks to Liberia.[65]

On July 4, 1827, slavery was abolished in New York State. Two African-American New Yorkers, Presbyterian minister Rev. Samuel F. Cornish and John B. Russworm, the first American black college graduate, had on March 16 begun publishing *Freedom's Journal,* the first African-American periodical. Their effort was inspired by a racist diatribe from Mordecai M. Noah, grand sachem of Tammany Hall and owner-editor of the *National Advocate,* the Tammany organ. Some time later, as a court of sessions judge, Noah instructed the New York grand jury to indict anyone at the American Anti-Slavery Convention who advocated the abolition of slavery. Noah was also conspicuous as the promoter of "Jim Crow" Daniel Rice, the first white clown in black face. In 1829, *Freedom's Journal,* mild in its protestation against colonization and slavery, was succeeded by the more militant *The Rights of All.*[66]

Artisans generally opposed African Americans' efforts to improve their lives. When the General Trades Union of the City of New York came into being in 1833, it elected Democratic Party stalwart and anti-abolitionist Ely Moore as president. With the exception of hackney coach drivers and the African-American chimney sweeps, all other licensed trades routinely practiced both segregation and the exclusion of recent immigrants like the Irish and the Germans. Successful blacks increasingly became targets of white violence. Pro-colonization whites spearheaded the anti-black riots of the 1830s, which would not be surpassed in intensity until the Civil War. In reaction, the city passed new regulations that forbade blacks to be employed as cartmen.[67]

In the 1830s and 1840s, mass participation in material consumption masked growing social inequalities. Nationally, slave ownership increased, albeit at a slower, more concentrated pace than earlier, while per capita land ownership declined. Public perception of that process was obscured by the proliferation of manufactured goods with many people plunging into a frenzy of selling themselves with their wares. The photograph on page 58 gives an idea of the resulting scene. It was, as Dickens recorded it, "a pantomime . . . where everybody is a merchant, resides above his store; so that many occupations are often carried on in one house and the whole front is covered with boards and inscriptions."[68]

Hudson Street c. 1865, from the collection of The New-York Historical Society.

THE LOCO FOCOS

Anti-bank, Anti-black, and Democratic Republican,
1828–1840

History affords many examples of nations struggling for their rights against priests and against kings, but this is the first instance of a people contending for its liberties against corporations.
"Thoughts on the Times," *United States Magazine and Democratic Review,* December 1839

The amount of depradations in various ways committed by the banks of the United States upon the people, far exceed what any invading army could have perpetrated, so far as property is considered only.
Fitzwilliam Byrdsall, *The History of the Loco-Foco or Equal Rights Party* (1842)

A great majority of our merchants are unformed men, placed in a situation of unusual temptation to discover the lower qualities, and there is no *collected* superior class to look them down, in the country.
James Fenimore Cooper to Horatio Greenough, July 1, 1838

If the law were to bind a free and independent citizen to keep his word with the public, what would become of liberty of the subject? Besides, it is the way of trade.
Charles Dickens, *American Notes* (1842)

DURING JACKSON'S PRESIDENCY, NORTHERN VISTAS WERE TRANS-
FORMED AS "COTTON MILLS AND RAILROADS REPLACED MOUNTAINS
and cataracts."[1] Southern horizons expanded with more land, more slaves, and more cotton—rendering the South ever more dependent on slavery and needy of Mexican territory and a war to gain it. The anti-slavery New York City Committee of Vigilance reported that "pro-slavery spirit pervaded the free states."[2]

was thick with praise for westward expansion, even if
. In this respect, he distinguished himself from Henry
who went to jail to protest the war that Whitman cele-
of the Democratic *Brooklyn Daily Eagle*, Whitman pro-
or the interest of mankind that its power and territory
ded—the farther the better. We claim these lands, thus by
to parchments and dry diplomatic rules."[3] His sentiments
of New York City Whig merchant Edward Tailer, who
confided to his diary, "America exists to reproach and reform the world.
. . . The rough and ready republicans expand themselves over a universe."[4]

Charles Dickens took issue with this democratic republican perspective. On his very first day in America, he denounced slavery as "that most
hideous blot and foul disgrace," and called for the restoration of "the
forest and the Indian village; in lieu of stars and stripes, let some poor
feather flutter in the breeze; replace the streets and squares by wigwams;
and though the death-song of a hundred haughty warriors fill the air, it
will be music to the shriek of one unhappy slave." From a railroad car
Dickens could see "great tracts where settlers had been burning down the
trees, and where their wounded bodies lay about, like those of murdered
creatures, while here and there some charred and blackened giant reared
aloft two withered arms, and seemed to call down curses on his foes."[5]

In a New York vaunting its textile products, halting the expansion of
Southern slavery was of no concern to immigrants beset by the need for
food and shelter.[6] Indeed, Tammany Hall claimed to publicly advance
immigrants' interests by actively promoting the idea that Southern slavery
created jobs for New Yorkers. No wonder most European Americans
supported slavery's expansion. Even James Fenimore Cooper, the most
renowned American author of the time, felt that freeing the slaves would
introduce into society "a body of men who had been nurtured in the
habits of slavery, with all their ignorance and animal qualities. . . ."[7]

Insecure immigrants and downwardly mobile artisans were encouraged
to believe that no matter how immiserated they became, psychological
satisfaction could be found in notions of white supremacy. Jackson's democracy strengthened this belief in racial "purity," while presiding over
the rise of a factory system that diminished artisan numbers and independence. Many journeymen and apprentices faced a bleak future indeed as
they saw their craft skills divvied up among factory workers. These fu-
tureless men were encouraged by Democratic Party activists to vent in-

dignation upon the most visible of scapegoats—free blacks—so that after 1830, racial segregation intensified in New York City. And so did support for slavery.[8]

Still, a small but distinguished body of northeasterners had determined that slavery must be abolished. Led by William Lloyd Garrison, they established the New England Anti-Slavery Society in January of 1832. Garrison's followers concentrated their efforts against the American Colonization Society, mentioned in the preceding chapter, which had been inspired by Thomas Jefferson and founded in 1816 to deport to Africa free blacks and aged slaves whom masters no longer cared to support. Future Whig leader Henry Clay presided over the American Colonization Society's inaugural meeting, while former President James Monroe, Chief Justice John Marshall, and Southern slaveholders lent their moral weight to the project.[9]

During 1833, a split developed between Northern and Southern members of the Colonization Society as overall cash donations dropped by two-thirds. This development should not be interpreted to mean that racism was on the decline. Rather, hostility to African Americans had grown to such proportions that any "assistance," even moving them out of the country to Liberia, no longer drew support from European Americans.

The Colonization Society's angry New York City members, spearheaded by James Watson Webb, editor of the *Courier and Enquirer*, determined to assault the inaugural meeting of the New York City Anti-Slavery Society scheduled for October 2. Webb denounced abolitionists for violating the Constitution and endangering the union of states. He led fifteen hundred New Yorkers in forcibly preventing abolitionists from convening at Clinton Hall. The anti-abolitionists then met at Tammany Hall to pass resolutions denouncing anti-slavery activity. Afterward, they rushed the Chatham Street Chapel where it was thought the abolitionists had reconvened. But the abolitionists had dispersed after electing silk merchant Arthur Tappan as their president. In frustration, the racists seized "a wretched looking old black" and forced him to preside over a mock session that passed a resolution demanding "immediate amalgamation."[10]

Fear of amalgamation, or racial intermarriage, was integral to the ideology of democratic republicanism, which felt challenged as well by Jackson's removal of federal funds from the National Bank to state banks. His action provoked a severe restriction of credit by National Bank director

Nicholas Biddle. The result was that investment declined and unemployment soared. Even so, fifty-six new banks were created in New York State from 1830 to 1834. Hone recorded that "the times are dreadfully hard." To handle the most recalcitrant of the hard-timers, New York City constructed the Tombs. Erected on the spot where the waters of the Collect Pond had shimmered in colonial times, this grim stone prison stood adjacent to Five Points, the slum that provided so many of the Tombs' victims. Iron-barred cells replaced the apartments of the old Bridewell Prison, and African-American prisoners were confined to the worst cells.[11]

Jackson's opponents, the National Republicans, characterized his actions as monarchical, a usurpation of legislative power by the executive. They changed their name to Whigs, in a historical allusion to the struggle that had taken place in late-eighteenth-century England when supporters of Parliament became Whigs in opposition to the king's men, or Tories. Although Democratic-Republicans and Whigs debated the status of the National Bank, they both agreed that abolitionists constituted a criminal nuisance.

The city's first popular mayoral election, conducted from April 8 to April 10, 1834, became a referendum on the National Bank when Democratic-Republican candidates for office signed an anti-monopoly pledge. *The Man,* a journalistic offshoot of the Workingmen's Party, extolled Andrew Jackson: "The Bank men are pestering the President . . . but the old General stands firm, as he did at New Orleans when he had a less subtle foe to contend with." *The Man's* editors were more concerned about banks than about slavery. They reported that almost three hundred of the city's few thousand cartmen had been induced by the "Paper Money Aristocracy" of the Whig Party "to oppose the removal of the deposites" from the National Bank. Yet they accepted without protest the removal of African-American New Yorkers to slavery in the South.[12]

For the three days of polling, the two parties each outfitted a ship on wheels, appropriately named *Constitution* and *Veto,* for use in transporting supporters to the polls. Whigs felt Jackson had violated the Constitution when he vetoed the National Bank, while *The Man* viewed the election as "clearly a contest of *Property* against *Poverty;* the rich against the poor; the Bank Aristocracy against the People." It added that,

THE MAN WHO CONTROLS A BANK, CONTROLS ALL WHO ARE INDEBTED TO THAT BANK; AND THUS BY SANCTIONING THE MERETRICIOUS UNION

OF MONEY WITH POWER, YOU DELIVER UP YOUR COUNTRY INTO CHAINS WHICH NOTHING BUT A DIVINE INTERPOSITION CAN EVER BREAK OR DISSOLVE.[13]

In its inaugural issue, *The Man* had inquired of its readers: *"What should be our condition as Republicans?* As republicans, we should legalize *no inequalities;* and recognize none but those of nature." In practice, this Lockean perspective relegated women, African Americans, and Native Americans to "separate spheres."[14]

On the afternoon of the first day of polling, a disturbance erupted in the Irish Democratic-Republican sixth ward. It began when pro-bank Whig clerks streamed from the first and second wards to the sixth ward, offering forty dollar voting bribes and vilifying anti-bank men.[15] When the clerks reached the sixth ward, fighting broke out, but property damage was minimal because city merchants, anticipating possible unrest, had closed their shops three days before.

The clerks then retreated to Masonic Hall and organized a new march into the sixth ward, led by the *Constitution* wagon. A brick-throwing crowd assailed the four horses drawing the wagon, and several injuries were sustained before both sides withdrew. The second day of polling took place without violent incident. On the morning of the third day, an Irishman was assaulted in front of Masonic Hall. An Irish crowd marched to Whig headquarters to avenge the beating, and hundreds took part in a bloody brawl. Whigs, hastily deputized and lacking badges and uniforms, quelled the riot. A number of these watchmen were badly hurt; one subsequently expired from his wounds. Whigs then ransacked the arsenal for guns. Thousands of men milled about. The mayor intervened and mustered the city militia, and the arms were returned. After the polls closed, the militia escorted the sixth-ward ballot box to city hall.[16]

When the results were announced on April 11, Democrat Cornelius Lawrence had defeated Gulian "Rag Money" Verplanck by 179 votes with 35,000 ballots cast, but the Whigs captured a majority of the Common Council. Hone blamed rich Democratic New Yorkers—bankers Preserved Fish and George D. Strong, merchant Abraham Le Roy, and Dr. John R. Rhinelander, among others—for instigating what he deemed an Irish attack. *The Man* attributed the disorders to the Whig leadership's "connection with the aristocracy, the Rothschilds and the Barings, of monarchical Europe, through the means of monied and trading monopolies. . . ."[17] However, these views did not alter the fact that the authority of the elite had not been effectively challenged; frustrations had been electorally channeled.

Three months later, the nation's worst anti-abolitionist riot began on the Fourth of July at Chatham Chapel when European-American workingmen broke up an abolitionist meeting. Abolitionists repulsed a second racist offensive on July 7, but not without some of their men being beaten and jailed. One of the black victims, Rev. Samuel Ringgold Ward, remarked in his autobiography that the attack had been "gathered and sustained by the leading commercial and political men and journals," who were imbued with the mobbish spirit of democratic republicanism and were zealous to stop even a legal public meeting of African Americans. His analysis is supported by Paul O. Weinbaum's readings of New York City's newspapers, which reveal the extent to which journalists concocted stories and editors instigated violence, with "almost the entire press not at first even condemning the rioting."[18]

Physical attacks against African Americans and their supporters raged from July 8 through 11. On the ninth, Bowery ruffians attacked abolitionists and also the Bowery Theater, because an English actor had allegedly disparaged Yankees; "anglophobia" reinforced a prime U.S. foreign policy objective, namely, the seizure of the Territory of Oregon from Great Britain. The same mob broke into the house of abolitionist silk merchant Lewis Tappan, forcing the mayor to personally intervene. On the tenth they marched down the Bowery to attack the Chatham Street Chapel. On the eleventh and twelfth, several thousand men, including many sailors stirred to violence by an anti-amalgamation speech that focused on black men and white women, demolished the African Episcopal Church. They then roamed Five Points singling out African-American homes for destruction. Out of fear or complicity, the white residents of Five Points placed candles in their windows to demonstrate support for the rioters. This gesture allowed the mob to single out African-American homes for destruction.[19]

A month later anti-black riots in Philadelphia followed a similar pattern. Bruce Laurie has established that the rioters were lower class in composition and leadership and that they enjoyed community support.[20] There is no reason to doubt that this was also the case in New York City. In both episodes, an interethnic, chauvinistic European-American coalition was active, one that would help define the American national character.

Years later, Rev. S. S. Jocelyn provided an eyewitness account of the

1834 anti-abolitionist riot that linked anti-black with anti-bank sentiment: "The mob had become more and more emboldened and reckless, seeking not only to wreak their vengeance upon obnoxious individuals, but to plunder the banks."[21]

Artisans had absorbed the Democratic Party's republicanism. They fought for the retention of their craftsmanship which, tragically for an individual's self-worth, represented an outmoded form of production standing in the way of the kind of machine-made production that led to American global power. These mechanics sought equitable land distribution and public control of the banks they assailed for eroding their control over enterprise and trade.[22]

In political behavior and social positioning, successful artisans became the chrysalis of the middle class as they set themselves off from the rich and the poor and from African Americans. By attacking anti-slavery societies, mechanics helped confine blacks to the bottom of the labor hierarchy, while at the same time promoting trade with the South.[23] The presence of slavery allowed artisans, who had traditionally employed slaves in colonial days, to perceive themselves as superior to the poor, while remaining suspicious of the rich, who thanks to preferential treatment by the banks, grew richer at the expense of the general population.

The bank issue divided Democrats from Whigs and provoked a split among Democrats into pro-bank Tammany and an independent anti-bank faction calling itself Loco Foco. Anti-bank Democrats conceived of the conflict in classic republican terms—as part of "the great struggle . . . betwixt '*might* and *right*'—betwixt *Aristocracy* and *Democracy*—betwixt *money* and *public virtue*—and betwixt *patriotism* and *avarice*. . . ." In contrast, Tammany accommodated itself to local and state banking interests. It led a street rally of city clerks against the National Bank, but did not attack the state banks because Martin Van Buren, Jackson's campaign manager and guru, relied on these "pet" banks to provide Jackson with crucial campaign funding. Van Buren's sponsorship of the state's safety-fund banking system in 1829 led to a proliferation of banks and rampant corruption in the state legislature.[24]

The growing reserves of the banks gave capitalists the financial leverage to undermine the control that artisans had formerly exercised over wages, prices, and labor. The increasing scale of capitalist-run enterprises allowed them to apply cost-cutting strategies that undercut the price artisans could afford to charge for making the same product, such as shoes.[25] Resulting artisan activist hostility was directed against bankers and abolitionists, both of whom were seeking to challenge the political hegemony of the democratic republican coalition between planters and artisans.

Artisans fostered traditional republican values based on agriculture existing in harmony with small-scale craft-based enterprises. They felt squeezed from the top by the bankers and undermined from below by abolitionist agitators. They strove to preserve their status. Hostility to the growing disparity of wealth and power led them to support the formation of the Workingmen's Party. Its more ambitious successor, the Equal Rights or Loco Foco Party, opposed banks, upheld Southern slavery, and favored restriction of rights for Northern African Americans.[26]

Like the Workingmen, the Loco Focos made banking the prime issue. Loco Focos did not differentiate between National Bank Whigs and state bank Democrats. They held that banks institutionalized as corporations would soon reduce Americans to dependent chattel, especially since the banks' lobbyists bribed the legislature to issue paper money, the value of which depreciated as a function of the amount in circulation.[27]

Loco Foco views fell within the parameters of the democratic republicanism of the Jefferson school, which regarded agrarian republicanism and bank monopoly as antithetical doctrines. The Loco Focos' position was often labeled "Agrarianism," a classical allusion to republican Rome's "Agrarian Law" that called for an equal division of agricultural land. Their views gained popular support in part because the relative position of the unskilled between 1820 and 1836 deteriorated with respect to industrial manufacturers, despite an increase in real wages.[28]

Anti-bank Democrats excluded bankers from their vision of society because bankers were nonproducers, and "*Capital* is not created by law, but by labor."[29] These Democrats had "very little sympathy with the deposite . . . whether it be a great incorporation with many branches, or an association of smaller ones—a colossal monopoly or an army of monopolisers."[30] They excoriated the "bank-nobility," this "paper money power":[31]

> The Aristocrats, alias Nationals; alias Independent Republicans; alias Whigs; alias anything else that will answer the purposes of deception . . . from Masonic Hall. Do the mechanicks and the labourers know, that every dollar which is paid in the discounting of uncurrent notes in Wall Street is filched out of their pockets?[32]

With Cassandra-like vision, an anti-bank Democrat provided the scenario for the next century when he detailed how this "paper money power" operated:

[It] led the projectors of an aristocratical class . . . to organize a system in avowed imitation of that of the mother country. The machinery of a national debt, in connexion with paper money banking, was established under the forms of law . . . creating corporations under the irresponsible control of a few individuals, with power to issue, without personal liability, the representative of the universal standard of value. The charter of such a corporation was held to be a vested right which could not be annulled by the power which created it. . . . When once obtained, by whatever means it was absolute and irresponsible. It enabled its managers to control the whole property of the country. A dollar belonging to them . . . might be represented by paper ten or twenty times over at their option. Such a currency among an enterprizing people could not fail to engender a general spirit of gambling.[33]

New York City had now replaced Philadelphia as the center of the nation's banking reserves, which was small consolation to the average New Yorker, who confronted legislative capitulation to the banks and inflation for the average workingman of 66 percent between April 1834 and October 1836. Resulting frustration lent substance to charges that "no charters are so shameless as corporations, and nothing is so easy to cheat as a state government."[34]

An important recipient of dissolved National Bank funds was the Manhattan Company, a successful bank, even though, as recounted in Chapter 2, the citizenry had been led to believe that its only purpose was to provide the city with water. Criticism soon mounted about the company's service, especially after the cholera epidemic of 1832 and an increase in fires blamed on malfunctioning Manhattan Company hydrants.[35]

With the passage of the Croton Aqueduct bill on May 2, 1834, the city entered a new era for its water supply. The legislation provided for the construction of an aqueduct to draw water from the 40-mile-distant Croton River through 165 miles of pipe. Late in the year, a referendum on the Croton project passed by a margin of more than three to one, with only the ninth, tenth, and thirteenth wards opposed because their wells remained relatively pure. Support was bipartisan and led to the adoption of large-scale, long-range planning by government leaders who sought to transcend the escalating political partisanship in the generation preceding the Civil War. Grandiose plans also, as Hone astutely remarked, "diverted the attention of the people from the vexed questions of the confused state of the national currency."[36]

Croton water flowed into the Yorkville Reservoir on June 27, 1842, five years and one month after construction began, and too late to prevent New York City's worst post–Revolutionary War fire. On the night of December 16, 1835, this fire consumed 19 blocks containing 674 buildings in the heart of the Wall Street district. Philip Hone suffered an 11,000 dollar personal loss in insurance company investments, and 300 people were arrested for looting. The ex-mayor castigated those who regarded the conflagration as a form of divine retribution against banker greed:

> [T]he miserable wretches who prowled about the ruins . . . beastly drunk on the champagne and other wines and liquors with which the streets and wharves were lined . . . exult in the misfortune . . . [with] "Ah! They'll make no more five per cent dividends!" and "This will make the aristocracy haul in their horns!" Poor deluded wretches, little do they know that their own horns "live and move and have their being" in these very horns of the aristocracy, as their instigators teach them to call it. This cant is the very text from which their leaders teach their deluded followers. It forms part of the warfare of the poor against the rich; a warfare . . . destined . . . to break the hearts of some of the politicians of Tammany Hall, who . . . find now that the dogs they have taught to bark will bite them as soon as their political opponents. . . .
>
> . . . this afternoon at the Bank for Savings. There was an evident run upon the bank by a gang of low Irishmen, who demanded their money in a peremptory and threatening manner. This class of men are the most ignorant . . . white men in the world . . . [who] sought to embarrass this excellent institution . . . established for the sole benefit of the poor. . . . These Irishmen, strangers among us, without . . . patriotism of affection in common with American citizens, decide the elections in the city of New York.[37]

Hone exemplified the patriarchal worldview of his class, members of which identified their personal interests with the destiny of the nation to the extent that the public would be made to assume the losses for which Hone's peers were responsible, thereby ensuring a handsome income for his heirs.

Such financial sleight of hand did not entirely escape the public eye. A case in point was again the Manhattan Company, which gained a more important resource than water when Secretary of the Treasury Roger B.

Taney began, on October 1, 1833, placing large federal deposits, the remains of the National Bank, into Manhattan Company vaults. The board
of directors then lent out these monies for stock purchases. Whig Hone
viewed these Democratic moves as taxing the people to support "Van
Buren's rotten bank system."[38] He was not far off the mark. Such public
subsidy of large private enterprise led Loco Focos to warn small producers of the necessity for "COMBINATION. . . . *Let them know their own
strength and resolve to be imposed upon no longer.*" The *Evening Post*
protested,

> Why are the producers of all the wealth of society the poorest, most
> despised and most downtrodden class of men? . . . because they are
> ignorant of their own strength. Let them combine together to de-
> mand whatever the plain principles of justice warrant, and we shall
> see what power there is which can deny them.[39]

Jackson's veto of the National Bank had galvanized the anti-monopoly
Democratic-Republicans who opposed the National Bank's intention to
centralize power in the federal government. The editors of the *Working
Man's Advocate,* George Henry Evans, and the *Evening Post,* William
Leggett, led the journalistic opposition. Anti-bank devotees of traditional
democratic republicanism also backed the *Democrat,* under the editor-
ship of William Hart, which ignored slavery and sentimentalized the role
of motherhood. The first issue polemically identified with the Irish republican cause; with Jackson, Whig leader Senator Henry Clay, Massachusetts industrial spokesman Daniel Webster, and Southern slavery
spokesman Senator John C. Calhoun; and with mechanics and laborers
deceived by men who "within the last thirty years" had called themselves
"National, Independent, and half a dozen other sorts of Republicans; but
who would willingly write themselves Federalists if they dare, [and] now
seek to trap you with professions of Democracy."[40]

For the April 1835 municipal election, Democratic-Republicans re-
named themselves the "Jeffersonian Anti-Monopoly Democrats."[41] Fresh
in these activists' minds was the June 1833 New York State Senate investi-
gatory commission that had disclosed how almost all of Tammany's leaders held bank stock. The stock came courtesy of the Seventh Ward Bank,
which had distributed shares to more than one hundred state and city
officials, including every Tammany state senator.

Party insurgents, the Equal Rights' Democracy, swore an anti-bank oath to thwart the designs of those they termed the "monopoly democracy," who were led by prominent party bankers like Gideon Lee and Preserved Fish. To retain control, the banker faction arrived early before a regular Tammany Hall session on the night of October 29, 1835. George D. Strong, president of the Commercial Bank, nominated future mayor and bank director Isaac L. Varian as party chairman.[42] Various resolutions were hurriedly passed and committee assignments made. Then, on schedule, the larger contingent of anti-bank Democratic-Republicans arrived. Under the leadership of workingman Joel Curtis, they moved to rout the undemocratic bank faction, whose supporters responded by extinguishing the hall's gaslights—whereupon, anti-bankers struck matches bearing the brand name Loco Foco, and the light was found by which to reverse the policies and political appointments made earlier that evening. For some time afterward, the shop that sold Loco Foco matches at the corner of William and Beekman did a brisk business in that brand. Nevertheless, since the banking faction edited party newspapers, its candidate lists were published, and the ward committees acquiesced.[43]

Loco Foco influence was widespread and appeared in unlikely places. Whig diarist George Templeton Strong was amazed that his former Columbia College teacher had become "a furiously enthusiastic Democrat":

> . . . an "every man himself-ocrat"—a man who believes in the utter perfectibility of the human race, and regards all law as an encumbrance, a shackle on the freedom which is the birthright of mankind. . . . Agrarianism, too, he supports. . . . In religion . . . not far from Deism—though he always speaks with respect of the Bible, and lives a moral life.[44]

In November, the *Evening Post* ceased serving as the journalistic organ of Democratic-Republicans. Tammany judged its editor William Leggett too extreme because he was the only Democratic newspaper editor to oppose the Democratic administration's ban on sending abolitionist literature through the U.S. mails.[45] The *Evening Post* also complained that party leaders had abandoned their anti-monopoly stance of 1834. Party leaders, the paper said, sanctioned monopolies,

> in Wall Street, the markets, the Ferries, and . . . a licensing system, which . . . bestows privileges on the one hand, deprives citizens of their rights on the other, and unconstitutionally establishes inequality in justice. . . . Of what use are our elections? We may as well

suffer a packed committee from each ward to assemble at Tammany Hall and say who are to be our representatives, and permit the Sachems a clique to be openly what they are secretly, an annual legislative directory. . . . The fear of federal rule has been the bug-bear for many years past, and has induced thousands to submit to the undemocratick practice of election by committee . . . the people find that the "clique" of the party were only crying out "wolf" in order the more securely to prey upon the community themselves. The democracy at length sees into the mystery of the inner temple of the party; that the "oldest and wisest," alias the *Bank gentry* are the same in principle and practice with their contemporary Bank Whigs; and to the great mass of the people it matters not which has the reins of government in their hands, they both pursue the same august, oppressive, and partial legislation and misrule.[46]

From June of 1835 through 1836, coincident with the rise of the Loco Focos, more racist attacks were conducted against anti-slavery men and women than at any time prior to the Civil War.[47] In part, this violence was a response to the rising militance of African Americans eager to exercise their human rights.

The same November that the *Evening Post* was denied Democratic support, the racially integrated Friends of Human Rights met on the twentieth and established the New York City Committee of Vigilance to prevent the kidnapping of African-American citizens for sale in the South. An African American need merely be accused of being a fugitive slave, and guilt was presumed, a jury trial denied. The hapless victim was rushed through a proceeding, "often without the aid of a friend or a counsellor," and deported south under the guard of the slaveowner's agent. The Committee of Vigilance reported that "the practice [was] so extensive that no colored man [or woman] is safe."[48] The right to property in the form of human beings took precedence over the Bill of Rights.

The resurgence of racism was reflected in the enhanced status of the Democratic Party. In December 1835, Tammany won majorities in all the wards. The following month, those Democrats disenchanted with Tammany's pro-bank position convened to nominate their own candidates, yet they professed to "utterly disclaim any intention or design of instituting any new party, but declare ourselves the original Democratic party. . . ."[49] At the same time, worker dissatisfaction reached new heights on New York City's docks, as a rise in interest rates to 24 percent precipi-

tated a slash in wages and violent protests. Troops protected strikebreakers as they unloaded ship cargoes. Such episodes, the *Herald* reported,
"may almost now be considered a settled element of American Character.
Occasionally the blame is thrown upon the poor devils of Irishmen, on
the popish religion, or on fanatics and abolitionists, but the unhappy trait
now developed is not confined to any section or to the season."[50] In
March 1836, the state legislature gave the mayor the sole right to call out
the militia.

That April, the municipal elections presented four slates to the public:
Tammany, Whig, Anti-Monopoly or Loco Foco, and Native American—
with the Loco Focos drawing support from Tammany Democrats, and
the Native Americans from the Whigs. But it was Tammany Hall and the
Whigs who divided the sixteen Common Council seats.

At their state convention in September, Loco Foco Democrats appealed to Southern supporters by seeking to have Colonel Samuel Young
run for governor. He had been the author of the anti-bank and anti-black
planks in the 1821 state constitution. Young turned the offer down because
he did not wish to further divide the "united Democracy."

Loco Focos then formed a third party called Equal Rights, which upheld the notion of natural rights as essential to "Republican government."
Delegates attacked state court rulings against unions, tarring them as un-
just and oppressive. This "Convention of Mechanics, Farmers and Working Men" favored gold and silver as the only legal tender, while
simultaneously stressing that "no human law can rightfully restrain free
men from fixing the wages of their own labor."[51] Their proposal rested
upon solid historical and constitutional grounds, for Chief Justice Marshall had led a unanimous 1819 decision, *Sturges v. Crowninshield*, in
ruling that gold and silver were the only acceptable legal tender.

Loco Foco Democrats held out for "the right to acquire property by
industry and honest enterprize, unimpeded by legislative restrictions or
monopolies." They opposed banking by incorporation and called for the
repeal of the restraining law, so that banking could be conducted "by
individuals and associations and a whole community on the watch." They
construed the legislature's attempt to create a banking system as "interference with the laws of trade."[52]

In 1836, the Equal Rights candidate for governor, Isaac S. Smith, declared in proto-Marxist language that

> All wealth is an accumulation of surplus labor, from which alone the
> expenses and burthens of government should be borne. No person

. . . can have a *moral* right to consume that which he does not . . . contribute to produce.

None of our institutions have so strong a tendency to create and perpetuate the odious distinctions betwixt the rich and the poor as the paper money banks. . . . the greatest cause of corruption in legislatures.

The worst feature . . . of the past legislatures, has been . . . the granting of charters for banks, with which to strengthen the hands of party leaders.

Yet Smith noted that unfortunately, "the great majority of the people have but little interest individually in these plunderings of the many for the benefit of the few. . . ."[53]

Perhaps their tepid response stemmed from the absurd solution that the Equal Rights Party put forth. The monopolization of the American people's assets by a new corporate class would be met by a call for universal public education, touted as the means whereby the gifted poor might rise to riches. In a "Letter to Mechanics, Farmers and Workingmen," the candidate for lieutenant governor on the Equal Rights ticket, Moses Jacques, stressed that "Those who produce all the wealth should not submit to have their families kept in ignorance and degradation, and the common schools held in disrepute, while the public bounty is showered upon those . . . aristocratical few. Too much cannot be done for common schools."[54] Jacques did not directly address the issue of poverty that remained to insistently remind all who were not poor of the perils of failing to persevere in one's trade, regardless of who set the rules.

The following year, Equal Rights men proposed a state constitution that mandated direct election by the people of all legislators, executives, and judges. It would prohibit the legislature both from chartering "any corporate or artificial body" and from conferring "on any individual" such a charter. Consistent with master-artisan values, these Loco Focos now opposed unions as well as corporations, on the grounds that unions were "artificial bodies." Loco Focos upheld equal opportunity in the marketplace, a notion first popularized by the Levelers in revolutionary seventeenth-century England and subsequently enshrined in Adam Smith's *Wealth of Nations*.[55] They stood for old-fashioned republican values:

We never had had, nor have we now, any desire to raise the standard of the poor against the rich, any further than may be necessary to the attainment of our natural and social rights . . . we complain that combinations of the rich, their corrupt influence and servile tools in the capitol, and on the bench . . . the leaders and the aristocracy of both the great political parties of the State, self-styled Federalists and Democrats, Whig or Tammanymen, have deceived the Workingmen by false pretenses of political honesty and justice . . . they are alike opposed to the "greatest good of the greatest number. . . ."

Let us combine before we go to the ballot boxes. . . . Remember that *combination* is our true remedy.[56]

Although anti–big business, Loco Focos were conspicuously silent about large land holdings. Indeed their leader, Fitzwilliam Byrdsall, frequently corresponded with John C. Calhoun, the philosopher-statesman of Southern plantation owners. To buttress their moral standing, Byrdsall and other Loco Focos called themselves Christian Democrats, for " 'God is no respecter of persons, all are equal in his sight,' we behold the universal equality of man." To directly appeal to the republican masses, Byrdsall proclaimed that "although we may live under the *cloak* of republicanism, we are in reality subjected to the worst of all tyrannies—an aristocracy of wealth. Our actual government, our real regulator of social rights and social intercourse, is money—the great heaps ruling the less."[57] Byrdsall shared Calhoun's and Jefferson's fears concerning the potential a banking corporation possessed to stifle the autonomy, if not the existence, of the republican farmer, large and small.[58] It is no political accident that all three men were Democratic-Republicans. Dirk Hoerder has found that mechanics' journals stressing an alliance between agriculture and labor were likely to be Democratic.[59]

On October 11, 1836, this "democracy of the city" assembled by ward to select three delegates who would in turn choose thirteen persons to represent the city in the senatorial convention held at Tammany Hall. Five persons from each ward constituted a nominating committee, which selected candidates for congress, state assembly, and other offices.[60] There seems no doubt that the Equal Rights Party contributed to the democratization of the ward system of the Democratic Party, as analyzed in Chapter 6.

The following year, on October 27, 1837, Tammany Hall nominated five of the Equal Rights candidates. The majority of Equal Rights men had united with Tammany Hall, believing that this move would sustain Van Buren in his contest against the banks. The following day, Equal

Rights candidates not nominated by Tammany withdrew from their political races, forced to do so by a vote of 171 to 22. But this "Union" or Tammany-Loco Foco ticket lost anyway. Democratic-Republicans had been occupying the White House for nine years, and the result, most voters believed, was the worst economic crisis in United States history. The public did not know that British investors had precipitously withdrawn from the American currency markets in response to what they deemed an American failure to curtail overinvestment by unregulated state banks.[61]

The Panic of 1837 "sadly . . . confirm[ed] the radicals' evil prophecies" about the robbery of the public by the banks.[62] The ensuing social misery engendered by the Panic of 1837 led, in David Reynolds's words, to "a volcanic protest literature produced by *radical democrats* who could describe modern America only in sarcastic, inverted terms, with bold social pariahs deemed preferable to hypocritical social rulers." Fifty thousand New Yorkers were unemployed, and two-thirds of the city's three hundred thousand inhabitants lacked adequate means of support. The city's labor unions were decimated.[63] In his satirical piece "The Business Man," Poe's protagonist defended his peers from any complicity in the economic collapse: "The frauds of the banks of course I couldn't help. Their suspension put me to ruinous inconvenience. These, however, are not individuals, but corporations; and corporations, it is very well known, have neither bodies to be kicked, nor souls to be damned."[64]

Loco Focos listed those whom they believed to be responsible:

First . . . the city corporation, with its hundred office holders in every ward, toiling and intriguing to preserve the ascendancy of the party whose patronage they enjoy.

Secondly . . . the moneyed power—the moneyed institutions . . . associations of men, who, with few exceptions, are enemies of the administration and the democracy.

Thirdly . . . the influence of the newspaper press, which, with the exception of two daily and one weekly paper, is hostile to the democratic party. . . .

Fourthly . . . the influence of a very large portion of the federal government in this city.[65]

Loco Focos then merged with the Democratic-Republican Party, whose name was changed to Democratic in time for the 1844 presidential election. Future New York City mayor Fernando Wood presided over the meeting that passed a resolution restoring the *Evening Post* as one of the official press organs of the Democratic-Republican Party.[66]

In New York City, Whigs could only win elections when the Democrats were divided or discredited by scandal. They sought to take advantage of the democratic movement by calling themselves the Democratic Whigs, opposed to the "Loco Foco managers at Tammany Hall."[67]

Democrats countered that the Whigs were plotting war to saddle the country with "permanent" national debt through "army and navy contracts, and contracts for loans . . . fluctuations of currency, and irregularity in the supply of commodities" that would "reduce the workingmen of America into as complete subjection as their brethren in England." Such Whig measures would make "the rich richer, and the poor poorer, the cardinal maxim of [Whig] political faith." Democrats worried that the United States would adopt the British system of deficit financing. Then, they warned, "where will be the limits of *our* national debt? . . . our bank nobility system . . . fastened upon us forever."[68]

In general, Democratic and Whig congressmen continued to divide strongly on public funding for banks. In the local elections of 1837, Whigs and a fractured Democratic Party split the wards. The Whigs took the first four, the seventh, the eighth, and fifteenth; the Democrats captured the rest, the seventeenth by just eight votes.[69]

That fall, the Loco Focos held their second convention to draft a new state constitution. "Regulation of the currency" was now the principal issue. In a convention address aimed at New York mechanics, Loco Foco leaders Levi Slamm (editor of the *Daily Plebeian*), inspector Alexander Ming, Byrdsall, and others excoriated banks as

> . . . combinations possessing the power to *expand* or *limit* trade and commerce, wages . . . prices of all commodities . . . the management of the value of every man's property and labor. They, with other *chartered combinations* are spread over our country like swarms of locusts, preying on the fruits of our industry; and lest these symbols of nobility without the name, should not . . . subject us in vassalage . . . the state itself has a workshop . . . to make the convicted felon the competitor to . . . ruin, the honest patriotick citizen.
>
> [While workingmen are prevented from organizing], capitalists and employers may combine together . . . not authorized by the constitution or the laws.

Trades Unions and Mechanicks Societies are only self-protective against the *countless combinations of aristocracy;* boards of banks and other chartered directories; boards of brokers . . . of trade and commerce; combinations of landlords, coal and wood dealers, monopolists, and all those who grasp at everything and produce nothing.[70]

While Whigs stressed national symbols, Democrats emphasized greater decentralization, even in commemorating Independence Day. They held no military parade or city corporation dinner, and during the first week in July, they lavished money and attention on a visit to the city by President Van Buren. Republican values were more important to Democrats than rituals linked to the Republic. They rejected being labeled Loco Foco or Agrarian. They preferred to be called Democrats, identifying with anti-bank forces and with the rural ethos that permeated republican consciousness.[71]

The Whigs attempted to capitalize on the fact that their political opposition defined itself as being both "republican" and "democrat" and asserted that these "DEMOCRATIC REPUBLICANS" identified too closely with local interests to afford effective national leadership. Whigs prided themselves on being an authentic political party, one they defined as "an organized union" based on "principle or a system of principles [that] proposes the good of the country." They regarded the Democrats as a faction that "confines its aims and objects within itself, 'its be all and end all' is self-aggrandizement."[72] Yet it was the very failure of the term *Whig* to capture the collective political imagination that played a role in the Whigs' effort to characterize all Democrats as Loco Focos.

Competition for the illegal riches of political office was intense. Dickens remarked that "the miserable strife of Party feeling had afflicted every aspect of American life."[73] The parties outdid each other in schemes to win election. Under pressure from "native" American associations who demanded a new law with stiff penalties for repeat voting, the board of aldermen in 1838 passed a resolution demanding formal registration of voters. The Common Council and Democratic-Republican ward committees attacked this measure as a violation of constitutional liberties, but that did not deter Whigs from flouting voting laws to limit the influence of the Catholic majority. Whigs equated control of the Catholic vote with the security of their property, and in New York City that property was an enormously profitable venture. For example, the richest man in America,

John Jacob Astor, had amassed even greater wealth by investing his fur-business profits in Manhattan real estate.

Landlord greed provided the incentive to modernize the city in helter-skelter fashion. Rich homeowners were "tempted with prices so high that none can resist," and landlords raised artisan proprietors' rents, forcing them out of their lower Manhattan home-work neighborhoods.[74] In a brilliant satire on the mercenary content of American republican values, James Fenimore Cooper pilloried the "speculator in town-lots," a Mr. Henry Halfacre, who possessed "a spirit for running in debt, and never shrunk from jeopardizing property that, in truth, belonged to his creditors."[75]

Speculative mania was fueled by generous fire insurance coverage. "How is it," Hone pondered while vacationing in London, "that fires are so frequent in New York and in this great city containing a million and a half of inhabitants, you never hear of one?" He subsequently discounted to his diary the fire insurance theory that had been publicly raised by foreign observers.[76] In another diary, the twenty-year-old fire buff George Templeton Strong, recorded the following:

> Really it's hard to tell exactly what we're coming to . . . this practice of merchants setting their stores on fire to get the insurance . . . is prevailing to such an extent in this community, and carries so small risk of detection, that if anybody is caught he ought to be operated on without benefit of clergy, *in terrorem.*[77]

Burning and demolishing were so common, Cooper reported, that while "in the early part of the century there were many buildings constructed prior to 1750, by mid-century nearly all had vanished."[78] In an address to the New-York Historical Society a decade later, Robert Benjamin Winthrop lamented, "It is far from an easy task to recall the objects of local interest which have so suddenly disappeared. As a people we have very little veneration for antiquity."[79]

The rapid pace of urban renewal and expansion led to the quadrupling of municipal expenses during the 1830s, with the brunt of the increase borne by the productive poor and middling classes. The Common Council contracted street cleaning to party benefactors, while sewage and street repair remained the responsibility of the private property owners who directly fronted thoroughfares. Cartmen protested a city corporation law requiring them to swear that each of them owned a good horse and cart not bound by debt, a restriction not imposed upon any other member of the commercial community.[80]

Work conditions were appalling. Stonecutters rioted over employment of Sing Sing convicts to construct the New York University on Washington Square. Hone was moved to protest in his diary that "Irishmen and horses are plenty enough in New York," but that something should be done to prevent terrible fires like the one that killed thirty-two horses and three hostlers at Twelfth Street and Third Avenue. Five days afterward, he applauded the harsh prison sentences meted out to journeyman tailors engaged in strike-related violence.[81] They were attempting to organize separately from masters who had combined to monopolize production.

Shortly thereafter, twenty-one journeyman tailors were indicted under a state supreme court edict that deemed it a criminal conspiracy for any two persons to meet to set a price upon their labor. Thousands of mechanics led by immigrant English labor organizers then demonstrated through their numbers the absurdity of this ruling. Hone presumed they were motivated by the opportunity to "villify [*sic*] Yankee judges and juries." In a climate of Americanization intolerant of ethnic pluralism, the demonstration failed to spark similar action by native tradesmen. Handbills denouncing "The Rich Against the Poor" did not presage seizure of political power, because American preindustrial trade unionists generally blamed their plight on "aristocrats," not capitalists. And as Cooper aptly observed, in America, "aristocracy . . . ranks as an eighth deadly sin, though no one seems to know precisely what it means." Many citizens were under the perennial delusion, encouraged by rich men and their journalistic sycophants, that "the luxuries of the rich give employment to the poor, and cause money to circulate."[82]

Beleaguered artisans were in no mood to consider African-American demands for parity in the marketplace. Richard Stott has concluded, "Blacks were 'nonpersons' to most white workers; in the letters, diaries, and reminiscences I examined, I did not see a single reference to an individual black person."[83]

Such social isolation compelled African Americans to organize their own mutual aid efforts. Although the 1836 United Anti-Slavery Society survived only one year, more lasting organizations were the Roger Williams Anti-Slavery Society in 1837, the Evangelical Union Anti-Slavery Society two years later, and the New York City Young Men's Anti-Slavery Society. Meanwhile, representatives of the *Colored American* fanned out from the city and across New York State seeking signers for a petition to the state legislature challenging the law that let less than one hundred black New Yorkers vote. The legislature refused to consider the petitions and their thousands of signatures.

In response, on October 11, 1838, blacks formed the Political Association of New York City, to mobilize against racist laws and to support progressive candidates for office. The association's efforts almost always translated by default into support for the Whig Party. Most African-American associations were adamantly opposed to colonization. When slavery was abolished in New York, colonization was not connected with its eradication.[84]

The "practical abolitionists," like the New York City Vigilance Committee, became the dominant abolitionist faction. More active than most anti-slavery societies, which merely lobbied Congress or commanded the pulpit on Sunday, the Vigilance Committee broke laws by both liberating those sent back to the South and aiding escaped slaves; it became part of the underground railroad. The Vigilance Committee characterized New York City police officers and judges who "send back the fugitive slaves to the chains and scourgings of the task-master" as "extraordinary samples of human depravity." Its leader, David Ruggles, was himself the target of kidnapping on at least two occasions, with a bounty of fifty thousand dollars reportedly placed on his head. Only in the United States, unlike Latin America, did being "one per cent African American" qualify one for the legally enforced status of being "black" and therefore a possible candidate for reenslavement. David Brion Davis has observed, "In no ancient society was the distinction between slavery and freedom so sharply drawn as in America."[85]

In the 1830s, after declining somewhat in the previous decade, kidnapping became more widespread than ever before. One notorious case was that of Jesse Collier, accused by a Southerner of being an escaped slave. In early September 1837, the city recorder, Richard Riker, Esq., ruled that because "a slave is held incapable of performing a voluntary act," Collier could not testify on his own behalf, even though he could prove through witnesses that he was not a fugitive. Collier had been arrested on August 28 and brought before the recorder the following day. Under the terms of the federally mandated Fugitive Slave Act of 1793, neither lawyer nor jury trial could legally be provided to the accused. Only "due process" need be followed, and that amounted to leaving the case's disposition to the recorder—in this instance, the pro-slavery Riker. Thus, after ten days of incarceration, Collier was transported to Maryland in chains to complete a life in slavery.[86]

Although the U.S. Constitution upheld slavery, it also contained a clause that banned the slave trade after 1808. However, that ban was honored in the breach by slave traders and owners. Any day of the week, slaves could be discovered stowed in the holds on board ships docked in New York harbor. They were brought from Africa, the West Indies, South America, and the American South, bound for reshipment to Southern plantations.[87] Many were headed for slaveholding Texas, until 1836 a province of Mexico, a country that otherwise tolerated no slavery. So long as the slaves did not set foot on city soil, few European Americans knew or cared about their plight. The ethics of sound business deals prevailed, with both Tammany and the Loco Focos outdoing each other in support of Southern slavery, while the chartering of banks continued to be the most serious issue of public disagreement between them.

In the fall of 1837, with the panic in full fury, Tammany reached a compromise with the Loco Focos in seeking their support for Van Buren's attempt to "separate Bank and State." The following year, the New York State legislature passed a general incorporation act that allowed anyone to start up a bank who agreed to abide by the terms of the safety-fund law. With the passage of New York's free banking act, debt liability was shifted from notes to deposits in a move that Bray Hammond termed "the most important event in American banking history." In Hammond's words, it "definitely helped the corporation replace the individual as an agent of free enterprise in the economy."[88] At the time, the leading Democratic journal of opinion predicted, with remarkable foresight, that it "must inevitably produce a more universal and degrading condition of dependence than the feudal system was ever able to effect!"[89]

Those who supported local banking interests diverted attention from the banks' speculations by focusing concern overseas. They warned that the United States could become dependent on Great Britain for capital if the safety fund were not approved. Five years earlier in 1833, when Jackson dismantled the Bank of the United States, *The Man* had defined the Bank of the United States as "the *modern* Colonial Government of British capitalist and British nobility." Hindsight demonstrates how well *The Man*'s editors played into the hands of the state banking establishment. Nationalistic Democrats portrayed Nicholas Biddle, president of the Bank of the United States, as "an aspiring clerk employed by a few capitalists abroad, and speculators at home, strutting forth from behind his desk with his pen behind his ear . . . dictating to the Legislature of the State of New York, and to the people of the Union at large, in such a pompous style of military grandiloquence."[90]

Even Hone displayed alarm: "All we undertake is predicated on the chance of borrowing money from John Locke . . . and the Bank of England becomes the arbiter of the American merchant." But he tempered those views when he extolled England as "the greatest nation in the world . . . in moral if not commercial force."[91]

In stark contrast, the *Evening Post* effectively distorted the situation when it proclaimed the following to its Democratic-Republican readers: "On one side is the BANK TICKET, the MONOPOLIST'S TICKET, the SPECULATOR'S TICKET. On the other is the DEMOCRATIC TICKET, the ANTI-MONOPOLISTS' TICKET, the PEOPLE'S TICKET."[92]

The transfer of deposits from the Bank of the United States to state banks had led to an orgy of uncontrolled speculation that precipitated the Panic of 1837. Banks controlled by influential Democrats failed. Loco Focos staged a rally on February 13, chanting, "Bread, Meat, Rent, and Fuel! The prices must come down!" At least one thousand men sacked prominent Democratic-Republican Party figure Eli Hart's large flour establishment. The mayor and several watchmen interceded but were immediately driven off. No better system of distribution of necessities to the poor resulted, only a call for "a more efficient police system" with which the poor "might be easily repressed." Also coerced were two Loco Foco members of the state assembly, cited for contempt after accusing their fellow assemblymen of legislative chicanery with respect to chartering banks and passing the bank-suspension law.[93]

Tammany was so shaken in political stature by the panic that it sent "a full deputation" to Washington Irving's Tarrytown home to inform the writer that he "had been unanimously and vociferously nominated Mayor." The Whig Irving declined the offer.[94] On a separate Loco Foco ticket, Moses Jacques ran for mayor and received four thousand votes, enough to throw the election to the Whigs.

Six weeks later, on May 7, there was a run on the banks for hard currency. The banks quickly petitioned the state legislature for a suspension law, and the lawmakers meekly complied. The banks had succeeded in their novel scheme to encourage debt so that they might profit. Once accepted, paper need not be redeemed for gold if the financiers persuaded the legislature not to do so.

Meanwhile, to boost political standing in their own neighborhoods,

Democratic ward leaders granted small but conspicuous favors to arriving immigrants that did little to reduce poverty. One influential party figure, John M. Bloodgood, lobbied to have bread and other foodstuffs distributed in poorer districts. As a police justice, Bloodgood was also in the fortunate position to finance this project with money extorted from prostitutes and criminals brought before his court.[95] Ward leaders hoped not only that new voters would be won over by such generosity, but that older ones could be wooed back from the Loco Foco Party. The Loco Focos' opposition to business incorporation was less attractive to the immigrant who desired job security, regardless of the kind of enterprise, than to the native craftsman whose independent livelihood and native traditions were threatened by ever larger corporately organized competition.

Democratic intellectuals like those editing the *United States Magazine and Democratic Review* clearly favored the artisans' position. They were explicit on this crucial point, writing that, "When *the institutions of the people* are mentioned, we do not understand private corporations established for individual profit drawn from the industry of the community." The *Evening Post* concurred:

> It is unquestionably necessary that the power of appropriating the property of the citizen to the use of the state in case of public need, resides in government. But it has been greatly questioned by our ablest jurists whether the state can delegate this right of eminent domain to individuals and corporations for the purpose of public improvement as a matter of private gain.[96]

However, the average politician's conscience had been sapped by the lure of easy riches. It thus fell to the Loco Focos, who did not control the state legislature, to oppose "public improvement as a matter of private gain." The vast majority of lawmakers took money in one disguised form or another from private entrepreneurs and voted both their pocketbooks.

To mask their intent lawmakers postured as reformers. Thus, Tammany appealed to skilled trades at its political gatherings, where "the shoemaker, tailor, hatter, clothier, silversmith, blacksmith, carver, gilder, shipwright, cabinet ware man, tinman . . . every one organized in active industry vied with each other in the expression of their hearty co-operation in the great work of Reform."[97]

Tammany adhered to its democratic republican roots when it excluded unskilled laborers from the category of producers.[98] In this respect, it was no different than the Equal Rights or Workingmen's Parties. Little evidence exists to support Herbert Gutman and Ira Berlin's assessment that, "In sum, prior to 1840, American wage earners had developed an indigenous ideology independent of and opposed to capitalism."[99]

The two-party system of the 1830s had demonstrated ideological elasticity in assimilating a generation's worth of third parties. According to Mike Walsh, leader of the Democratic Spartan Association, the Loco Focos had admirable beginnings, but were subsequently bribed into compliance by Van Buren through his skillful covert distribution of customs house positions. Illustrative of the ease with which Loco Foco leaders could be transformed into Tammany stalwarts is Elijah F. Purdy, characterized by the *Evening Post* in 1836 as the "bane of the monopolists." After serving as New York City mayor and grand sachem of the Tammany Society, he became the model for future Tammany bosses in the late 1840s; and as Cooper noted, "boss" was "only a republican word for master."[100]

The transitory nature of "equal rights" parties testified to the diminishing role artisans played in the city's economy and to the social resilience of the emerging capitalist order. Whereas servants in the 1830s preferred to be called "help," and policemen resisted wearing uniforms because it smacked of an aristocratic order, the wrenching class stratification that accompanied the increasing industrial division of labor, rendered servants "servants" and uniforms compulsory by the time of the Civil War.[101] Although the two-party system absorbed equal rights parties with relative ease, a hopeful note was raised at the close of the 1840s when the anti-slavery Liberty Party, formed in 1839, extended the notion of equal rights to include slaves. New York City African-American leader Samuel Ringgold Ward proclaimed, "I go for Equal Rights; the Equal Rights of *all men*—not as a mere abstract, practical theory, but as a great speculative idea, to be realized in the workings, and recognized as the subject, and aim of Civil Government."[102] The rhetoric of the Equal Rights Party, although not designed to further African-American rights, had nonetheless presented those opposed to slavery with an opportunity to carry equal rights polemics to their logical conclusion.

The ban on any discussion of slavery that the U.S. Congress had voted on itself between 1836 and 1844 gave the Liberty Party a monopoly on public discussion of this issue. At this third party's first nominating convention in 1840, former slaveowner James G. Birney was nominated for president. A few years later, the party split and dissolved, and a successor, the Free Soil Party, took its place. In 1848, both Samuel Ringgold Ward and Frederick Douglass attended the Free Soil Party's first presidential convention in Buffalo, New York. The Free Soilers caused the Democrats to become more identified with slavery, and it helped to destroy the Whigs and create the Republicans in 1854.

This final Republican Party emerged at the historical moment when Hawthorne, Thoreau, Melville, Whitman, and Stowe generated a literary blaze of light. Between 1850 and 1855, *Moby-Dick, The Scarlet Letter, The House of the Seven Gables, Uncle Tom's Cabin, Leaves of Grass, Walden,* and *Civil Disobedience,* were all published, and Emily Dickinson began composing her poetry. All of these authors, as well as Irving, Cooper, and Poe, were comfortable neither with the kind of democracy America had produced nor with the commercial culture that came to dominate New York City life in the 1840s. They possessed only their powerful moral imaginations with which to confront a turbulent social atmosphere where the economic cutthroat was praised by national leaders as a demigod.[103]

✦ 5 ✦

THE INDUSTRIALIZATION OF
POLITICS AND CULTURE
1828–1850

And our literature!—Oh, when will it breathe the spirit of our republican institutions?

"The Great Nation of Futurity," *United States Magazine and Democratic Review*, 1839

Money makes both beauty and distinction in this part of the world.

James Fenimore Cooper, "Autobiography of a Pocket-Handkerchief" (1843)

The fact of aristocracy, with its two weapons of wealth and manners, is as commanding a feature of the nineteenth century, and the American republic, as of old Rome, or mother England.

Ralph Waldo Emerson, "Lectures on the Times," *The Dial*, July 1842

———

THE SECOND PARTY SYSTEM'S RELIANCE ON MASS ELECTORAL INVOLVEMENT ACCOMPANIED THE RISE OF A POPULAR CULTURE OF "artificial wants." This culture obscured the legislatively manipulated transfer of economic control from artisans, the holders of productive skills, to financiers, the holders of capital. Critics of this new commercialization, like Cooper and Poe, were not so easily fooled. They recognized that "artificial wants"—the product, in Herbert Marcuse's words, of "the technological veil [that] conceals the reproduction of inequality and enslavement"—distinguished this new mass consumer society from its first-party-system predecessor.[1]

Public consumption would now compensate for the loss of artisan control over production standards. Consumer taste became confused with political choice, so that democracy appeared on the rise when in fact a man's control over his work was being taken away by a new order of capitalists and financiers. Cultural entrepreneurs like P. T. Barnum and

George Ripley sold spectacles and fantasies to immigrant factory operatives who worked long hours. Even if they had the time, these workers could not replicate their old culture because work and home occupied different spaces, neither of which they owned.

Factory work differed from its agricultural counterpart in that the product was expropriated entirely by the factory owner, who partially returned its value in the form of a wage. Part of this wage was used to buy a culture not produced by the factory workers themselves. On a European farm, peasants kept at least part of what they grew to produce their own culture, giving rise to the distinctive national identities of Europe.

In New York City, the public eye was diverted from the disintegration of the artisanal code of conduct, with its rigid controls of craft skills, to the penny-press creation "Mose the B'hoy"—a violent, politically impotent republican whose misogyny and racism drew upon the legacy of John Locke. The b'hoy, the urban social equivalent to the cowboy, became a stock confection of American popular writers and sensation mongers. Frustrated Irish journeymen could assume the b'hoy persona on the Old Bowery of the 1830s by coiffuring their hair in soap-locks and purchasing, as Dickens pictured them, "long-tailed blue coats . . . bright buttons, and . . . drab trousers. . . ." The b'hoys then tangled in gang wars with American-born mechanics who also sported a distinctive style of dress. Native and immigrant gangs could join forces and attack their favorite target—African Americans.[2]

A democratic politics had given the b'hoy, a contraction of Bowery Boy, status and social recognition spread by the violent, punning penny dreadfuls that celebrated the "cunning and duplicity" of the "likeable criminal" over the "institutionalized criminality masked by law and religion." It was a character form also developed by Melville in his novels *Redburn* and *Whitejacket* and popularized by Ned Buntline in *The G'hals of New York*.[3]

Is it any wonder, then, that crime rose in a marketplace that culturally sanctioned outlaw stereotypes? Marketing this "new man" advanced modernization, because it substituted the opportunist, eager to follow the vagaries of the new fashion industry, for the artisan and his homespun.

The b'hoy was one social type among many, the offspring of the symbiosis between the fashion industry and yellow journalism, as much a creation of a mercenary media as anything else. Contemporary observer George Foster wrote,

The b'hoy of the Bowery, the rowdy of Philadelphia, the Hoosier of the Mississippi, the trapper of the Rocky Mountains, and the gold-hunter of California are so much alike that an unpracticed hand could not distinguish one from the other; while the "Lize" of the Chatham Theater and the belle of a Wisconsin ball-room are absolutely identical, and might change places without any body being the wiser.[4]

In fact, this American "radical democrat" differed little from the English "plebeian" of a generation earlier.[5] Rather than standing in as a collective assertion of working-class autonomy, the b'hoy merely represented the first formal detachments of working-class elements from traditional republican politics, a stylized rendering of a young worker by an elitist-controlled commercial press vying for readers through cleverly conceived sensation. The b'hoys' "butt-ender" assaults lent mass politics a violent flavor that erupted in reactionary outbursts like the attack on foreign workers in the Gashouse Riot, the Independence Day battle between Irish and Anglo-American workers that left four dead in 1838, and the 1840 New Year's Eve Anglo-American assault on Germans. Such events demonstrated the impotence of the city's watchmen as well as the inability of New York City labor to behave in a unified fashion. Of the watchmen, Hone observed, "They are appointed . . . as a reward for party services performed at the polls, not to quell riots created by the very fellows who assisted to place the men in office from whom they derive their support."[6]

Although Whitman's 1842 *Aurora* editorials defended nativist riots as evidence of working-class spunk, b'hoy anglophobia was readily channeled and marketed by both sympathizers and debunkers of working-class vitality. Philip Hone, no lover of the working class, displayed an American populist noblesse oblige by sponsoring the release of several men and boys jailed for shattering the windows of the Park Theater when an English actor who insulted "Yankees" appeared on stage. Hone recorded that "the American and tricolored flags were exhibited from the upper windows to appease the populace, which served to allay the tumult."[7] This die-hard nationalism would later be put to good use by Northern civic leaders during the Civil War when they hired substitutes to man the battle lines in their stead.

The new cultural entrepreneurs popularized working-class leisure activities like boxing matches. This sport distilled commonly shared frustrations on the job and class tensions into a bloody contest that heightened enthusiasm on the part of onlookers, an enthusiasm that could rarely be mustered for the workaday world.

Hone commented on the spread of prize fighting during the 1830s from England to New York City, where it rapidly became "one of the fashionable abominations of our loafer-ridden city." He described a bout of two hours forty-three minutes and 119 rounds that was won by a boxer who killed his opponent with one hundred "square blows" and eighty-one knockdowns. Debates over prize fighting had become a national obsession, an "artificial want" that diverted attention from the burning issues of the day being settled by social and political elites.[8]

To cater to the debased needs of men in a burgeoning capitalist society, "New York experienced a kind of sexual revolution, as commercial sex became widespread" after 1820. "By midcentury, New York had become the carnal showcase of the Western world." Prostitutes had displayed considerable autonomy over their craft in the first quarter of the nineteenth century but were battered into submission, literally in some cases, during the Jacksonian era. By 1850, they were controlled by pimps, their party bosses.[9]

The two distinct gender subcultures of lower-class prostitutes and b'hoys, along with the higher-class adjunct of sportsmen and dandies, arose in a milieu where "intercourse was only one of many sexual activities organized around commerce, exchange, and consumption."[10] The integrated but scattered prostitution of blacks and whites was replaced in the 1820s by a segregated sexual-entertainment district around Broadway north of Canal Street, which was run by entrepreneurs with the connivance of public officials who accepted bribes as a routine professional perk.

A parallel African-American culture had also evolved. Unlike the gender subcultures, it possessed the potential to evolve into a distinctly American culture, primarily because of its strengths in music and dance. In New York City in the wake of the War of 1812, African-American culture struggled to maintain itself in a closely knit community of less than eleven thousand blacks in a city with eleven times that population. By 1821, the African Grove Theatre, at Bleeker and Mercer Streets, had become its cultural mecca. One could see a waiter from the City Hotel play a richly costumed Plantagenet in *Richard III*,[11] or view works like *Shotoway or the Insurrection of the Caribs of St. Domingo*, written by the stage manager William Henry Brown, a retired ship steward. But on the night of January 9, 1822, city watchmen raided the theater under the pretext that the building posed a fire hazard. The actors were jailed. In his defense, Brown pointed out to the judge that the nearby, newly re-opened Park Theater at Bleeker and Astor Place could not withstand the competition, especially since Brown's productions drew white patrons and featured the brilliant Ira Aldridge, soon to become an expatriate and a renowned European Shakespearean actor. The African Grove Theater reopened but was finally forced to close in 1823, the year the European-American Edwin Forrest popularized a Southern plantation black man whose character became the prototype for the minstrel show. In 1836, the Loco Focos approached Forrest to be their candidate for the U.S. Senate, but he declined. Subsequently, Forrest became a stage hero to the Astor Place rioters, while minstrelsy became the most popular form of commercial entertainment through the Civil War period. It was the basis for vaudeville, which thrived on the cultural expressions of the black experience.[12] Thus did talented immigrant white entertainers mine a black tradition whose creators were socially isolated and economically exploited by white entrepreneurs in a form of cultural slavery.

Minstrelsy combined the appropriation of black music and dance with a satire on African-American pretensions to equality with whites. Its roots can be traced to 1820s lithographs showing white Masons caricaturing their black counterparts. In a cruel twist to poetic justice, the most talented minstrel performer, African-American New Yorker William Henry Lane, had to disguise himself as a white in black face when he entertained outside of the Five Points, where he impressed Dickens on the author's 1842 tour of the United States. Lane was such a breathtaking dancer that in 1844, when he went on tour in the United States and Europe, he could stop pretending he was white. He was the exception.[13]

Denying blacks the right to portray themselves constituted acknowledgment on the part of their white counterparts that American identity was too fragile to tolerate even recognition, let alone acceptance, of the contributions African Americans had made to the formation of a national character. Minstrelsy became the culturally sanctioned, exclusively racist means to express this uncomfortable truth. Its gross social caricatures also reflected the strong opposition to interracial sex of upper-class reformers, journalists, ministers, and abolitionists.[14]

That black culture was at the core of American national identity was recognized at the time. Henry C. Watson, music critic of the *Broadway*

Journal, which he coedited with Poe, wrote of New York City's popular music in 1845:

> Last summer, Plantation Niggers threatened to overthrow Rossini himself. In truth, the Ethiopian is our only national music . . . This school of music, for such it is fast becoming, is *truly national and truly democratic* [my italics]. It has its home among the slaves, and fairly represents their amusements, character, and social condition.[15]

To grant autonomy to the culture of a people who constituted the most oppressed segment of the workforce would jeopardize the social control the authorities sought over all—black and white—who labored in order to live. Blacks could therefore not be allowed to control the marketing or, as minstrelsy demonstrated, even the expression of their own creations. The mandate for slavery had been reinforced both by the granting of statehood to the Black Belt states of Mississippi, Alabama, and Louisiana and by the 1820 Missouri Compromise, which legally guaranteed the expansion of slavery. And so economic and social pressures against African Americans intensified, as did the onslaught against their cultural autonomy.[16] To most whites, the ideal black man was a contented, obedient being whose sole goal in life was to serve his master.[17] That such a type was rare did not diminish the power of this image and the need to assiduously promote it through the new commercial culture.

While the last vestiges of slavery died out in the North, the minstrel emerged as an important cultural persona for affirming the black's inferior status. Those blacks who would not or could not conform to this white lie were deemed threats to the social order, or worse. African-controlled ventures like the African Grove Theater were suppressed, while Seneca Village, a thriving African-American community, was obliterated in the 1850s to make way for Central Park.[18]

During this critical period of American cultural formation, the African Company's dramatic interpretations of Shakespeare were on a par with the best theater America had to offer at the time. Yet they were not accepted on their own merits because slavery's growing importance to the American economy demanded an appropriate cultural equivalent to bondage and inferiority. Freedom was a necessary precondition for acceptance, and so the African Company was driven from its public stage to be replaced by the minstrel show.[19] The pathological rationale for doing so was provided by the contemporary John McGinn, upon whom

Melville drew for background material in "Bartleby, The Scrivener: A Story of Wall-Street." McGinn wrote of the black man:

> Keep him underneath your feet, and make him grovel in the mire of his own natural and inherent degradation, and he is the most obsequious hound in the world, ready and eager to obey your slightest nod, and fawning around you with all the servility of a dog. But take the same nigger and treat him with something like equality—put him in some petty situation of responsibility or trust, and Cuffee instantly becomes a great man, far too big for his boots. Imitating white people and white fashions with all the faithful mimicry of a monkey, Cuffee becomes insolent and forgets his proper place. The only way, then, to bring him to his senses, is to kick him on the most sensitive part of his skin, or pull his wool until he promises amendment. New York boys, generally speaking, will not tolerate a darkey, as many a dandy nigger, who has been whitened with flour while going along the streets, can testify. How easy it is to distinguish the Southern negro from one born and bred in the North! Sambo from the South, when he enters a bar-room, respectfully uncovers his head, and stands near the door until he is perceived by the barkeeper, who carries him his liquor, for which Sambo pays and feels grateful. Not for the world would he approach the bar—for he *knows his place* and *keeps it*. What a contrast does the conduct of the Northern negro present! He swaggers into a bar-room with the air of a nabob, and calls for his liquor in a loud tone of authority. . . . The Southern negro is obedient, humble, docile, humorous and witty. He looks up to the white man as his natural superior and master—in fact, as his protector. But *Mister Caesar Augustus Johnson*, a dandy Northern nigger who has retired from the patent boot-blacking profession, is pompous, saucy, stupid, ignorant, in every way disgusting. His impertinence frequently deserves the application of a horse-whip.[20]

Whatever redeeming qualities blacks were thought to possess came as the consequence of white "culture and blood." On the eve of the Civil War, Julia Ward Howe—who wrote the words to the "Battle Hymn of the Republic"—offered a less violent racist perspective in the *Atlantic Monthly*:

> The negro of the North is the ideal Negro; it is the negro refined by white culture, elevated by white blood, instructed even by white

iniquity; the negro among negroes is a coarse, grinning, flat-footed, thick-skinned creature, ugly as Caliban, lazy as the laziest of brutes, chiefly ambitious to be of no use to any in the world. View him as you will, his stock in trade is small;—he has but the tangible instinct of all creatures,—love of life, of ease, and of offspring. For all else, he must go to school to the white race, and his discipline must be long and laborious.[21]

The print media thrived on the popularization of such negative stereotypes. When the *New York Sun* in 1833 introduced a journalism that offered titillating revelations of personal misfortune and scandal along with racial caricatures, it became a commercial success.[22] Newspapers were now manufactured more quickly, thanks to technical innovations that in two years allowed the number of copies run off in an hour to rise from two hundred to fifty-five hundred. As Poe had predicted, factory-made falsehoods impacted upon popular consciousness "probably beyond all calculation."[23]

A new factory proletariat with little, if any, formal education, and little appetite for their European heritage other than different habits of food preparation and religious orientation, found on-the-job disappointments alleviated through a mass-based culture that required only a small part of one's wage to absorb. Whether located in factories or in the declining artisan trades, unskilled and semiskilled workers would make up the bulk of the city's workforce by the mid-1850s.[24] Organized sports helped channel their social identification toward elite-dominated pursuits. New technologies assisted in accustoming the populace to identify with "Yankee ingenuity."

Labor's frustrations were released in specially designed public spaces like Barnum's theater and Ripley's emporium. Barnum and Ripley provided temporary psychic relief within a fantasized space. In a grotesque parody of America as a melting pot, Barnum proposed "to secure a man and a woman, as perfect as could be procured, from every accessible people, civilized and barbarous, on the face of the globe."[25] Melville aesthetically realized this human panorama on board the *Pequod* in *Moby-Dick*, where despite a multiplicity of tongues and skin colors, there was no escape from the madman who led all but Ishmael to their doom. Barnum's first entrepreneurial venture as a showman was a traveling road show featuring a 161-year-old slave who had been owned by George Washington's father and who was allegedly present at "the father of our country's" birth. Barnum made so much money from this hoax that he proclaimed he "had at last found my true vocation." His next venture was "an Italian." Soon he had purchased and refurbished the American Museum, located, appropriately enough, across the street from his main spiritual competition, St. Paul's church. The museum's eclectic hodge-podge of skeletons, stuffed birds, wax historical figures, global artifacts, peep-show dioramas, live animals, and the first public aquarium in America was enhanced by the "Lecture Room," arguably as fine a theater as could be found in the city. The American Museum swiftly became the most popular commercial attraction in the world.[26]

Industrial capitalism had generated a consumer playland that reflected the bifurcation of culture into middle-class and working-class variants, roughly championed by and corresponding to Whig nativist Republican, and Democratic Republican immigrant. Consumption gradually advanced purchasing power as a substitute for political power. Psychic stress promoted by increasingly alienated labor led to a need to consume that was reinforced by the wage system.

Duller work and longer hours of work laid emphasis on material enjoyment outside the workplace. Rest had to be made sweeter if not healthier. While Barnum and Ripley provided psychic escape within a fantasized space, Frederick Law Olmsted's Republican park replaced the republican vistas of Jefferson. Visions of homesteads for all workingmen were replaced by a "central" park where little republicans might mingle with big Republicans[27] and be safely socialized by the latter in a manner that reinforced economic subservience. Outside Central Park, the landscape itself was being transformed into "mile after mile of stunted trees."[28] For the cities, planners had landscaped an oasis of green onto a concrete and asphalt grid.

Price substituted for spiritual values, as the marketplace spuriously distinguished between good and bad men. For centuries, men had been imprisoned for going into debt. Since private entrepreneurs forced the state itself to go into debt by bribing the state legislature to fund their operations, debt was no longer deemed a crime, and imprisonment for debt was abolished in 1837 in New York State, just as the panic struck.

The economic boom of the 1830s accelerated this deterioration of financial integrity. It created in Cooper's words, a subclass:

nouveaux riches, who are as certain to succeed an old and displaced class of superiors, as hungry flies to follow them with bellies, [and] would have been much more apt to run into extravagance and folly, than persons always accustomed to money, and who did not depend on its exhibition for their importance.[29]

The more intellectually pretentious of these *nouveaux riches* sponsored literary impresarios who sought to create a cultural caste through magazines that became armories of good taste; they also condemned works like *Moby-Dick* for offending same. Their literary magazines, in Perry Miller's words, "constructed funeral pyres in 1851 and 1852 for that original genius of America they had, in their several ways, expected to emerge in the 1840s."[30] This new middle class "craved not challenge but reassurance."[31] Fiction that forced readers to think about the role they played in society was ignored; so Hawthorne's and especially Melville's reputations, small as they were with the general public, declined to irrelevance.

The professional intellectual removed himself from public life when the first party system's "civic culture," as Thomas Bender has termed it, succumbed to the incipient consumerism of the second.[32] Prior to the development of this consumerism, Europeans did not perceive America as possessing its own cultural identity, and even, as Cooper wrote, confounded America with South America "and with the aborigines."[33] This did have at least one unintended effect: the great bird painter John James Audubon was an immediate success in England, while in the United States he was ignored for a long time.

In the generation during which the second party system was in existence, Europeans came to identify consumer culture with America. During the first party system, there had been no uniquely marketed American culture. European culture was readily expropriated and rendered intelligible to all classes and ethnic groups, as exemplified by the wide audience given Shakespeare and Italian opera. After the Civil War, with culture more stratified along class lines, Shakespeare and Italian opera became "highbrow." But even before the Civil War, this process of cultural divorce was facilitated by American commentators, like George Foster, who touted the superiority of the culture of the streets over European civilization.[34]

The American emphasis on the material and impulsive displeased the literati clustered around the *Knickerbocker Magazine*. They sought to create a safe social distance from mass culture, rather than a precarious social alternative to it. Their quest for British literary models to civilize the masses accorded with support for British bankers and industrialists, whose investments in America, aside from keeping America's expansion fueled by adequate credit, reinforced social ties with the American ruling elite.

The literary impresarios set standards of refinement that rankled writers of the first rank, like Cooper, who supported the Democrats, now in the midst of a presidential campaign. Democrats attacked Whigs for intending to saddle the United States with a two hundred million dollar debt to "the fundmongers of London,"[35] and for allowing Great Britain to hold onto Oregon. Cooper charged that

> England holds the character of almost every man in the nation at her mercy. . . . Look at my own case—I had exceeding popularity in this country, until I wrote *The Travelling Bachelor*—This book displeased the English; they abused me, and even those who had known me from childhood began to look on me with distrustful eyes. Any falsehood that the English chose to circulate was repeated at home, and believed.[36]

Even Irving, the most anglophilic among prominent American writers, complained about "the vast influx of British literature, aided by the state of our Copy wright law, render[ing] it hard for Native writers to get their heads above the surface."[37]

As the literary vehicle for New York City's anglophiles, the *Knickerbocker Magazine*, launched in 1833 in New York City, quickly became the nation's most important literary journal. Until the Civil War, the *Knickerbocker* stood for New York "high" society. Episcopalian Whig Lewis Gaylord Clark was its tyrannical captain of good taste—in the words of Perry Miller, "vain, feline, vindictive . . . in person and in print, disgustingly smug, all the time parading as hail-fellow-well-met,"[38] a veritable Machiavellian. Clark tacked to the new national class with a view of "Nature" in patriotic service to an America stretching "from sea to shining sea."

In friendly competition, the *United States Magazine and Democratic Review* emerged in 1837. As the literary journal of American frontier nationalism, it became cultural home to the Loco Focos and to their militant auxiliary, the Young America movement.[39] Its editor, John L. O'Sullivan, was a New York City Protestant Tammany assemblyman who believed, like Madison, that landed expansion held the key to giving European men, native and immigrant, a stake in the American dream. Africans and their abolitionist supporters were excluded. The inaugural issue proclaimed belief "in the principle of democratic republicanism, in its strongest and purest sense . . . in the virtue, intelligence, and full capacity for self-government, of the great mass of our people—our industrious, honest, manly, intelligent millions of freemen."

Democracy was equated with republicanism, "for the republican principle . . ." is "the supremacy of the will of the majority. . . ." And given that two-thirds of the commercial press was "anti-democratic . . . the vital principle of an American national literature must be democracy." O'Sullivan exhorted American writers to free themselves from "the past and present literature of England. All history has to be re-written; political science and the whole scope of all moral truth have to be considered and illustrated in the light of the democratic principle."[40]

The *United States Magazine and Democratic Review* integrated into its ranks Paineite organs like the *Working Man's Advocate*, whose masthead proudly proclaimed its devotion "to the political and social Advancement of the Masses." In its concern for "farmers and workingmen," the *Working Man's Advocate* chastised the dominant parties for following the principle that the "Government take care of the rich, and the rich will manage the poor." Placing the interests of the farmers first meant that plantation owners were included in this Jeffersonian axis.[41]

The *Knickerbocker Magazine* and the *United States Magazine and Democratic Review* complemented one another—journalistic wings to transport the American imperial eagle westward. As every patriot sacrificed himself for his country, so nature was made to sacrifice herself to the American entrepreneurs' notion of progress, popularized by New Yorker Walt Whitman in his masterwork *Leaves of Grass*. Whitman, a rare literary apostle of industrialism, placed man on an equal plane with nature because of "all this mighty, many-threaded wealth and industry concentrated here."[42] In *Leaves of Grass*, he approvingly cataloged the mechanical novelty that Poe perceived as sapping the spiritual integrity of the individual.[43]

In stark contrast, Poe, who lived for much of his literary career in New York City, felt science denied the mystery of life at the core of our sensual experience. In "Sonnet—To Science," he objected to science wrenching nature from its setting to satisfy human ambition:

> Science! true daughter of Old Time thou art!
> Who alterest all things with thy peering eyes.

Why prey'st thou thus upon the poet's heart,
    Vulture, whose wings are dull realities?
How should he love thee? or how deem thee wise,
    Who wouldst not leave him in his wandering
To seek for treasure in the jewelled skies,
    Albeit he soared with an undaunted wing?
Hast thou not torn the Naiad from her flood,
The elfin from the green grass, and from me
The summer dream beneath the tamarind tree?[44]

Poe was publicly scorned, while Whitman became a celebrated public figure. Whitman recognized that America's cultural role rested with "the average, the bodily, the concrete, the dramatic, the popular, in which all the superstructures of the future are to permanently rest."[45] Still, he claimed to yearn for a more spiritual culture, something Henry David Thoreau actively sought to embody in his lifestyle as well as in his writings. In contrast to Spain and France, in America, Thoreau observed,

> Utility is the rallying word with us; we are a nation of speculators, stock-holders, and money-changers; we do everything by steam, because it is most expeditious, and cheapest in the long run. . . . The question with us is whether a book will take—will sell well, not whether it is worth taking, or worth selling. . . .[46]

Through the literary journal *The Dial*, Margaret Fuller sought to give more literary substance to the newly formed American commercial identity that so alienated Poe. She provided an aesthetic as well as a moral alternative to rampant utilitarianism. At the same time, her transcendentalist feminism threatened the standing of a paternalist patrician like George Templeton Strong because she did not subordinate her intellect to "womanly impulse," as he put it.[47]

Strong was assisted in his misogyny by the growing strength of capital, which allowed a new Republican like himself to link national integrity with industrial progress led by tycoons, members of a distinctively male occupation. These entrepreneurs distinguished themselves from slaveholders by treating men's labor, rather than the actual men themselves, as a commodity. They asserted that every man's liberty was at risk from the Southern slaveholder.[48] Liberty and freedom became so obsessively heralded in this political environment that one Dickensian character quipped, "They're so fond of Liberty in this part of the globe, that they buy her and sell her and carry her to market with 'em. They've such a passion for Liberty, that they can't help taking liberties with her."[49]

Before the 1820s, theater had provided entertainment for rich men, poor women in need of their money, and artisans and workmen out to vent their frustrations on both. Afterward, it became an arena of public display for the working class. Celebrities publicly outshone economic elites but did not challenge the latter's easy access to public resources. The first celebrities were thespians, radiating glamour to divert attention away from control of the means of production and toward frivolous consumer concerns that possessed vast marketing potential. By the 1850s, the theatrical scene had bifurcated to reflect growing class divisions, with the rich patronizing theaters on Broadway while workers frequented vaudeville houses on the Lower East Side. Certainly, the right to recreation was a more important issue for the working class than the right of the slaves to be free.

The economic elite's discomfort with popular politics intensified with the rise of celebrities led by divas Fanny Ellser and Jenny Lind in the 1840s. Hone was uneasy when he encountered a *Herald* reporter at a "Fancy Ball." He recorded in his diary that "this kind of surveillance is getting to be intolerable, and nothing but the force of public opinion will correct the insolence, which, it is to be feared, will never be applied as long as . . . gentlemen make this Mr. Attree 'hail fellow well met,' as they did on this occasion."[50]

The rich responded by withdrawing into newly created private clubs, which provided sanctuary for their schemes of private enrichment at public expense. They transformed their more publicly accessible partnerships into abstract incorporated entities that deflected public attention from the principal figures engaged in peculation or usury.

The social impact of the celebrity can be measured by tracing the changes in placement of theater seating. The family circle designed for women and children coincided with the disappearance of the notorious third tier for prostitutes. The old space had pandered to merchants and lawyers who, as the theatergoing elite, had grown accustomed to dropping their public reserve in the off-stage areas during the main event.

In the new consumer realm of domestic comforts, a market arose for carpets and cheap furniture for working-class homes—a phenomenon unknown in Europe. Poe designated the carpet "the soul of the apartment," and found much to deride in the dwellings of the "rabble" who equated taste with cost.[51] The introduction of central heating and hot and cold water to the best boardinghouses and upper-class homes provided incentive for workers to labor harder. Ready-made clothes were purchased by a wage-earning class dependent on domestic manufacturing capitalistically organized. Workers had shoes and ate more meat than today's Americans. In 1841, 39 percent of the food budget went to meat, 25 percent to grain, 22 percent to dairy products, and only 14 percent to vegetables and fruits. Yet for the period from 1843 to 1856, while average per capita income increased in the city's richest wards from 281 to 581 dollars, in the three poorest wards, the increase was only 41 dollars—from 21 to 62 dollars.[52] The richest wards were now more than nine times richer than the poorer ones, as opposed to seven times richer in 1843.

The commercialization of culture assisted in the erosion of values upheld since the founding of the colonies, values enshrined by John Bunyan, who in his dislike of the haughty rich and the desperate poor stood for classic republican virtues. In his masterwork, *The Pilgrim's Progress,* placed next to the *Bible* on countless bedside tables, Bunyan had written of a Town of Vanity with a Fair that displayed "all such Merchandise sold, as houses, lands, trades, places, honours, preferments, titles, countries, kingdoms, lusts, pleasures, and delights of all sorts," including "thefts, murders, adulteries, [and] false-swearers." The pilgrims who dared to "buy the truth" behind the appearance of this material glut were judged "bedlams and mad. . . . Therefore they . . . beat them . . . and . . . put them in a cage that they might be made a spectacle to all the men of the fair." Their fate is reminiscent of "the discerning few" in Machiavelli's *The Prince,* who are made into a dire object lesson and "are isolated when the majority and the government are at one." The popularity of *The Pilgrim's Progress* evaporated as its message became irrelevant to the consumer-oriented needs of a dynamic industrial capitalism.

In a defense of consumerism, *Putnam's Monthly Magazine* proclaimed, "We reject the Spartan theory of republican life, which simply leads us back to the barbarities of Spartan or Puritan despotism. . . . We like to be amused, we are only too happy to be entertained."[53]

Those who challenged this Whig-Republican *novus ordo seclorum* were subjected to campaigns of vilification, especially if they were nationally distinguished like Cooper. Whig editors and politicians Park Benjamin, Horace Greeley, James Watson Webb, and Thurlow Weed all libeled or slandered Cooper because of the latter's revealing portrait of America in his work *Home As Found.* So intense was their journalistic barrage that

Cooper despaired of ever being able to prosecute them all. He concluded of the United States:

[It] is the only country in which I have found it a positive personal disadvantage to be a writer. A century is wanting to advance the country far enough to appreciate the rights of authors . . . in my case, the press publicly insists on its right to libel me, under the pretence of supporting the inviolability of criticism. . . . When I appeal to the laws for protection against falsehood and calumny, conspiring to destroy me, and profess a willingness to put the issue on the truth, I am met with the answer, that you are public property, and we can and will publish to the world, in newspapers, truely or falsely, what we please of you . . . in no other country, claiming to be civilized, would men be found who dared to hold such a doctrine.[54]

Still, Cooper managed to be one of the handful of American writers of quality who was able to support himself through his writings. When Cooper began his career in the 1820s, the literary marketplace was such that he received from 30 to 45 percent of the proceeds of his sales. By 1840, his net American income per book had been reduced by almost 90 percent. One presidential election later, Cooper complained, "The book-trade is in such a condition now, that booksellers will take no ink, unless they can reap all the profits. . . ." Hawthorne and Melville, and especially Poe, fared worse.[55]

The anti-Cooper campaign was masterminded by Weed, who officially headed up the brilliant 1840 Whig presidential electoral strategy. Weed successfully portrayed the Democrats as aristocrats and his party as more democratic. Whigs put up a 50-by-100-foot log cabin "of unhewn logs, in the most primitive style" to appeal to the aesthetic of the average man;[56] in fact, their candidate, William Henry Harrison, dubbed a "log cabin and hard cider" man, had been born in a mansion and drank bourbon. Hone candidly summed up the Machiavellian Whig recipe for presidential success when he wrote that the "Whigs had learned to abandon their elitist principles in public in favor of a campaign of appearances that would get them into office where they might rule as usual."[57]

Harrison inspired European Americans through his conquests of "inferior" peoples. His fictive apotheosis was Colonel A. B. C. Smith of the Poe short story, "The Man That Was Used Up."[58] In this tale, the reporter protagonist went beyond appearances to the dressing room that revealed the broken man behind the heroic image. The ready-made clothing industry was but one industrial manifestation necessary to the success of the colonel's disguise. A new model for American national politics had been set for the few who could feel beyond appearance. By satirizing past, present, and future military presidents for fulfilling his personal political horror at how their parts added up to more than the whole of their appearance—in A.[ll] B.[ut] C.[omplete] Smith—Poe lent substance to Machiavelli's justly famous remark that "everyone can see what you appear to be, whereas few have direct experience of what you really are, and those few will not dare to challenge the popular view. . . ."[59]

The first Colonel A. B. C. Smith had been Andrew Jackson. His innovative style had transformed political campaigning. Jackson's powers as president were so unprecedented that National Republicans were politically unprepared for his popularity. In response, they appealed to the progressive element in Anglo-Saxon political tradition by changing their name to Whigs. They felt the average voter knew that the Whigs had led the struggle against the tyrannical policies of the seventeenth-century divine-right monarchs, with whom they sought to identify Andrew Jackson.

The political embers that the Whigs of 1834 vainly stirred had once blazed in the American Revolution with such rhetoric as, "the candidate for my Vote must be a Whig, . . . Zealous for the Glorious Revolution . . . To Despotism in the Ruler, or Licentiousness in the People as equally destructive to Liberty, he must be utterly averse. . . ."

Seventy years after the Revolution the revival resonated poorly. Democrats gauged correctly that "the Whigs are imitative, and ready to take any method of catching popularity. . . ."[60] Instead of firing the political imaginations of the people, the change of name from National Republican to Whig only contributed to the Whigs' extinguishment as a party just a score of years afterward.[61]

Democratic consumption substituted for the decline in small-scale enterprises as production became more of a mass collective effort where a relatively small number of capitalists exercised effective control. This incipient "totalitarian" society—defined by Marcuse as "a non-terroristic economic-technical coordination which operates through the manipulation of needs by vested interests"[62]—would ultimately castrate the labor movement. The anesthetic would be Poe's gas-and-glass consumerism, as passive spectacle substituted for active drama. Barnum's pioneering Jenny

Lind mass concerts catered to all classes and joined them pacifically at moments of public consumption.[63] But on the job, immigrant workers and their new capitalist bosses shared only the mutual antagonism bred by the alienating environment of the workplace. Acting in concert on the stage of republican society was replaced by actors in concert on a vaudevillian stage that Americanized immigrants. Spectacles choreographed and advertised by Barnum were presented as evidence of a vibrant democracy.[64] Industrialization allowed for the marketing of a new identity for the working classes that involved them in a merry-go-round of fashion changes and personality cults, while depriving them of the right to participate in setting the national economic agenda. A few financially successful artisans ceased to support the mercantilism that produced artisans, and instead became capitalists, encouraged by a loosening of the standards for establishing corporations.

Material gloss proliferated, thanks to mechanization. The newest hotel lobbies housed fancy shops that sported the latest machine-spun wares. Poe summed up the new commercial aesthetic when he exclaimed, "We are violently enamored of gas and of glass. . . . We have adopted it, partly on account of its *flashiness*, but principally on account of its *greater cost*." The "almighty dollar" ruled.[65]

In the aftermath of the Panic of 1837, illusion became a much sought after commodity, an insensate reality alien to the temperament of an aesthete like Poe. In a trenchant satire, "The Philosophy of Furniture," Poe brilliantly assessed all this novelty as,

> but the wicked invention of a race of time-servers and money-lovers—children of Baal and worshippers of Mammon—Benthams, who, to spare thought and economize fancy, first cruelly invented the Kaleidoscope, and then established joint-stock companies to twirl it by steam.[66]

American industry, through its journalistic agents, promoted mass culture as more and more artisans lost control over the sale of their product. More deracinated individuals lost themselves in ever larger crowds. New York City became "the theatre of humbugs," as one contemporary observer put it, with its "motley population," many of whom "spend their time in nothing else, but in searching after some new thing."[67] Poe believed that "we live in an age so enlightened that no such thing as an individual is supposed to exist. It is the mass for which the true Humanity cares."[68]

The shift in political values precipitated by this market revolution was illuminated in the contrasts provided by Washington Irving and James Fenimore Cooper,[69] and in a literary apostle of industrialism, the patent intellectual and transcendentalist Ralph Waldo Emerson, in his 1844 lecture, "The Young American." Emerson was the most pragmatic of visionaries, one who epitomized the artisan middle-class desire for reform.[70] In *The Confidence-Man: His Masquerade*, Melville satirized Emerson through the character of Mark Winsome, who rhapsodized, "Mystery is in the morning, and mystery in the night, and the beauty of mystery is everywhere; but still the plain truth remains, that worth and purse must be filled." Emerson was the pathfinder of the middle class, concerned with "the relations of man to the objects around him."[71] The relations of man to man could be left to the statesmen Jefferson Davis and Abraham Lincoln, who helped wrench New York City from its devotion to the Southern cause.

With Cooper, Hawthorne, Melville, and Poe, an American literature attained immortality that arose from an acute sense of place.[72] This facility was not achieved until the mass-based second party system generated values that fictional characters could embody. The literary results constitute masterworks of disillusionment in Hawthorne and Melville, escape in Thoreau, or the horrific amalgam of the two in Poe.

Among the many trials at which Cooper was compelled to endure spit in his literary eye was one at the town of Fonda, which he satirized in *Home As Found*. As Cooper subsequently reported in a letter to Cornelius Matthews and Augustus Ducykinck—a pair of editors who consciously strove to publish a bowdlerized American literature—the townspeople "discovered they did not know things that stood daily before their eyes, had not read straight, and, in short, were all wrong. What is still more remarkable, they do not hesitate to say it."[73] In *Martin Chuzzlewit*, Dickens presented the rich abolitionist Norrises as hypocrites when it came to socially associating with blacks and with whites like Martin Chuzzlewit, who were not rich; for the Norrises

> were the bright particular stars of an exalted New York sphere. There were other fashionable spheres above them, and none of the stars in any of these spheres had anything to say to the stars in any other of these spheres. But, through all the spheres it would go forth, that the Norrises, deceived by gentlemanly manners and appearances, had, falling from their high estate, 'received' a dollarless

and unknown man. O guardian eagle of the pure Republic, had they lived for this![74]

Business success became the acme of individuality and spawned its own pulp literature to sugarcoat materialism. Parvenus attended concerts and lectures entitled, "The Philosophy of the Soul," "The Philosophy of Crime," and "The Philosophy of Vegetables," to "escape . . . monotony; look at each other's clothes; and come home again." Poe was amused to see how many New York City oyster cellars, hats, gloves, and walking canes could be named after James Polk, the slaveholding Democratic presidential candidate.[75]

Work had become less creative, more fragmented, yet routine, and subject to the steely control of financiers and capitalists. Consumerism was the trade-off, and a politics of the mass was consumerism's reflection and reinforcement. So captivating was the material allure of this "wonderfully inventive age"[76] that even a poet of the stature of Walt Whitman, the Andrew Jackson of American literature, smoothed the rough course by glamorizing in his *Leaves of Grass* the myriad types of objects and persons generated by the industrialization of society through the second party system.

THE ROARING FORTIES

Democrats Extend Their Turf,
1840–1849

Society [is divided] into two classes—whereof, one, the great mass, asserts a spurious independence, most miserably dependent for its mean existence on the disregard of humanising conventionalities of manner and social custom, so that the coarser a man is, the more distinctly it shall appeal to his taste; while the other, disgusted with the low standard thus set up and made adaptable to everything, takes refuge among the graces and refinements it can bring to bear on private life, and leaves the public weal to such fortune as may betide it in the press and uproar of a general scramble.

Charles Dickens, *Martin Chuzzlewit* (1843)

Whenever a theory is put forth, which threatens, if carried into practice, to abridge the power of the rich—to lessen their means of preying upon the poor, and to elevate the unfortunate victims of their unrelenting avarice and oppression, it is sure to be associated with the most bitter and untiring malignity.

Mike Walsh, "Agrarianism," *Subterranean*, February 24, 1844

I du believe wutever trash
　　'll keep the people in blindness,—
Thet we the Mexicuns can thrash
　　Right inter brotherly kindness,
Thet bombshells, grape, an' powder 'n' ball
　　Air good-will's strongest magnets,
Thet peace, to make it stick at all.
　　Must be druv in with bagnets.

James Russell Lowell, "The Pious Editor's Creed" (1847)

New York City Democrats made themselves responsible for the political acculturation of the increasing flow of European immigrants who replaced the native artisans as the body of New York City's working class by 1850. With New York City absorbing 22 percent of all immigration to the United States, four times as many immigrants arrived from 1845 to 1860 as had done so in the previous quarter century, yielding the greatest rate of urbanization in United States history. Many found jobs in New York, as the city's share of U.S. imports rose from one-quarter in the 1790s to two-thirds a half century later.[1]

The economic growth fueled by immigrant labor promoted corruption among bankers and the politicians they bribed; the corruption helped precipitate the Panic of 1837. Nine years later, the state legislature sought to curtail the widespread practice of having depreciated stocks act as security for circulating notes. Banking bill no. 322 passed the assembly by a vote of ninety-two to five. When it reached the senate floor, George F. Curtis, a banker subsequently prominent in New York State Republican politics, wrote to New York City state senator George Folsom, "I could not myself be a director for five minutes with such a law." Curtis feared that "Banking will be in the wrong hands," namely, subject to public oversight. He felt especially vulnerable to a provision that made even "unintentional" violations of the law subject to imprisonment. Thanks to Folsom and five other senators, the bill lost on May 13, 1846. The vote in the thirty-two-man senate was twenty in favor and six opposed. Because it was an act to amend a banking law, a two-thirds vote had been required.[2]

The investment favored by bankers during the second party system was the railroad, which soon dwarfed in size the printing and clothing industries. Whereas textiles reigned as the most important industry economically during the first third of the nineteenth century, speculation in railroad securities accounted for most of the growth in the New York Stock Exchange during the 1830s.[3]

The railroad having the greatest impact on New York City's development in the antebellum period was the Erie, chartered in 1832. Four years later, the Erie received a 3 million dollar loan from the state legislature without repayment being specified. When the Panic of 1837 set in, the Erie proposed to offer employment to three thousand men in exchange for the city advancing it credit. While the Whigs supported the proposal, the Democrats opposed it. When the city refused to advance credit, the

Erie again petitioned the state legislature, which rejected its appeal on the grounds that the state could not afford to subsidize this enterprise. By 1842 the Erie had exhausted its credit, owed 12.5 million dollars, and had laid only 470 miles of track. Then, in an about-face, the Democratic-controlled legislature approved a charter. Soon afterward, the Erie declared bankruptcy, defaulted on 5 million dollars worth of stock, and saddled the state with interest to pay on that stock.[4]

This default helped make taxation a permanent feature of state government. Passage of the Stop and Tax Act in 1842 suspended internal improvements and initiated taxation of real and personal property. L. Ray Gunn has noted that this law appealed to traditional republican values, while at the same time, it initiated "a modern, rational, financial system." By 1845, the state had given up its claim to recover the original 3 million dollars.[5]

The taxpayer was now legally obligated to finance enterprise without owning it. Other railroads, like the New York and Harlem, following in the tracks of the Erie, soon proved to be lucrative ventures for their owners because they had the benefit of public subsidy without public control, a pattern that flourishes in the present to the detriment of the public interest.[6]

In terms of providing employment, railroads replaced the canal building of a generation earlier. Immigrant Irishmen would continue to provide the labor. Their need to escape materially and psychologically from the holocaust that English imperialism inflicted on their homeland made them ideal receptors for the new mass culture that provided a sensory palliative for dangerous canal or railroad work.

Commercial cultural spectacles diverted attention from the growing disparity in the distribution of wealth. The new Republican Party would in the 1850s redefine republicanism to exclude questions of economic equality from political consideration, instead stressing questions of state. Without counting wealth owned by nonresidents, the wealthiest 4 percent of New York City's population increased its share of noncorporate wealth from 63 to 80 percent between 1828 and 1845.[7]

Many of the remaining 96 percent of New Yorkers were foreign born and lived in dreadful circumstances that allowed the Whigs to target immigrants as the principal threat to an American culture identified with English tradition. Ex-mayor Philip Hone was alarmed that this "great animated, overwhelming material . . . cannot make a living at home . . .

increase our taxes, eat our bread, and encumber our streets, and not one in twenty is competent to keep himself."[8]

In his satire on the future, "Mellonta Tauta," Poe observed,

> a fellow named *Mob* . . . set up a despotism. This Mob [a foreigner by birth] is said to have been the most odious of all men that ever encumbered the earth. He was a giant in stature—insolent, rapacious, filthy; had the gall of a bullock with the heart of a hyena and the brains of a peacock. . . . As for Republicanism, no analogy could be found for it upon the face of the earth—unless we except the case of the "prairie dogs," an exception which serves to demonstrate, if anything, that democracy is a very admirable form of government— for dogs.[9]

Unlike Poe, New York City Whigs could not politically afford to openly resist democracy or immigration, because foreign labor powered the new factory system. During the 1840s and early 1850s, they covertly supported the nativist, mainly European Protestant American Republicans, a precursor to the Know Nothings of the 1850s. Founded in 1843 and made up mainly of ex-Whigs, this reform party's program essentially consisted of restricting immigrant rights through enforced inclusion, rather than outright exclusion. Whigs wanted immigrants to conform to "American" standards, or else face the wrath of the law. Like the Workingmen of the late 1820s, American Republicans reacted against the mass employment of less skilled labor. Their anti-Catholic rhetoric disguised class bias because American Republicans vilified the less skilled Irish, rather than the more skilled German.[10]

American Republicans and Whigs were more anti-immigrant than anti-African, labeling themselves "native American" republican as opposed to "democratic" republican.[11] Since Africans had been present in large numbers in the seventeenth century they could be considered native. African Americans were no political threat to the elite Whigs' sense of mission. They could be utilized as agents of American national promise, so long as their role remained subservient.

The adoption of rigorous entry requirements for immigrants that was at the core of American Republican precepts weakened the Whig Party in New York City. Only when opposition to the expansion of slavery became the critical issue in the 1850s did many Whigs develop the moral momentum suited to their national aspirations. But this new vigor came at a price—the destruction of their party when the new Republican Party absorbed them as well as the American Republicans and Free Soilers.

Through the new commercial culture, the Republican Party promoted entrepreneurial values as "American values." Through Abraham Lincoln they produced the most powerful chief executive the United States had ever known. He relied on the war industry, the most dynamic sector of the economy during his presidency, to create a more centralized federal government.

Even before the Civil War, New York City's government reflected this trend toward concentration of authority in fewer hands, though passing through the city's streets, one might easily believe otherwise. By 1850, the city's population had increased 800 percent in a half century, to 516,000. Municipally run fire districts needed to be established, if only because volunteer-company engine houses had become, in too many instances, "places of debauchery; boys pass the nights there, and are corrupted and initiated to bad courses." They were also schools for racism and notorious for their anti-abolitionist fervor.[12]

In the meantime, the middle and upper classes moved north of Bleeker Street but could commute to work thanks to the introduction of horse-drawn omnibuses and of railroads. Urban growth amplified opportunities for self-aggrandizement through advance knowledge of city land purchases or, more frequently, city land sales to pay for municipal services.

In the long run, leasing would have been sounder for the city's fiscal health. Instead, long-term public stability was sacrificed to short-term personal profit and the financial security of New York City's most socially prominent families, whose investments in new forms of communication, transportation, and utilities were richly rewarded through city contracts. For instance, the Common Council gave the city's first gas company the exclusive right, gratis, to illuminate all thoroughfares south of Grand Street for thirty years, while Tammany officials were the incorporators of the New York and Harlem Railroad.[13] In 1844, when American Republican mayor and publisher James Harper, who opposed this Tammany railroad as well as the Irish and Germans, failed to halt railroad service on Sundays, Poe noted "loud complaints, on the part of the 'original Natives' that the new authorities have made nearly all the appointments from the ranks of the Whigs. There can be no doubt that patriotism (well paid) is a capital thing."[14]

Even before the Great Famine, the Irish were a powerful social and political presence in New York City. By 1840, the sixth ward, site of

Tammany Hall, was the largest Irish community in the nation. The miserable condition of its Irish prompted the city to seek poor relief from the state government for the first time. This unprecedented event demonstrated the failure of the charitable efforts of well-to-do New Yorkers like Hone and Strong, whose philanthropy from the sanctity of their townhouses was a mainstay of their public as well as personal identity and sense of self-worth. That their benevolence had proven insufficient only made the social elite more eager to blame the victims suffering in their shanties. These mainly Anglo-Dutch Protestants feared the loss of Whig electoral control to Catholic newcomers, now caricatured in the press as physically grotesque louts being manipulated by corrupt Democratic politicians. Smug Whigs like Strong castigated Democrats for possessing an "agrarian, disorganizing, law-defying character."[15]

In Philadelphia, riots had occurred in 1844 when nativist artisans set upon Catholic immigrants; twelve persons were killed.[16] These murderous feelings were exacerbated a year later by an influx of hundreds of thousands of impoverished Irish uprooted by the Great Famine. Profound differences in expectations and personal outlook toward work stemmed from the immigrants' accustomed role in production and from an intellectual horizon that had been limited by concern for mere survival. These differences had been transmuted into religious and cultural bigotry on both sides.

The vast Irish influx ensured the dominance of New York City Democrats. Taking advantage of Whig-controlled Common Council harassment of immigrants, Tammany Hall established a naturalization bureau to inculcate new citizens on the workings of a Democratic marketplace in which everything was for sale, including votes. In less than four months in early 1840, almost nine hundred aliens took the oath of citizenship before judges friendly to Tammany. Jealous at the success of this judicial innovation, Whigs countered with a bill mandating formal registration of voters, which the Democrats opposed to the point of noncompliance.[17]

The potential for voter fraud expanded when wards were divided into election districts, each containing approximately five hundred voters, and in April 1840, Democrats captured the same twelve wards they had controlled before the election. To win over the Democratic voter, Whig Governor William Seward, subsequently a principal founder of the Republican Party, proposed during his 1840 state of the state address that schools employ teachers with the same religious and cultural background as their students. His plan was opposed by the Anglo-Dutch citizens who ran the Public School Society. They contended that the immigrant influx lowered the quality of life for all. Bishop John Hughes's political organization, Carroll Hall, provided political grist for the nativist crusade. It refused to endorse any Tammany man who did not support Seward's proposal, and the three Democrats who did not receive the bishop's blessing lost their contests in the fall of 1841.[18] The bishop's interference in political affairs prompted Tammany to mobilize the labor movement in the 1844 election.

Immigrants, drawn from the social landscape of a ravaged peasantry, embraced the Democratic values of small property ownership in a city "black with dirt and putridness," where "a thin, noisome vapour reeked up from the cellars which were stowed with human beings, packed like Africans in the hold of a slave ship."[19] Many of the more recent arrivals fared better, confined to boardinghouses and tenements, the architectural innovation of the 1840s.[20] Catholic immigrants alienated the xenophobic American Republicans, who came to power in New York City in 1844 on a platform of reform that targeted immigrants as the source of urban blight. A board of aldermen report estimated that ten thousand prostitutes—mainly immigrants, some not yet teenagers—conducted their trade in 1844. But the new "reform" party chose to explicitly ignore their plight, instead pledging to elect only the native born.[21] Since Whigs were closely identified with Americans of Anglo-Dutch background, the American Republican Party's nativist appeal could only cost Whigs votes.

In the three-way mayoral race in 1844, American Republicans received 49 percent of the vote, with Democrats getting 41 percent. The Whigs' 10 percent showing brought into serious question the party's continued existence as a dominant political force. For New York City, the social composition of the Whigs has yet to be examined with precision. What is clear is that American Republican anti-immigrant animus drew largely from Whig ranks, and not from Democrats as the Workingmen had done in the early 1830s. The Democratic Party had become the party of non-Protestant immigrants, race supremacists, and artisans who opposed the spread of incorporated enterprises. That the American Republican Party did not draw from Democratic ranks was widely known at the time. The staunchly Democratic Irish labor leader Mike Walsh, in characteristically racist language, found "Native American democrats" as common as "honest thieves or white darkies."[22]

Even though they presented themselves as a "reform" party, the American Republicans proved no more resistant than others to charges of corruption. Ironically, only when they were ousted from office in 1845 was New York City able to establish a uniformed police force to take the place of the old watch, a legacy of colonial times.[23] That year, the American Republicans joined the nationally based Native American Party, dedicated to a "defense of American institutions against the encroachments of foreign influence, open or concealed."[24] They were ultimately absorbed into the new Republican Party, whose anti-Catholic bias proved attractive to native Protestant artisans unwilling to attack the emerging capitalist order.

By 1845, with the city population at more than 400,000 and growing at the rate of 20,000 per year, 300,000 people lived on a dollar a week per person.[25] Most of these poor were Irish Catholics of whom the overwhelming majority voted Democratic.

In the 1840s, the Democrats made political history by developing the most socially representative political organization on earth. It was a team effort by rash men of muscle whose political impatience on land was reinforced by courage at sea. No other sailing vessels ever equaled the fabled Yankee clippers of this era. Just as the clipper captain and sailors triumphantly plied the sea lanes, merchant and artisans rode a Democratic Party opposed to the centripetal state tendencies that corporate capitalism was engendering.

Analysis of New York City Democrats in 1844 reveals that more than 950 members of the 2,391-man party were skilled and unskilled workers.[26] In a time of small-scale production, this made the party larger than any other urban institution and vital to the maintenance of public order and economic growth.

Political power in the New York City "Democracy" centered in the General Committee of fifty-one men elected from each of the city's seventeen wards. The General Committee overlapped with the Tammany Society, whose steering committee, the Council of Sachems, owned the building where the party met. The sachems decided which faction could use its facilities.[27] Paralleling the General Committee was the Young Men's general committee, a stepping stone to higher party office, to which men under thirty years old belonged. The Tammany Society, the Democratic General Committee, and the Young Men's general committee were the most important agencies of the party.

Below these groups stood the ward committees, which mediated between the party elite and the mass of voters. They served as the party's organizational building blocks. At their meeting halls, men gathered to share the Democratic experience.[28] Each ward committee consisted of thirteen to twenty-five men who, in turn, elected three representatives to the General Committee. In practice, fewer than half the General Committee members attended meetings, and a caucus of the General Committee leadership nominated party officials.

Wards, in turn, consisted of election districts that varied in number from two in the second and twelfth wards, to eight in the eighth. The election district was the smallest political unit; each contained a polling place supervised by a voting inspector.[29] Votes were cast for ward aldermen and assistant aldermen. These men served on the Common Council, whose legislative enactments were subject to mayoral veto. Each ward also elected a tax collector, two assessors, and two constables. Groups of wards constituted the four districts for congressional seats, while one senator and thirteen assemblymen represented the city in the state legislature. Assembly-district boundaries differed from those of wards in this period, as state politicians sought to control city politics through gerrymandering.

Because the wards acted as the link between people and party, they possessed a complex infrastructure of subcommittees and auxiliary organizations. Subcommittees nominated candidates for primaries and carried out party directives. In addition, some forty-seven separate organizations,[30] including colorfully designated auxiliary clubs like the Butt-End Coon Hunters and the Fearnot Club, extended the influence of the party at the grassroots level by offering both political and social activity, such as fancy dress balls held during the winter months.[31] This political culture was not as exclusive as it would later become.[32]

In the days before gaslight, the different Democratic clubs promised "brilliant illuminations" at their outdoor evening meetings. Potential voters, many of whom did not regularly read newspapers, became aware of the party's presence on the streets. Meetings, like the one conducted on September 23 by the ninth ward for "Associations, Clubs, Cartmen, Butchers, and Democrats generally," focused public attention on the party's concern for tradesmen. The corresponding committee of the Democratic Party General Committee made itself available in the Democratic Republican reading room to "answer any and all friendly questions" that immigrants and tradesmen might have concerning the party's stance on various issues.[33]

What sort of men gave increasing amounts of time to building and maintaining the Democracy? Lawyers made up the largest group (163 out of the 1,432 men for whom occupations could be found, in a universe of 2,391 individuals). But clubs such as the all-important Democratic-Republican butchers, watchmen and lamplighters, cabinetmakers, grocers, and journeymen printers indicate that native and immigrant European-American male artisans and tradesmen also played an active role.[34] Of 1,052 organization men, 23 percent were professionals or businessmen, 38 percent were lesser white-collar, 33 percent were skilled workers, and 6 percent were unskilled.[35]

Though rate of involvement was found to be proportional to socioeconomic status, a remarkably high percentage of the most active members of the party—33 percent—were skilled workers. Of civic officials, 25 percent were also skilled workers, with all but three of these occupying medium- or top-rank positions.[36]

Of the 153 ward committee members whose occupations could be ascertained, only 16 percent were professionals or businessmen, as contrasted with 48 percent white-collar, 30 percent skilled workers, and 6 percent unskilled.[37] In fact, in no other level of the party were professionals or businessmen so poorly represented. The wards favored men of modest socioeconomic status, consistent with the small-producer values of American democratic republicanism. Also consistent with these political tenets was the fact that not one woman or African American was among the 2,391 activists uncovered.

If class determined one's rank within the Democracy, ethnicity did not. The party attracted new Americans; 22 percent had Irish surnames, almost identical to their 20 percent of the population.[38] Irishmen in the top organizational level were represented in proportion to their numbers in the population. Twenty-seven percent of the Tammany Society, General Committee, and Young Men's general committee were Irish, 64 percent were old-stock Americans (British and Dutch), while 7 percent were German.[39]

Analysis of party personnel also demonstrates that old-stock Americans did not dominate the party hierarchy.[40] Nor was ethnicity associated with the rate of party activity.[41] Ethnic representation in both areas, as well as in the ward committees, mirrored the Irish and German proportion in the population at large,[42] although the Irish were more strongly represented at the top of the party structure than at the bottom, indicating the value placed on visibly displaying the party as the champion of immigrant interests.

Old-stock Democrats were, however, more likely to be present in citywide party associations than were the Irish, a reflection, perhaps, of their broader and growing corporate business ties.[43] Among those Democrats holding elective or appointive office, ethnic affiliation was somewhat more important,[44] though as noted, men of rank clearly dominated the party's upper reaches.

Newspapers are rich in information that confirms these findings and tell us much about grassroots activity, for this period was the golden age of the printed word. In 1850, New York City boasted fourteen dailies with a combined circulation of 150,000, for a per capita readership of one paper for every 4.5 inhabitants, the highest point it would ever reach. A contemporary observer noted, "America is the only country where everybody reads."[45]

Many of these newspapers were sensationalist. In *Martin Chuzzlewit*, Dickens presented a graphic scene of newsboys on city streets hawking papers with names like the *New York Sewer*, *New York Stabber*, or *New York Family Spy*. The *Evening Post* condemned the novel by claiming that Dickens "knew little about New York City." In a lead article, entitled, "An English cockney," Mike Walsh reported that *Martin Chuzzlewit* had been "written at the direction of the British government, for the purpose of depreciating Republican institutions by turning them into ridicule." He also added, betraying his own feudal tastes, that Dickens was inferior in talent to Sir Walter Scott, the most popular author in the American South.[46] The ideological blinders of democratic republicanism prevented both Walsh and the *Evening Post* from appreciating Dickens's stinging portrait.

Nonetheless, since the Democrats retained little archival material of value, it is fortunate that in the nineteenth century, newspapers typically served as party informational and ideological organs, with managing editors often assuming party leadership roles. Partisanship, however, did not diminish reliability, because partisan newspapers were obligated to record party business.[47]

The newspapers reveal a sophisticated network of occupational and ethnic groupings that made the party a social as well as a political movement.[48] Party newspapers catered to specific groups. On September 18, the Loco Foco *Daily Plebeian* published a petition by ninety-nine shoemakers who attacked the tariff as a "special privilege to a few overgrown capitalists to the detriment of the country." The petition summarized the plight to which the skilled worker and yeoman farmer had been driven by the growth of business monopolies, and it anticipated the political rallying cries of factory workers and small farmers in the 1870s and 1880s. The next day, in language that echoed Thomas Paine, another mechanic petition placed the interests of the farmer above all others in society. Unlike Paine though, the petitioners ignored slavery, once again demonstrating that urban craftsmen, threatened by industrialization and victimized by monopolistic practices, were politically allied with the pro-slavery agriculture interests that dominated the Democratic Party on the national level.[49]

New York City artisans recognized that slavery in Southern agriculture posed little economic threat to Northern artisanal manufacturers. They were grounded in the Jeffersonian tradition, which regarded the tariff as a national pricing mechanism aiding the growth of monopolies, while simultaneously depriving the planter of national political hegemony by sapping his economic power because it raised the cost of the many imported goods the South required.[50]

Although New York City had become "the distribution center for the East, South and West," commerce occupied the energies of but 10 percent of the workers. A third of the labor force engaged in manufacturing, with women operatives equal in numbers to men. The service sector commanded the major share, as had been the case in colonial times. Half the country's imports and a third of its exports passed through New York City, bounded in 1844 by Fourteenth Street on the west side of Manhattan Island and Eighth Street on the east. Cotton made up half the exports.[51] Merchants accounted for less than 1 percent of city officials and only 5 percent of the Democratic Party activists, but they lent powerful ideological support to slavery.[52] This linkage no doubt contributed to the general business climate, which Emerson scathingly described: "The ways of trade grow selfish to the borders of theft, and supple to the borders [if not beyond the borders] of fraud."[53]

Slavery proved to be the most divisive issue within the Democratic Party in 1844, when ex-president Van Buren tried to run for president. To trumpet his availability for another term, supporters had organized Van Buren Associations in each of the city's wards. However, New York's most powerful political leader since Alexander Hamilton lost the nomination at the national convention because he opposed the annexation of Texas.

Democrats stood for any species of land expansion, provided slavery was not explicitly prohibited. This translated into war against Mexico over Texas. It also brought heated rhetoric against Great Britain over its control of Oregon, but that called for bluster rather than bullets, owing to the need for a continued infusion of British capital.[54]

Democrats linked settlement in the West with immigration in the East, for it was feared that without immigration, the West would drain labor from the East.[55] They maintained, according to O'Sullivan's *United States Magazine and Democratic Review*, that "the chief evil of Europe, that which oppresses England, and destroys Ireland, is the exclusion of the people from the soil." At a Grand Meeting of Workingmen on the Subject of Public Lands, a likely precursor to the Industrial Congress of 1850, New Yorkers rallied "to save land from speculators"; for out West the native American and "the poor white squatter and his family" had been driven from the land owing to the "wicked agency of government." In the eastern coastal cities, the "mechanic" was "rendered yearly more dependent and deplorable by the increasing power of machinery and capital"; providing demographic support for this political assessment was the acceleration of inequality between the classes from 1844 to 1856.[56]

The economically fanciful solution to the dilemma of growing economic inequality was to call for giving free public lands to the actual tillers of the soil. Democratic leaders believed that this action would enhance the power and standard of living of the eastern worker because "the surplus population of our cities will be rapidly drained off to the far west."[57] Such reasoning led Captain Isaiah Rynders's immigrant-based Empire Club to actively support Texas annexation. Its members hooted down opposing speakers and, on horseback, physically attacked rival political processions in a style that combined pageantry with cowboy machismo.[58]

For most of the late colonial period and until the Civil War, the Bowery was used for cattle drives that ended, for the drovers, at the Bull's Head Tavern on Canal Street, and for the cattle, in slaughterhouses situated on Chrystie, Elizabeth, and Forsyth Streets. The violence inflicted on animals provided inspiration for the violence men inflicted on one another. For example, in 1846, a pet bull terrier broke its chain as it was riding atop an omnibus, dashed into a herd of cattle being driven up the Bowery, and seized a young bull by the nose. The bull, maddened by the attack, ran wildly up the street, trying to shake the dog from its snout. Finally, a group of men subdued the bull. To their amazement, the dog was dead and had to be pried loose from the bull's nose. It was later learned that a man residing in the sixth ward had refused an offer of two hundred dollars for the dog, which was prized for his fighting ability.[59]

The dog's owner was the kind of fighting type Rynders and Mike Walsh hoped to attract to the Democratic banner.

Later commentators have stigmatized the German-Irish Rynders as an early example of the unsavory tie between New York City politics and organized crime. Herbert Asbury characterized him as "the political boss of the Sixth Ward and as such King of the Five Points gangsters."[60] As proprietor of the Arena saloon at 28 Park Row, where the Empire Club met upstairs, Rynders extorted money from brothels and saloon keepers, who in turn extended him political support. "Sporting man" Rynders became a political fixture; he was the only 1844 Democratic Party leader still in the party forty years later—by that time a revered, almost mythic figure. The Empire Club, less reform-minded than the independent Spartans led by the demagogic Mike Walsh, strove to channel the hostility that arose from oppression in Ireland and New York City into a fighting force for the Democratic Party—one that could be used against the party's political opponents or against anti-slavery Mexico and the Native Americans. Rynders flexed this political muscle in leading the cries of "Polk and Dallas, Texas, Oregon, and Fifty-four forty, or fight."[61]

The other political organization the press identified as mainly working class was Walsh's republican Spartan Association, which also supported slavery and denial of any civil rights to New York City's freed blacks, consistent with the democratic republican creed. Walsh maintained that "there can be no such thing in this country!" as a third party.[62] He was solidly in the Democratic camp.

A public image of political militancy rendered him attractive to the newly arrived, exploited Irish immigrant, and to the Democratic Party leadership who assisted Walsh's followers in securing their share of the political spoils. Walsh hated Van Buren and touted slaveowner John C. Calhoun for Democratic standard-bearer. In fact, the first biographical sketch of any individual presented in Walsh's newspaper, the *Subterranean*, was of Calhoun, and it stressed his Irish heritage and promoted him as "a friend to working-men and mechanics . . . anxious to have all labor rewarded." Walsh turned a blind eye to the fact that Calhoun had resolved the contradiction between labor and capital by making the laborer a slave. When Walsh did allude to African Americans, he cast them in the most unsympathetic and vicious light, as in his article on the "insanity of the Negro race."[63]

Walsh sought to champion the Irish by characterizing Dutch working-men as "hoe-boys" and linking them with "negro prostitutes." His views helped divide Irish from German workers. In the spring of 1846, the middle-class New York German Society sponsored German scabs in an Irish strike on the Brooklyn waterfront. After one German laborer was killed and others injured, the state militia was summoned.[64]

In rhetoric, Walsh was anti-capitalist, or perhaps precapitalist is a better term, given his disparaging attacks on fellow workers who were not of Irish extraction and his inability to present a concrete program for dealing with capitalism, other than support of the South and attacks on monopolies, both of which qualified him to be a Loco Foco.[65] Sometimes, however, his political analysis could be acute. For instance:

> If a number of lazy, plundering, wealthy capitalists, get themselves incorporated into a chartered monopoly, by the legislature, they can contract debts to an almost unlimited amount—swindle the community, then laugh at, and look down upon the people with contempt, while luxuriating in the fortunes out of which they have defrauded them, but if a poor man steals a loaf of bread to lull to sleep the starvation which has been brought upon himself and family by the plundering depradations of these speculating scoundrels, he is sentenced, not unfrequently, without even that mockery of a trial. . . .
>
> When the chartered company fails, and entails ruin upon thousands of industrious poor families, they plead as they did at the general suspension—*Necessity*—, and this excuse must be taken, even though each stockholder's pockets contain thousands of surplus dollars, which had been realized from the previous profits of the defunct institution. But how unavailable is the plea of necessity when urged by the poor man.[66]

Too often though, Walsh's intemperate politics led him to expend energy on attacking individuals rather than raising issues. This conduct led him frequently into court on charges of libel, and even assault. Running as a Democrat, Walsh served three terms in the state legislature—in 1847, 1848, and 1851—and one in Congress beginning the following year, where he prated about the "white slavery" of laborers. The tragedy of Walsh and his ideological soul mates is that their racist politics guaranteed that the oppressive conditions of, as Thoreau put it, "a hundred Irishmen, with Yankee overseers"[67] would not inspire a broader-based movement.

In a more tranquil vein, Democratic Young Hickory associations staged rallies centering around the planting of hickory trees. Elected party officials, who customarily responded to a petition emanating from among the ward's young Democrats, authorized their placement. So many were planted that a coordinating body, the Young Men's Central Hickory Association, was established. Under supervision of the "committee appointed to serve and conduct the raising," the tree plantings involved intricate ceremonies that linked the party in the public's mind with the masculine frontier image of "Old Hickory" Andrew Jackson.[68]

The most spectacular political rallies the city had ever seen took place just prior to the presidential election of 1844. They were marked by campaign rhetoric that combined appeals to material interests with notions of racial superiority and the need for national expansion.[69]

One such rally, held in and around Tammany Hall on the evening of September 16, was billed as the largest political gathering in the city's history. Since the crowd spread further than the range of the human voice, speakers simultaneously addressed separate gatherings in front of city hall, the registry office, and even Whig Horace Greeley's *Tribune* headquarters. In all, there were ten groupings to this huge assemblage, including one composed exclusively of four to five thousand Germans. At one of these gatherings the crowd mockingly serenaded Clay:

> O coony, coony Clay
> O coony, coony Clay
> You never can be President
> So all the people say[70]

While the crowd sang, the *Daily Plebeian* reporter observed,

> an attempt was made to submerge an exquisite who, with an open glass in hand, was scrutinizing the personal appearance of the chairman with sundry Whig explanations. The gentleman Whig, however, escaped without injury, except a wet foot and slight soiling of one of the ruffles of his shirt.

The largest gathering of all—some 6,500 persons—massed in front of Tammany Hall for Thomas Carr's attack on the Whigs' temporizing on Texas: "[the Whigs] opposed it because they mistook the popular will. . . . Then [Henry Clay] was in favor of it "niggers and all. . . ." Carr championed Texas annexation on economic grounds:

> Texas was a cotton country [cheers]. . . . England had a direct interest in procuring that country [cheers] . . . she could coerce the

United States by commercial regulations with the assistance of Texas if she should remain an independent country [cheers]. . . . Texas would furnish a market for Northern manufacturers and Northern agricultural products.

Clinton De Witt then accused the National Bank of contributing to inflation that lowered living standards for "every poor man" and concluded "with a most pathetic appeal to the working classes in favor of the working man's candidate . . . Polk of Tennessee."[71]

Newspapers do not mention ward committees convening after September 27, 1844. It is likely that energies had shifted to bringing out the vote. The city's most prominent labor leader, Ely Moore, assumed an active role. He extolled "municipal reform" as "a great Movement of the people," and "the Democracy" as "alive to the Vital Interests of the Enlightened Freemen."[72]

Moore's earlier career as a printer culminated in the presidency of the Typographical Society, a position that gave him the necessary credentials to act as the spokesman for labor within the Democratic Party. Moore had been an important figure in the Equal Rights Party, running for Congress on their ticket in 1836. He was vehemently anti-abolitionist.[73]

In the final days before the election, political rivals were beating up each other and smashing windows at each other's party headquarters. The Democratic Party did little to cool the situation. One auxiliary, the Butt-End Coon Hunters, even announced a "Grand National Coon Hunt":

Resolved . . . the Butt-End Coon Hunters . . . join in the general chase . . . to take place in November next . . .

Resolved, that we go for Oregon because she is ours; and for Texas because she wants to be; and if California and Canada wish to join us, we shall not object; because the old Coon Hunters of the Revolution deemed it Democratic to *enlarge the boundaries of Freedom.*

Resolved: that each hunter keep his flint picked, his powder dry, and when they see the white of the eye—let split!

Resolved, that the Coon will be so dead in November next that all the *resurrectionists* in the Union can't bring him to life.[74]

This combativeness also extended to local edicts. Party celebrants openly flouted a Common Council resolution of September 22 "prohibiting the Democracy from celebrating Democratic victories with cannon in the Park," under penalty of a fifty dollar fine (an exorbitant sum in those days). Captain John Order was thanked "for his present to the Club of three hundred 'Young Hickory' walking sticks, intended for use of the members when on chase of the 'varmint.' "[75]

The Democratic Party fueled this political culture of violence, which reached its antebellum peak in May 1849 with the Astor Place Riots, in which twenty-two lives were lost. This bloody clash was triggered by a long-standing stage rivalry between English actor William C. Macready and his American counterpart Edwin Forrest, the most famous actors in their respective countries. For a week preceding, the city press, led by James Bennett's Democratic *Herald*, had energetically promoted their rivalry. On the night of May 7, while Forrest was performing as Macbeth at the Broadway Theater, Macready made his stage entrance as Macbeth at the city's most elegant theater, the Astor Place Opera House, on Eighth and Lafayette Streets. The performance was interrupted by a group of the b'hoys described in Chapter 5. These downwardly mobile journeymen and apprentices were led by journalist Ned Buntline and identified with the Order of United Americans, potential Know Nothings. The b'hoys hurled eggs and chairs onto the stage while Democratic leaders Isaiah Rynders and Edward Strahan goaded the crowd. No arrests were made. Washington Irving and Herman Melville, among others, then signed a petition for a second performance.[76] In response, Buntline's group designated itself the American Committee and posted placards citywide that read, "WORKINGMEN Shall Americans or English Rule in this City?" To halt Macready's appearance on the evening of the tenth, several hundred men tried to enter the theater, which was guarded by three hundred policemen. The few who succeeded in forcing their way in were seized by plainclothesmen.

Outside, a mob estimated at upward of ten thousand men and boys began hurling paving stones through the windows. Inside, theater patrons rushed from their seats to seek protection close to the walls. The police sought to arrest the stone throwers but suffered numerous injuries and were driven into the theater. Nevertheless, the stage performance continued. Two regiments of soldiers were summoned, and the mob directed its wrath against the assembled infantry as the play ended. After projectiles struck down the general in command and injured other soldiers, and after several warnings had been issued but evidently not heard through the tumult, the troops fired three volleys, hitting mostly innocent bystanders of various classes and races from the rioters. Seventeen men died that night of wounds from military bullets, and five more expired subsequently from the same cause.[77]

The next day, thousands of men gathered to hear Democratic stalwarts Edward Strahan, Isaiah Rynders, and Mike Walsh denounce the actions of the mayor, police, and military in strong democratic republican language. At one point, Rynders exclaimed, "I hope you will prove by your conduct this evening, that the working men of our city are as orderly as the aristocracy," even though military force had been used "to revenge the aristocracy of this city against the working classes." The crowd listened in stony silence, and when resolutions were "put to a vote," they roared their "acclamation." Several thousand persons then marched to the scene of the fatal rioting before finally disbanding in the face of a large contingent of soldiers and police. The Democratic Party had provided the margin of peace.[78]

For Philip Hone, "the fact has been established that law and order can be maintained under a Republican form of government." His reading of republicanism stressed the Republic, the nation-state aspect of the concept. This point would be exploited by the Republican Party against the Democrats, whose fiery street leader Ned Buntline served as the commercial cultural spokesman for the "people's right" to riot and as an instigator of the event itself. Buntline sought to place himself squarely in the artisan mechanic tradition as head of the pro-slavery Order of United American Mechanics (OUAM). He affected a vigilante stance, armed as he was with twin long-handled six-shooters, his own invention. Buntline denounced the "cod-fish aristocracy" and sensationalized the degradation of the poor in his magazine, *Ned Buntline's Own*, which he financed by blackmailing gamblers whose payments ensured that their names would not be published. Buntline claimed to authentically present the perspectives of "the dandy, the artisan, and the beggar" in his journal.[79]

The violence that marred the political scene of the 1840s dismayed both domestic and foreign observers. Literary entrepreneurs seized upon its commercial possibilities, especially since New York City hotels and rooming houses did a brisk business with sailors and soldiers bound for the Mexican War. In an analysis of "Davy Crockett Almanacs" published in various American cities between 1835 and 1856, David Reynolds recounted one anecdote in which Crockett's wife wore a pair of earrings to church that were made out of dried human eyes gouged out by her husband.[80] Crockett's favorite eye-gouging targets were African and Native

Americans, in keeping with his manly, straightforward democratic republican values. He was no foppish Whig deceiver.

The week of the 1844 presidential election, the *Daily Plebeian* carried an article headed by a picture of an upraised arm clenching a hammer, by which the people "confirmed" the nomination of Polk at Tammany Hall. This confirmation was followed by the "grand Democratic Torchlight Procession" or "Seven Miles of Democrats" featuring "mechanics and Workingmen." The slogan was martial—"Polk and Dallas, Oregon and Texas, and Down with the British"—and effective—Polk beat Clay. The *Richmond Enquirer* observed that "*there was no single individual* to whom the Union was more indebted" than John Louis O'Sullivan, editor of both the *United States Magazine and Democratic Review* and a local New York City newspaper, the *Morning News*, which began publication in August to support the propaganda blitz on behalf of Polk.[81]

The Democrats had rebounded to victory from their resounding defeat in April local elections. A five-thousand-vote lead in New York State, which included a two-thousand-vote win in New York City, was the margin between Polk and his Whig opponent. It represented a stunning victory "for this perverse leveling generation," as Hone termed it.[82] Democrats had fashioned a political organization in which significant numbers of Irish and German workers participated as party activists and civic officials. Their continued participation within the party was linked to a politics that reflected the nature and scale of production.

An artisan politics corresponded to the city's artisan-based economy. Richard Stott found for 1820 that 68 of 101 firms centered in New York City had 10 or fewer workers. This tendency toward smallness persisted until the Civil War because soaring land prices forced factories to relocate from the city, while "differences *within* trades were as large as differences *between* trades." From 1820 to 1850, the average New York City shop grew from 14.7 to 25 workers, but the number then stagnated and declined, so that by 1890, 14 workers was the average. Although the skilled workforce was about 650 percent larger in 1860 than in 1820, the workforce as a whole was somewhat less skilled than before,[83] with the number of skilled barely keeping pace with the rise in New York City's population.

So long as economic enterprise had remained relatively small, decentralized, and technologically backward, resting to a high degree upon skilled labor, the Democracy could be classed as democratic for adult European-American males. In a day when many artisans and tradesmen lived where they worked, the wards were ideally suited as local political sounding boards.

European-American workers believed slavery posed no competitive threat so long as it was confined to the South, and so long as the slaves were primarily involved in the growing of cotton. The Texas issue, on the other hand, forced men to take a stand on whether it was worth shedding their blood on behalf of the slaveholder.[84] Whitman celebrated the American position: "What has miserable, inefficient Mexico . . . to do with the great mission of peopling the New World with a noble race? Be it ours, to achieve that mission!" Emerson decried the conflict with Mexico:

> But who is he that prates
> Of the culture of mankind
> Of better arts and life?
> Go, blindworm, go,
> Behold the famous States
> Harrying Mexico
> With rifle and with knife![85]

But Emerson's concerns were overwhelmed by land fever.

George Henry Evans, "the intellectual father of the land reform movement," and Hermann Kriege and Wilhelm Weitling, communist leaders of German-American workers, all ranked wage "slavery" ahead of the abolition of African-American slavery in importance. Evans exhorted his democratic republican followers to "emancipate the white laborer, *by restoring his natural right to the soil.*" He declared that land reform prevented class conflict and violent attacks on property, and he appealed to Congress to provide a homestead for each family who requested it. Evans steadfastly maintained that "land is not property, and therefore, should not be transferable like the products of man's labor."[86]

Though wooed by Whig free labor advocate Horace Greeley, both Kriege and Weitling joined the Democratic Party.[87] They no doubt recognized that sectional labor segmentation benefited New York laborers: engaged as they were in activities associated with the cotton trade, as well as in the manufacture of goods destined for the South. New York workers' tasks complemented and reinforced the slave system.

This delicate but cruel social balance was reflected in a Democratic Party ideology that might just as well be termed planter-artisan republicanism as democratic republicanism.[88] It would come apart as technology advanced, manufacturing became more important, and many unskilled immigrants became New York citizens. But in 1844, in this transitional political phase, no political party in the world could match the Democrats in terms of their heterogeneous class and ethnic makeup and organizational sophistication in a city that, as a public corporation, embraced more private interests than any private corporation in the country.[89]

This equation of scale changed at the close of the 1840s and was marked by the introduction of the foreman who mirrored the ward and party boss with respect to the power he wielded. The city's largest clothing firms then rivaled political parties in size, with the largest firm, Lewis and Hanford Clothiers of the second ward, employing over four thousand people. The metalworking trades exhibited a similar, although less pronounced, pattern of consolidation.[90]

As manufacturing grew in scale and complexity, so did the political organization of the city. Aldermen continued to perform municipal services, even though the city's Charter of 1830 had established separate executive departments. In 1845, the election of sugar baron William Havemeyer brought to power a strong chief executive. Tammany had boosted him as a "native New Yorker" to steal political thunder from the American Republicans Party. Havemeyer sought to limit the Common Council's powers, in favor of an independent mayor. He acted as a political harbinger of the Progressive movement forty years later, when upperclass reformers lobbied to reorganize city government along the lines of the modern corporation. By that time, workers would no longer be activists in the party, but in unions.[91]

The 1846 revision of the state constitution did limit the Common Council's powers, but not in the manner favored by Havemeyer. Instead of transferring authority to the mayor, it left the choice of city department heads to the voters. The charter revision incorporated many of the fiduciary demands of Democratic workingmen spokesmen, but it continued to deny African Americans the right to vote because it retained the three-year state residency requirement and 250 dollar property qualification for them, as opposed to one year and no property qualification for whites.[92] In the entire state, only about five hundred African-American adult males remained eligible to vote, out of a total black population of forty-five thousand persons. Horace Greeley had been fearful that the charter convention would have to be canceled because in New York City nearly all the "Adopted Citizens" were induced to vote against the convention by

Democratic chants of "Niggers Voting."[93] Withholding the vote from the African enhanced the value of the franchise to the European.

With the Whig vote split between their candidate and a Native American, Tammany elected Andrew Mickle, "one of the b'hoys," who was born in an Irish shanty in "the bloody-ould Sixth" and died a millionaire. Later that year, in a demonstration of African-American resolve, an adolescent was judicially freed from the clutches of slave catchers and a celebration held, in Hone's disparaging words, by "a mob of all colors, from dirty white to shiny black."[94]

In New York State, Democrats split into "Hard" Hunker and "Soft" Barnburner factions. In 1844 and 1845, Barnburners sided with the landlords during the anti-rent rebellion of tenant farmers. As Barnburner leader, Van Buren withheld support from free homesteads and opposed assumption of state debts for internal improvements.

Only when the Democratic Party's internal wrangling led to multicandidate races could the opposition take power in New York City. This happened in 1847 when a party split over slavery's extension allowed Whig millionaire silversmith William V. Brady to capture the mayoralty and his party to gain control of the Common Council. But in April 1848, Democrats managed briefly to patch up their differences and once again barely elected Havemeyer as mayor, this time over the incumbent Brady. Later that year, Barnburners sent their own delegates to the Democratic National Convention.

During the 1848 presidential election, regular Democrats continued to be called Loco Focos by their Whig detractors, to distinguish them from the Van Buren Democrats. The latter's opposition to the dominant proslavery wing of the party rested on the assumption that the "inviolable concomitant" of slavery was "the social and political degradation of the white laborer."[95] Barnburners formed their own General Committee and met on Lispenard Street, opposing the pro-slavery Hunkers supported by Mike Walsh, who favored popular sovereignty. A year later, the Whigs celebrated their biggest landslide, capturing the mayoralty, thirteen of the eighteen aldermen seats, and fourteen assistant aldermen seats.

Very soon, though, a clever twist to the land reform issue would transform the political war against monopoly into a military crusade against slave expansion, led by political apologists for the industrial consolidators.[96] These new Republicans would exacerbate the divisions in New York City's working class on the issues of race, ethnicity, and gender.

⊶ 7 ⊷

THE NEW
REPUBLICANISM
1849–1857

The most immoral *moral* of the story, if it has any moral at all, seems to be the impracticability of virtue.

From the *Literary World* review of Herman Melville's *Pierre* (1857)

Who believes that Whites and Blacks can ever amalgamate in America? Or who wishes it to happen? Nature has set an impossible seal against it. Besides, is not America for the Whites? And is it not better so?

Walt Whitman in *Brooklyn Daily Times*, May 6, 1858

What separates the enlightened man from the savage? Is civilization a thing distinct, or is it an advanced stage of barbarism?

Herman Melville, *Israel Potter* (1851)

———

IN JANUARY 1854, DEMOCRATIC PARTY LEADER STEPHEN DOUGLAS UPSET THE FRAGILE BOUNDARY BETWEEN FREE AND SLAVE SOIL drawn by the 1820 Missouri Compromise, which had "forever" banned slavery in new states north of the 36°30′ line of latitude. His "popular sovereignty" doctrine now left it to the settlers of a given region to decide whether they wanted slaves in their midst. Kansas-Nebraska, the test case, swiftly degenerated to a battleground as pro- and anti-slavery partisans waged guerrilla warfare in a dress rehearsal for the Civil War.

Popular sovereignty constituted a political response to a growing realization that slave ownership was an option that fewer and fewer whites could successfully afford. James Fenimore Cooper wrote to his most intimate friend, William Branford Shubrick:

[T]he idea of an equilibrium (between slave and free states) is preposterous. It infers that whenever freedom gets ahead of slavery, she must halt, and aid the last in getting up with her. It requires no prophet to say that freedom will do no such thing. The fact is, that the south, by means of political machinery, has controlled this Union; the power is now passing toward the north, and the present commotion is no more than the throes of the south in being delivered.[1]

Popular sovereignty appealed to "Young America," the youthful wing of a nationalistic Democratic Party flushed with victory in the Mexican-American War[2] and eager to gloss "ruthless democracy"[3] with patriotic gilt. The military conquest of the northern third of Mexico, which added vast new territories to the United States, allowed Young America's political idol Douglas to co-opt the *Working Man's Advocate* platform plank of "Lands free to Actual Settlers." He then bowed to the pressure of pro-banking Northern railroad interests by ignoring the "No Bank" pledge of the Loco Focos or "Hard" Democrats. Douglas was blamed for the armed skirmishes that soon erupted throughout Kansas, because he had not offered guarantees to either side on the slavery question. "Bleeding Kansas," as the territory was soon known, split the Democratic Party on the national level more seriously than ever before.[4]

Popular sovereignty alienated the "independent Democrats," made up mainly of the remnants of the Barnburners. The Whig *Tribune*, the principal unofficial press spokesman for these Democrats in New York City, presented a South scheming to enslave all labor. The independents criticized Douglas for his failure to offer a vision of community that did not include the expansion of slavery. Bleeding Kansas galvanized these independent Democrats, many of whom joined the newly formed national Republican Party, established in 1854 as the successor to the Whigs in the two-party system. Independent Democrats were drawn to the stance of former New York governor and leader of the Republican Party William Henry Seward, who sought to train public attention on plantation owners as the "Dominant Class in the Republic,"[5] deflecting attention from their Northern industrial capitalist counterparts who were his party's staunchest financial supporters.

This renewed focus on slavery did not yield support for African-American rights. *Tribune* editor Horace Greeley and Arthur Brisbane, the principal advocate of Fourier socialism in America, advocated racial segregation. They reflected the sociology of the marketplace, from which blacks were virtually excluded. Eric Foner has concluded that by the

1850s, many Northern blacks had forsaken active participation within American life. The *United States Magazine and Democratic Review* spoke for the majority of European Americans when it cited the "fact" that "the dark races are utterly incapable of attaining to that intellectual superiority which marks the white race."[6] Even the Whiggish Irving concurred: "I wish to heavens, nature would restore to the poor negroes their tails and settle them in their proper place in the scale of creation. It would be a great relief to both them and the abolitionists, and I see no other way of settling the question effectively."[7]

And Charles Dickens had no room for the African American in his cast of characters: "Free of course he ought to be; but the stupendous absurdity of making him a voter glares out of every roll of his eye, stretch of his mouth, and bump of his head. I have a strong impression that the race must fade out of the States very fast."[8]

Why then should New York City labor Democrats be any different? The Workingmen's Democratic Republican Association upheld the rights of white workers only, while favoring the gradual abolition of slavery. In its newspaper, the *Iron Platform*, British trade was blamed for soup houses and for making "slaves of white men and their children."[9] It seconded the *Herald*'s assessment that "We have played second-fiddle to the debt-ridden, tax-ridden nations of Europe long enough. . . . With natural resources unsurpassed . . . there is no reason in the world why we should not . . . free ourselves from the thralldom of foreign capitalists."[10] In its inaugural issue, the *Iron Platform* protested that slavery imposed "helpless degradation . . . upon the free labor of white men who are not fortunate enough to be the owners of plantations and gangs of slaves"; the solution became "the establishment of manufactures in the South to uplift white labor,"[11] not the abolition of slavery.

Most whites, even the most downtrodden, felt uplifted by the permanently degraded status of the black man. A contemporary British observer, Charles Mackay wrote,

> The Irishman is seldom long in America before he, too, begins to assert the supremacy of his white blood, and to come out of what he considers the degrading ranks of "science." . . . The Irishwomen fall willingly at first into domestic service, but the public opinion around them soon indoctrinates them with the aristocratic idea that black men and women are the only proper servants.[12]

So deep ran the current of racism fostered by the Democratic Party that the new Republican Party chose to address the issue of land reform, rather than slavery, to gain national standing. These republicans of the Republic celebrated "the laborer's legal self-ownership and autonomy," and demanded that future states be bound by free labor statutes. They appealed to both the landless and to the industrialists, while excluding slave and female labor from protection, lending credence to Jonathan A. Glickstein's assessment that free labor ideology was "implicitly sexist and patriarchal, and it shared widely held middle-class notions that the competitive marketplace was an inappropriate field for female activity."[13]

Free labor ideology carried with it the weight of historical and religious tradition. Since the Bible had been written, men had widely invoked its wisdom, especially that contained in the Old Testament, to defend both slavery and the subjugation of women.[14] Stephanie McCurry has convincingly argued that

> proslavery spokesmen returned repeatedly to gender relations . . . [which] enabled proslavery spokesmen to tap beliefs about the legitimacy of inequality that go so deep in the individual psyche and social structure that for most historians they are still unrecognized as the subject of history.[15]

In America, organized religion provided the most powerful apologia for African-American slavery.[16] While Protestants, Catholics, and Jews actively supported Southern slavery, in the realm of heavenly zeal, evangelical ministers outdid their godly brethren by producing more than half the pro-slavery tracts ever written in the United States.[17] More generally, David Brion Davis has concluded that enslavement after Christ was tied to the spread of religion, that slavery was "a creation of the most progressive peoples and forces in Europe—Italian merchants; Iberian explorers; Jewish inventors, traders, and cartographers; Dutch, German, and British investors and bankers." Davis stresses how widespread was the "belief that Christianization justified inhumanity."[18]

Although the new Republican Party referred to slavery as a "relic of barbarism," this did not mean the party was pro-black. To the contrary, most Republicans were racists who did not believe in social equality of the races.

It was left to African Americans to continue to take the lead in opposing racism. In New York City, the Committee of Thirteen had been organized by the African-American leadership to oppose the implementation of the Fugitive Slave Act.[19] It met to denounce the "ignorance and wickedness" of New York State Governor Washington Hunt's January 1852 proposal to provide public funds for the American Colonization Society. Hunt had merely been acting on behalf of the public will. If Irish Democrats and Anglo-Dutch Know Nothings agreed on anything, it was on denying African Americans "equal rights." To make its anti-slavery politically respectable, even New York State's Free Soil Party was forced to delete the commitment to equal rights from its platform.[20]

Even if it were included in political discourse, equal rights rhetoric proved elastic enough to serve opposing classes. A rich George Templeton Strong fancied himself an indignant revolutionary. "I belong," he boasted, "to the insurgent plebeians of the North arming against a twopenny South Carolina aristocracy." This did not mean that he was pro–African American. Absent from his analysis is any appreciation of the positive role that African Americans might play in their own liberation: "there are germs of insurrection among the 'poor trash,' the plebeians who don't own niggers. Such a movement once formed and recognized must triumph sooner or later, and nigger emancipation and the downfall of the nigger-breeding (and mulatto-breeding) aristocracy of those states must follow."[21] So long as political debate could be framed by such American plutocrats, the issue of public control of a privately owned economy could never be a factor in political calculation, and racism, sexism, and ethnic bigotry would continue to poison human relations.

While Democrats struggled to preserve an atavistic republicanism, Republicans attacked them for jeopardizing U.S. material progress by restricting labor's rights, either by politically embracing the Catholic Church, which accepted cash payments from capitalists to assist in worker pacification, or by strengthening slavery in the South. In New York City, outnumbered Anglo-Dutch long-term residents wanted "NO UNION BETWEEN CHURCH AND STATE." The American Party perceived that the Catholic Church was violating this credo of the Founding Fathers by seeking to "create an Inquisition on American soil, and fatten the land with American blood." At the same time, they rationalized their sense of superiority over the Irish by defining themselves as being more "American." One Republican observer wrote of his peers: "They want a Paddy hunt and on a Paddy hunt they will go."[22]

The Catholic Irish confronted a gargantuan alien metropolis, not the walking city of a generation earlier. Yet because 52.3 percent of the population was foreign born and two-thirds of the city's labor force was un-skilled by 1855, unskilled immigrants constituted a potentially powerful political force. By that year, labor's real wages were 80 percent of what they had been in 1844. For the first time in the city's history, whole neighborhoods, like the Lower East Side, had become solidly working class. This trend frightened middle-class citizens as well as native work-ers. So many immigrants had arrived that no ward was without a substan-tial number. For the 1850s, Richard Stott estimates that possibly 1,650,000 people moved into the city and 1,415,000 left, accounting for a net population increase of 257,000.[23]

Such demographic volatility heightened social anxiety within a Protes-tant establishment already shaken by the reactionary turn of events in Europe after the 1848 revolutions.[24] The reaction to 1848 threatened to jeopardize the adoption of marketplace laws that promoted American business interests abroad. Members of the American Party redoubled their efforts at sponsoring temperance and free public schools to compete with taverns and parochial schools not under their control. They em-braced the anti-slavery movement because it served the emerging capi-talist order. Their leader might well have been Colonel Diver, the Dickensian editor of the *New York Rowdy Journal*, "the organ of our aristocracy," composed of "intelligence and virtue. And of their necessary consequence in this republic. Dollars."[25]

In 1850, American Republican Party remnants reconstituted them-selves as the Order of the Star-Spangled Banner. As described in Chapter 6, their leader Ned Buntline had the year before helped spark the Astor Place Riots.[26] Sworn to an oath of secrecy that if pressed they would claim to "know nothing," these Know Nothings, as party members now designated themselves, resembled the Masonic Order. Local lodges sup-plied delegates to a state grand council, which in turn selected an agenda-setting national body.

Simultaneously, by the end of 1853 every Northern state boasted a Republican Party state council with a membership limited to adult non-Catholic males who swore to having no Catholic relations of either a personal or business nature. Officially, the New York Republican Party frowned on the Know Nothings. Party officials publicly castigated Know Nothings for "secret contributions, oaths, rituals, and organizations," for disagreeing "with the liberal principles of our free Government," and for being "anti-republican"; yet Republicans acknowledged that when

". . . *combined*, Know-Nothingism and Anti Slavery can sweep the country."[27]

Although Democrats had long since thrown in their lot with Catholic victims of discrimination, their job was made more difficult by the church's anti-republican campaign, which antagonized North America's Protestant majority. A journey to the United States by the pope's personal emissary provoked anti-Catholic riots in several cities, leading to the emissary's secret and swift departure from New York City back to Rome.[28]

The political activism of the Roman Catholic clergy had helped make nativism the most important variable in determining political choice in the 1854 elections. Nativism arose in a context of labor segmentation that reflected differences in the national origins and capabilities of the new immigration of the 1840s; for instance, Germans tended to come from a more skilled background than the Irish. In New York City, the conflict between native and immigrant crystallized when bare-knuckle boxing champion Irish John Morrissey's henchmen, one of them an ex-policeman, killed saloon keeper Bill "the Butcher" Poole. The March 1854 funeral was the biggest New York City had ever seen. Two years later, nativism had been modified by the Free-Soil movement, which allowed greater numbers of Germans to feel comfortable enough about the Republican Party to enlist in its ranks.[29] Still, such voting shifts proved insufficient to defeat a united national Democratic Party in the 1856 presidential election.

The victor, James Buchanan, immediately signaled his pro-slavery supporters that he would not enforce laws against outfitting slave ships when he made Isaiah Rynders the United States Marshal for the Southern District of New York.[30] Although Captain Rynders did not have a wooden leg, his violent temperament and ownership of a small schooner in the 1830s made him seem a parallel for Captain Ahab—demonized by the kind of politics that nearly sank the American ship of state.

On the eve of the Civil War, pro-slavery sentiment remained very strong among New York City labor, especially since the shipping industry recovered from the Panic of 1857 by supplying vessels for the slave trade. The *London Times* reported that Gotham had become "the greatest slave-trading mart in the world." Against this economic background, even the communist Joseph Wedemeyer could not treat slavery as a separate issue, but had to link the anti-slavery movement with free land. As late as 1857, Wedemeyer would not mention slavery for fear of alienating many in his allegedly progressive labor movement. Interestingly enough, though,

Germans schooled in European socialist republican values produced no anti-African spokesmen. Frederick Douglass even went so far as to exclaim, "A German has only to be a German to be utterly opposed to slavery."[31]

In 1847, the abolitionist reformer Wendell Phillips had differentiated between Southern slavery and Northern wage slaves:

> Except in a few crowded cities and a few manufacturing towns, I believe the terms "wage slavery" and "white slavery" would be utterly unintelligible to an audience of laboring people, as applied to themselves. . . . First, the laborers, as a class, are neither wronged nor oppressed: and secondly, if they were, they possess ample power to defend themselves by the exercise of their own acknowledged rights. Does legislation bear hard upon them? Their votes can alter it. Does capital wrong them? *Economy will make them capitalists.* [my italics] Does the crowded competition of cities reduce their wages? They have only to stay at home, devoted to other pursuits, and soon diminished supply will bring the remedy. . . . To economy, self-denial, temperance, education, and moral and religious character, the laboring class, and every other class in this country, must owe its elevation and improvement.[32]

This naive faith in collective self-improvement grew for the first generation that experienced the social dislocation wrought by industrialization. That is, it grew during the second quarter of the nineteenth century, when no factory employed more operatives than the biggest plantations and Democrats enlisted a plurality of artisan activists. Neither the plantation nor the factory yielded men of character. Ownership of these enterprises corrupted a man, while work in them degraded his spirit.

Melville lamented this denigration of the individual and the corresponding attempts by prominent men of his era to offer what amounted to self-serving solutions. In *The Confidence-Man: His Masquerade*, a sort of updated *Pilgrim's Progress*, deception of this sort assumed many guises. Until the 1840s, America had African-American music, tall tales from the Southwest, Niagara Falls, and Cooper's frontier. Now national attributes could be marketed and social identities manufactured for private gain.

The nationalization of civic society made the *appearance* of being *American* more vital to political identity than being *republican*, the significant attribute of pre-1840 American political culture. Republicanism was losing value as a term able to stand for the *citizen* ideology of small producers. In popular parlance, the term *citizen* would now come to distinguish between those immigrants who had been here for two centuries, like the Dutch and the English, and the recently arrived southern and eastern Europeans, for whom the Irish would serve as political brokers in New York City.

From Cicero to Rousseau, the highest service had been considered service to the public good. America had developed no such tradition; rather, private gain, when legitimized by law, was considered a public good. This interpretation of republicanism became, in the hands of the new Republican Party, the doctrine for entrepreneurially minded individuals who required an *American Republic* to protect their wider corporate interests. They benefited from Democratic failure to deal with the need for a common *national* identity that would bring unity.

In an attempt to restrict Tammany's power, the Whig-controlled state legislature in 1849 passed radical reforms of the city charter that formally prohibited civic officials from becoming involved in city contracts and created nine new municipal departments. Persistent Tammany infighting allowed the Whigs, a year later, to capture thirteen of sixteen assembly seats and three out of four congressional seats. The Whigs amended the election law to lengthen the mayor's term to two years instead of one, with elections scheduled for the same day in November as state and national contests.

While parrying these Whig thrusts at the Democracy, a Loco Foco ex-mayor, Grand Sachem Elijah F. Purdy, attempted to forge party unity by seeking safety in numbers. He invited 142 members to join Tammany in 1850; for the two preceding years only 24 new members had been recruited to the society's rolls. Purdy tightened his control over the party when the General Committee adopted the convention system of nominations and arrogated from the ward committees the right to choose election inspectors. Prior to this change, Rynders and Walsh had used their bully-boys to pack meetings in order to influence the outcome.

As party boss, Purdy worked hard to prevent Rynders and Walsh from fomenting public strife. However, the party's pro-South, anti-black values had so pervaded the rank and file that he had difficulty doing so. With the city's business elite looking to the party leader to ensure public peace, enhancement of the party leader came at a price—the demagoguery of Fernando Wood and the extortion of William Tweed.

In between the political reign of these two politicians, an army of the Republic, the Union army, would channel the frustrations of a self-armed republican people and unite native artisan with immigrant semiskilled under one Union banner. Republicans of a nationalistic Republican Party would be fighting Democrat republicans of the South. "American Republicanism" would become a rejuvenating force, as the stirring rhythms of the "Battle Hymn of the Republic" suggest.[33]

The new Republican Party's desire to extend the principle of wage labor to all workers was consistent with the goals of Northern capitalists who sought a national market for their products. Their political caution in publicly proclaiming devotion to an emerging industrial order was based in part on recognition that agricultural pursuits still commanded the majority of the nation's voters.[34] Sound political strategy therefore dictated that emphasis be placed on land reform and opposing the extension of slavery.

This free-soil platform appealed to many New York State farmers. It allowed the New York Republican Party in 1856, the third year of its existence, to place first, 24 percentage points ahead of the nativist American Party's 21 percent, while the Democrats split their votes between Hards (14 percent) and Softs (21 percent). In marked contrast to the Democrats, Republican supporters at presidential candidate John Fremont's meetings included women in numbers proportionate to the general population.[35] This sexual equality was in keeping with a more progressive or liberal conception of republicanism, the antecedents of which lay in the Federalist tendency to treat all labor—male and female, black and white—as equally subservient. Democrats continued to exclude women as a result of time-worn notions of dependence, cultivated through the semirural and religious values of immigrants in cities like New York, and reinforced by farmers in the country's vast hinterlands.

The Democracy provided islands of reassurance for newly arrived immigrants in a turbulent urban ocean of frustrated expectations. New York City was a Democratic fortress whenever the party was able to muster a united front, a circumstance rarely achieved in the 1850s. Party leaders mediated between private entrepreneurs and a rapidly developing, highly unstable proletariat made up mainly of immigrants and a few older artisans. The latter, like the journeyman tailor who did not possess the requisite capital to start up a shop of his own, were often reduced to factory-worker status.[36]

In response to this decline in worker autonomy, the skilled trades met in June 1850 at New York City's first Industrial Congress. The main agenda item was land reform, which Tammany Hall eagerly embraced. Land reform had traditionally served in the exceptional circumstances of a land-rich America as the key component of antebellum Democratic ideology.[37] But when President James Buchanan vetoed a free-homestead bill that would have granted land to actual settlers, which he did because Southerners feared western migration would lower their land values, both the New York and national Republican Parties opted to make the Homestead Act central to Lincoln's successful 1860 presidential campaign. This act sought "to secure homesteads to actual settlers on the public domain." By making non-slave western expansion the answer to urban social problems, the new Republican Party gained backing from midwestern farmers whose support for the South had diminished.[38]

Labor's concern for land hardly made workers radical. For land to become a politically radicalizing agent, its redistribution from one class to another has to be the focus of popular will, as it was in the genuinely radical French Revolution. In the United States, where land was widely assumed to exist in unlimited quantities, albeit occupied by Native Americans, land hunger was successfully channeled through nonradical modes of political discourse. The result was obsessive hatred of the American Indian, not of the aristocracy that was the target in France during its revolution.

From Jefferson to Jackson, from the War of 1812 to the Mexican War and Southern filibustering expeditions against Nicaragua and Cuba, landed expansion became the cornerstone of a virulently racist Democratic ideology. Politically active sectors of New York City's working classes strategically supported this ideology. So did Walt Whitman, the leading literary booster of American democracy, who proudly predicted that by 1976, "there will be some forty to fifty states, among them Canada and Cuba . . . the Pacific Ocean will be ours, and the Atlantic mainly ours." When Ned Buntline lectured on "Liberty in Cuba" and "Americanism at Home," he meant that Cuba would be "freed" from Spanish rule to become a new slaveholding state of the United States.[39]

Land reform contributed to the lack of a working-class party by providing the prospect of an escape from the working class. In 1850, at the high point of antebellum labor organizing, the New York City Industrial Congress put forth several demands. The first three dealt with land reform; no mention was made of slavery. Although Wilentz has asserted that in June 1851 the Industrial Congress "finally put political action for land reform before all other questions," it had always done so.[40]

In response to the segregated organizing strategy of the European-American trades, African Americans, led by Frederick Douglass and Samuel Ringgold Ward, formed the American League of Colored Labourers in July 1850.[41] They aimed to subsidize black-owned businesses, support the skilled trades, and sponsor an industrial fair for May 1852 to exhibit the products of "colored mechanics, artisans and agriculturalists." Evidence of what transpired there is yet to be discovered. We do know that the New York City fair held in 1853 at the Crystal Palace excluded African Americans, while Democratic workingmen continued to attack Whigs and their Republican successors for " 'reduce[ing] white men to a forbidden level with negroes.' "[42]

Precisely because the Democratic Party had such deep social and organizational roots in New York City's working class, it could not lose local political hegemony to the Republicans. It successfully galvanized the political ambitions of the racist Industrial Congress leadership, who capitulated to the values of an incorporating America by relegating labor to an organized lobby rather than an independent political party. While the Industrial Congress limited its membership to crafts like cabinetmakers and turners, the Democratic Party's organizational efforts reached out to the foreign-born 75 percent of the workers in the larger, less skilled trades.

The bureaucratic organization of the Industrial Congress, with its proliferation of nomination and vigilance committees, mirrored the Democrats of 1844. All delegate credentials had to be formally screened. No unaccredited delegates were received in plenum. "Benevolent, protective, associative and cooperative Societies, for benefit and protection" of the workers revolved around the issue of land reform; so did the ward associations.[43] Control of the means of production was left to parochial trade interests, which meant that in a manner consistent with democratic republican notions of democracy, no solidarity was shown with African Americans, the unskilled, or women workers.

Cooperatives became the agreed-upon utopian solution to the erosion of the skilled trades' control over production. Each trade was called upon to organize as follows:

> a corporation or partnership . . . providing capital by taking stock
> in the concern . . . receiving dividends . . . according to their several

investments, and being paid for their work according to a predetermined scale based on the actual value of the product. Each company or corporation should be composed of persons known to and confiding in each other, and should choose its foreman, agent, treasurer, & c. by a general vote. . . . In process of time, each trade or corporation would come to supply the wants of its members by wholesale purchases from other trades.[44]

Similar gatherings took place in Pittsburgh and Washington, among other cities. Chicago's Industrial Congress predicted,

[T]he U.S. Congress . . . will soon act on the great question of Land Reform, by donating the public domain to actual settlers . . . as would guarantee a good homestead to the hardy pioneer, and the panting immigrant, who is driven to our shores by the gigantic curse of Land Monopoly, the source of so much misery, degradation and poverty.[45]

Such sentiments were consistent with Madison's *Federalist* No. 10, which conceived imperial expansion, rather than wealth redistribution, as the means of channeling the threat to the rule of large landowners. These ideas demonstrate the potential basis for union between the Northeast and the West, as perceived by a political party that twelve years later, in the midst of civil war, would enact a homestead law as a way to shore up dwindling support for the war effort.

The moral bankruptcy of the Industrial Congress was revealed by its failure even to mention African-American slavery. The congress stood for an artisanal labor aristocracy, and as such, was the precursor to the American Federation of Labor.

While skilled trades industriously built social walls around themselves—like the housepainters whose "secret order" instituted "measures for mutual protection"—increasingly frustrated unskilled or apprentice newcomers vented their anger on African Americans. Illustrative of their behavior in New York City was the near riot they caused in May 1850 at an abolitionist convention open to "all ages, sexes and complexions." William Lloyd Garrison, president of the American Anti-Slavery Society, provoked a heated response from some of the European-American men in the audience by proclaiming, "The whole of the Churches are incompetent in their work. They are a standing satire on Christianity and Humanity. . . . We stood where Moses stood, where Christ and Luther took their positions . . . against the Church and against the State of their time."[46]

His attack on President Zachary Taylor's pro-slavery position riled Captain Rynders, the Democratic Empire Club leader, who "backed by a posse," rushed the platform. "Ladies became frightened—children screamed." When order was restored, Frederick Douglass and Rev. Samuel Ringgold Ward spoke. Douglass regarded Ward as peerless, as he would make clear in his autobiography:

> As an orator and thinker he was vastly superior, I thought, to any of us, and being perfectly black and of unmixed African descent, the splendors of his intellect went directly to the glory of his race. In depth of thought, fluency of speech, readiness of wit, logical exactness, and general intelligence, Samuel R. Ward has left no successor among the colored men amongst us . . . .[47]

Ward had been pastor to a white church in Cortland, New York; to the *Tribune* reporter, he was "one of the blackest and most eloquent sons of Boanerges now in the ministry."[48]

On the convention's second day, about 250 persons attended, of whom half were either female, African American, or both. Such gender and race integration, rare among Whigs, was unheard of among Democrats. Once again, the "Law and Order" party, as Captain Rynders's rowdy band was designated, defended "Republican Freedom" by harassing these abolitionists. The rowdies chanted for Stephen Douglas when a resolution was passed condemning Daniel Webster for supporting the Fugitive Slave Act, which made it a federal crime to assist a runaway slave in any free state.

One heckler cried out, "Ha, old Garrison, are you Jesus?" When the abolitionist C. C. Burleigh, with his shoulder-length hair, rose to speak, another racist derided, "Go pay yer barber's bill!" Still another yelled, "S-a-a-y! Did anybody ever take you for a man?"

Rynders then mounted the stage to shouts of "White niggers," "Give the niggers a sight!" and "Oh, hell let's go and drink!" He demanded of Garrison, "Why don't the abolitionists buy the slaves?" He then quoted from Christ's reply to the rich man who asked what he should do to be saved. A colleague, an ex-policeman dismissed from the force for being found drunk in a whorehouse, then read an anti-abolitionist statement. Finally, the police arrived and adjourned the meeting.

The following day, the Anti-Slavery Society was forced to meet in closed session at the Sailors' Home on Cherry Street. The mayor, chief of police, and high sheriff had not protected the rights of the abolitionists to be heard. They did less to protect African Americans thirteen years later during the city's infamous draft riots. For now, sixth ward alderman John Kelley, who would become Tammany boss in the 1880s, introduced a resolution in the city council that called for Anti-Slavery Society meetings to be "suppress[ed]" owing to their "blasphemous and irreligious" nature. The resolution failed of passage by an eight-to-six vote.[49]

Five months later, a United States Marshal took James Hamlet back in chains from New York City to Baltimore. The first victim of a stiffened Fugitive Slave Act, Hamlet had been captured under false pretenses, denied legal counsel, and not allowed to say goodbye to his wife and children. Even some Democrats were outraged, on the grounds of states' rights, by this federal intervention in New York City affairs. But it was African-American New Yorkers who raised the eight hundred dollars that Hamlet's master demanded in exchange for his freedom. Hamlet was lucky; he returned a week later to a victory celebration arranged by the Committee of Thirteen. Not so fortunate was Henry Long, sent south in December after the New York State Supreme Court ruled against his plea to remain in the state. He never came back. There were also the publicized cases in 1854 of Horace Preston, whose freedom was ultimately purchased after he was sent to Baltimore, and Stephen Pembroke.[50]

In 1855, an anti-slavery convention appointed a Committee of Seven to mobilize blacks to vote for candidates who supported black suffrage. A year later, an African-American state convention decided to support the Republican Party, especially since the Democrats had recruited the Irish who, in the words of black abolitionist leader Henry Highland Garnet, "once naturalized, are the loudest shouters for . . . slavery extension, and the bitterest foes of the negro."[51]

In the 1850s the Democratic Party split over the spoils of office. "Hardshells" and "Softshells" formed separate general committees in 1853 after Tammany sachems on January 15, 1853, laid down rules for certification to General Committee membership that gave the Hards a minority of seats. The Hards withdrew and established a rival organization known as the Stuyvesant Institute Democracy, with auxiliary Young Men's Democratic national clubs to muster the physical force necessary to return fugitive slaves to their owners. The split widened to the state level at September's Syracuse convention.[52]

A grand jury report in February 1853 detailing corrupt practices by both parties further weakened public confidence in the political system. The investigation had been initiated after a lobbyist testified that a ring within the board of aldermen was demanding bribes for city contracts. The report implicated all Democratic and Whig factions in accepting hush money from the railroads. There was even an attempt to overcharge the city for the black crepe paper used at Henry Clay's memorial service. These timely disclosures were used by the Whig-dominated state legislature to justify replacement of the entire city council with sixty members who would now be chosen annually from districts other than the wards. Tammany's political infrastructure had been shaken.

The ward system, the most democratic feature of New York City's political system, suffered irreparable damage. Under the guise of preventing corruption, the *Evening Post* rationalized these moves:

> So prodigious had been the growth of the city, so various and large are the interests—and so numerous and craftily laid are the plans for pillaging the treasury, that a man who might have filled the office of Mayor quite respectably ten . . . years ago, is . . . unfit . . . at the present time.[53]

Fear of one-man rule led some among the economic elite to organize the Civic Reform Party. Iron manufacturer and philanthropist Peter Cooper, and his fellow patricians W. F. Havemeyer, Alexander Ming, Jr., and Theodore Tomlinson, wryly designated themselves the American Democracy.[54] Enough of the voting public was persuaded so that the Civic Reform Party, the first "reformist" party not explicitly nativist, won the 1853 fall elections. But like the American Republican Party of a decade earlier, the Civic Reformers proved unable or unwilling to confront the social problems resulting from the city's unprecedented growth and so expired as an independent political force.

The failure of reformers and the temporary disgrace of Tammany created a political vacuum that pro-slavery chandler, real estate speculator, and Democratic politician Fernando Wood sought to fill. Wood exuded personal charm in dealing with New York's men of wealth and conspicuously contributed to Irish Catholic relief agencies, while simultaneously buying up the land on which these immigrants rented their housing. Before first becoming mayor in 1854, Wood had long identified with Loco Foco policies.[55] A Wood supporter characterized the mayor's opponents as "a heterogenous conglomeration of Abolitionists, Fourierites, Kansas-shriekers, Know-Nothings, Shoulder-hitters, Women's Rights Advocates, Infidels, and Atheists."[56] This future millionaire won the 1854 election as mayor with 33.6 percent of the popular vote. In the four-man race, Wood beat by fifteen hundred votes the teetotaler small businessman James W. Barker, who represented the anti-Catholic Know Nothings. Wood was strongly endorsed by the two largest ethnic newspapers, the *Irish-American* and the *New Yorker Staatszeitung*. He portrayed himself in his inaugural address as "a man of honor, a friend of labor and industry, and a protector of the poor," now the largest segment of the city's population; and he concluded on a class note: "Do not let it be said that labor, which produces everything, gets nothing, and dies of hunger in our midst; while capital, which produces nothing, gets everything, and pampers in luxury and plenty."[57]

If Mike Walsh acted the part of labor's spokesman for the 1840s, Fernando Wood parlayed that role into immense political power in the subsequent decade. No mayor had enjoyed such overwhelming support from Irish and German immigrants. In a move calculated to allay the fears of his wealthy benefactors, Wood, as one member of the three-man police commission, ordered individual policemen to report personally to him on any violations of the law. He also linked station houses together with a telegraph system for the first time. A "Model Mayor" image soon made Wood, according to the governor of Ohio, the most popular man west of the Alleghenies and popular with the ladies. Wood capitalized on opposition to the draconian 1855 Prohibitory Act against alcohol, which was passed by the New York State legislature and antagonized his mainly immigrant constituency. The act directed various bizarre class-biased measures against intoxicants; one confined a public drunkard to prison until he named his source of alcohol, usually beer or whiskey, but exempted those intoxicated thanks to imported liquors like fine wines. Ten thousand persons signed a petition calling for mass protest, while the municipal police force refused to enforce this prohibition, later declared unconstitutional.[58]

The specter of a city openly defying the state liquor law exacerbated the differences between New York and Albany. Upstate canal and railroad interests sought to reduce the city's influence in party affairs. They believed that private enterprise best served the public interest because the private sector "rendered men accountable to one another, to law, and to nature for their actions." At the same time, Wood's ambitious program appealed to the city's social and cultural elite because it included better sanitation and housing, a municipal university for women as well as men that would rank with the great universities of Europe, and a veto of a Common Council resolution to reduce the size of Central Park.[59]

Wood took advantage of the solid support of almost a hundred conservative businessmen who urged him to run for mayor again.[60] He centralized control in his hands by establishing an executive committee to appoint those election inspectors about whom the General Committee could not agree. Despite charges that he required a kickback from would-be policemen, and even though the two other members of the police commission had accused him of providing police officers with time off to campaign, Wood's formal political opposition remained divided among Republican, American, and Reform tickets. Then, just before the 1856 election, a formidable detractor, the charismatic young lion and leader of the Hards Lorenzo Shepard, died. Thus, good fortune and strong financing, skill in politicking and bullyboying, had combined to give Wood another victory, with a 45 percent plurality.

For the first time in six years, the Democrats held a majority on the Common Council. Wood now ran Tammany Hall and boasted in a letter to President Buchanan that "We have *one* organization for the first time since 1848." He continued, however, to be stymied in his efforts to control the Tammany Society's right to designate which rival faction could form the official General Committee. Both Hards and Softs soon united within the Tammany Society against the one-man rule of Wood. In a seven-to-five vote, the Council of Sachems challenged Wood's control of the ward primary system by establishing electoral districts charged with running primary elections and by creating a new union general committee. Wood, who felt he had President Buchanan's confidence, was disappointed when the president gave anti-Wood men the bulk of federal spoils.[61]

In the state legislature, Republicans took advantage of Democratic divisions and designed the 1857 New York City charter to reorganize municipal departments. Five departments became three: Croton Aqueduct, street inspector, and city inspector. The mayor appointed the heads, subject to aldermanic approval. Grand jury members were selected by the mayor, the first judge of common pleas, and the chief justice of the superior court. Two-thirds of the aldermen could now override a mayoral veto. Comptroller, corporation counsel, recorder, register, surrogate, and eighteen judges of different courts would be popularly elected. The mayor no longer controlled the board of education, almshouse, or fire and health departments. The Common Council was in charge of contracts. The date for a new mayoral election was set for December 1, 1857, thereby separating that race from all other national and state contests. The state took over municipal projects. The governor appointed state commissions to oversee construction of Central Park, a new city hall, and Harlem Bridge and to control piers, wharves, and harbor pilots. Out of 4,644 city jobs, the mayor now shared control of those held by only 29 men who appointed 223 subordinates. Most importantly, wards were replaced by 17 aldermanic districts and a 24-man Common Council elected from the city's four state senatorial districts.

If the wards were the most politically democratic institutions in the world in the 1840s, their dismantling in the 1850s represented a major step backward in the evolution of political democracy. Unlike the charter revisions of 1849 and 1853, the 1857 charter was not submitted to the people for approval; nor was state control of the police force, to be discussed momentarily. The New York City Democracy had been formally crippled by the state-dominant Republican Party. The *Times* approved of the anti-democratic movement, commenting that "Most of the objects of a city administration are far better carried out . . . by a vigorous and arbitrary police system than by a representative assembly."[62]

On April 15, 1857, the same day the new municipal charter was enacted, the legislature created the Metropolitan Police for New York, Kings, Westchester and Richmond Counties to rival Wood's municipal force. Control of this body was assigned to a five-man state-appointed board, of which Wood was merely an ex officio member. A day later, the despised Excise Law, curtailing alcohol sales, was enacted. Strong characterized the new police bill as designed "to take power out of the paws of Mayor Wood and get it into those of the other scoundrels at Albany." Strong designated them the "two gangs," and waited "with perfect resignation for the Court of Appeals to decide which horde has the legal right to be supported by public plunder."[63] He penned these words the day after the municipal police denied the new gubernatorially appointed street commissioner access to his office. When a state supreme court judge ordered Mayor Wood's arrest, municipals blocked metropolitans from serving the warrant. Street fighting between the two police forces led the superior court to call for assistance from the 7th Regiment. Wood then arranged for his own arrest by a friendly judge, who released him on a writ of *habeas corpus*, thereby legally outflanking a politically antagonistic superior court. A year later the court of appeals ruled that Governor John King's move against Wood had been illegal.

On July 2, 1857, the state court of appeals upheld the new police act, contrary to the expectations of Wood and his mainly Irish constituency. The next day, Wood disbanded the municipal police. At 1:30 A.M. on July 4th, a crowd of Irish men and boys in the sixth ward attacked some metropolitans, who thereupon sought refuge in the saloon that was headquarters to the English-American Bowery Boys gang. At that point the Irish Dead-Rabbits, youthful Wood supporters with blue stripes on their pantaloons, set upon the English Bowery Boy group known as the Roach Guards, who wore red-striped trousers. After a metropolitan was beaten and reinforcements summoned, both gangs turned on the officers, and two policemen were killed, leading Tailer to call for arming the police with guns.[64] The Empire Club's Captain Rynders attempted to calm the rioters. He had gained mythical notoriety for, among other "political" acts, his aggressive exploits on behalf of Polk in the 1844 presidential election and the 1850 attack on the abolitionists. Failing to restore calm, Rynders recommended use of the military. The 71st and 8th Regiments were rushed in to pacify the community, but not before twelve men had died and many more had been injured, mostly by gunshot wounds.

Widespread local bitterness ensued, especially among Wood's Irish supporters. For some time afterward, the mere presence of a man in uniform was enough to provoke community rage, so the police were kept out of this predominantly Irish ward.[65] Sporadic violence directed against both the new state-appointed police and state-legislated temperance laws persisted for several weeks afterward, and engaged German immigrants as well.

The October Panic of 1857 set off New York City's next political crisis. The panic itself was the result of "railroad fever," that is, of eastern bankers' losses in western railroads and land deals, both adversely affected by the fighting in Kansas. With thirty-five thousand New Yorkers losing their jobs, Wood forestalled a bread riot when he put comparatively few of these men to work on Central Park and other public works projects. The Common Council agreed to the hiring of only eleven hundred men, and only after a November 5 march by six thousand unemployed mechanics and laborers through Wall Street to city hall, where the participants stressed the connection between capitalism and unemployment. The gentlemen of the state-appointed board overseeing the Central Park project, the largest public works project in the city's history, made sure that the jobs generated would be under their control and not the Democratic Party's. In August 1858, the board gave Frederick Law Olmsted the right to personally select the thousands of day laborers who would build the park. As Roy Rosenzweig and Elizabeth Blackmar point out, ". . . if the board failed to abolish patronage, it did succeed in consolidating and centralizing management in a way never previously tried in a public works project." Every effort was made not to hire any of the November 5 protesters.[66]

When it came to the business of men hiring prostitutes, there was no abatement of commercial activity, and virtually no prosecution either, because both real estate and hotel interests profited. In 1855, prostitution was the second largest enterprise in the city after the garment industry. In the next four years, only one criminal case was prosecuted against the thirty-four brothels listed in city directories.[67] One supposes that economic conditions would have been considerably worse without this trade.

Strong described the Panic of 1857 as "far the worst period of public calamity and distress I've ever seen, and I fear it is but the beginning."[68] As one descended the American social ladder, conditions grew bleaker. For the eleven thousand African Americans residing in New York City, rampant racism rendered their plight bleakest of all. Wood then repeated his 1854 assessment that "Truly may it be said that in New York those who produce everything get nothing, and those who produce nothing get everything." The Democratic Party's General Committee responded to Wood's declaration by pledging opposition to any member who "sows dissensions among the rich and the poor." The *Times* editorialized, "Mr. Wood raises the banner of the most fiery communism."[69] Such a Manichaean perception helped fuse Wood's divided opposition. Wood did not help his cause with the poor when he employed the metropolitans to guard city hall after the hungry attacked bakers' wagons to get bread.

In the 1857 mayoral race, Tammany Democrats and Republicans united as the People's Party and chose as their candidate the wealthy German-American paint manufacturer and former Free-Soiler Daniel F. Tiemann, who defeated Wood on December 1 by a margin of 2,327 votes out of a record 84,105 cast.[70] Following his defeat, Wood sought to purge from the party the leadership of his opposition within Tammany. On the first vote, he succeeded by a margin of 63 to 34, but this outcome was swiftly rescinded by another ballot, which went 51 to 43 against Wood. Two years later, however, facing a divided opposition in the 1859 mayoral election, Wood made a successful comeback against Tammany sugar baron Havemeyer and Republican merchant George Opdyke.

To help alleviate the economic depression gripping the city, Democrats invoked the Monroe Doctrine to call for the annexation of Cuba to secure more slaves for Southern plantations. Such an outcome would bring profit to New York City merchants and jobs for the city's dockworkers. In the meantime, the *Times* judged the drinking habits of the working classes to be distasteful, and suggested alternatives: "Cheap amusements were an antidote to crime and strong drink . . . licensing hand organs, instituting cheap concerts, cheapening literature and newspapers, were all valuable means for conquering drunkeness. . . ." And, the paper added, so was Central Park.[71]

The new Republicans had difficulty keeping temperance and nativism from taking center stage away from slavery, although startling technological advances such as the transatlantic cable enhanced their global economic strategy. In New York City, middle-class Republicans stereotyped Irish whiskey drinkers and German beer guzzlers as responsible for the social disorder wrought by the new industrial order. As usual, most men judged matters by appearances and blamed the victims. By 1855, with the foreign-born majority of New York City's population making up 75 percent of the workforce, even the formerly Whig and elite first ward now had a significant slum district, with the third highest percentage of immigrants (68.4 percent) of all the wards.[72]

Mercantile hegemony over the marketplace was being challenged by industrial capital, and so Democratic merchants and their employees became bolder in defending political ties to Southern planters.[73] They commanded the organizational resources to politically educate workers on the economic necessity of maintaining close relations with the South. New York County was the only county in the state to give the Democrats a political majority in 1856, and in no county was racism more overtly expressed than in Manhattan.

It was a Pyrrhic victory. As economic polarity between the classes grew, neither the Democratic nor the Republican Party held out any salvation for Union without bloodshed; neither demonstrated a capacity for moral leadership. There were no statesmen, only men of their respective states and men of the national state. This dismal course of political events turned the prominent men who argued otherwise into fit subjects for satire, as Melville demonstrated in *The Confidence-Man: His Masquer-*

ade.[74] In this parable of slavery's ill effects on American character, Melville demonstrated the corollary of those effects—that no confidence should be placed in any of the men who held out hope for reform. They were either dissemblers or impotent to avert national cataclysm.

⊸ 8 ⊶

THE TRIUMPHAL
DEBACLE OF DEMOCRATIC
REPUBLICANISM
1857–1863

There is no State in the American Union wherein there were not free and
independent democratic republicans, and *soi-disant* Christians, 'ready, aye
ready' to aid in overpowering a runaway, *for pay.*

> Samuel Ringgold Ward, *Autobiography* (1855)

The Romans worshipped their standards, and the Roman standard happened to be an eagle. Our standard is only one-tenth of an Eagle—a Dollar—but we make all even by adoring it with ten-fold devotion.

> Edgar A. Poe, *Southern Literary Messenger* (June 1849)

The best class we show, is but a mob of fashionably dress'd speculators
and vulgarians.

> Walt Whitman, *Democratic Vistas* (1870)

Set men face to face, with weapons in their hands, and they are as ready
to slaughter one another now, after playing at peace and good-will for so
many years, as in the rudest ages, that never heard of peace-societies, and
thought no wine so delicious as what they quaffed from an enemy's skull.

> Nathaniel Hawthorne, "Chiefly About War-Matters,"
> *Atlantic Monthly,* July 1862

———

ON THE EVE OF THE CIVIL WAR, MORE THAN TWO-THIRDS OF NEW
YORK CITY'S ELECTORATE CAST THEIR BALLOTS FOR THE DEMO-
cratic Party. This did not, however, translate into political hegemony for
the Democrats, because the Republicans controlled a state legislature that
wielded growing power over the city. Republicans perceived their own

party as essential to the maintenance of social order. They held Democrats politically responsible for the Irish, whose high crime rate was considered proof of their racial degeneracy. That this crime rate could be directly correlated with poverty went generally unappreciated. In likeminded fashion, Democrats overlooked that a high crime rate among blacks was but a function of racism and their poverty.

Democrats were also saddled by identification with "filibustering pirates"[1]—Southern plantation owners who financed marauding expeditions against Cuba and Nicaragua to seize slaves. These "fire-eaters" spearheaded a similar effort to force Kansas to become a slave state. Their New York City defenders engaged in violent acts that provided a convenient rationale for the anti-democratic effort conducted by the Republican state legislature to centralize power in its hands, as just discussed in Chapter 7.[2] Republicans were assisted by upstate Democratic canal and railroad men[3] whose regional interests outweighed party allegiance.

During March and April of 1858, the Tammany Society inducted new braves to pack Tammany and deny Wood control. Their success prompted Wood to form a rival political organization, Mozart Hall, which zealously professed to defend free white labor. Mozart Hall assembled twenty-two "Democratic Societies of Regulars" to correspond with each of the wards. They in turn elected delegates to a Mozart general committee.

Wood was the closest New York City had come to having a party boss, a man who could not have existed prior to 1845, a time when most workers were artisans who strove to be their own bosses. Long before their counterparts in Europe, New York City Irish and German artisans possessed the vote and were absorbed into dominant-party ranks, from which they in turn counseled immigrants to work within the established two-party system. These artisan citizens were ideologically set apart from Parisian red republicans, who boasted a century-old tradition of revolutionary protest against the denial of the vote to the male majority.[4] Parisian artisans had even organized their own radical party. For New York City artisans in an expanding economy, the ballot box had become "the coffin of class consciousness," to employ Alan Dawley's felicitous phrasing.[5] Unlike those in Paris, or Frankfurt or Dublin for that matter, New York City artisans had by 1855 been replaced by less skilled foreign workers who now composed the bulk of the workforce. These new immigrants represented more of a volatile social threat than did their artisan predecessors, while generally identifying with the Democratic Party.

The political crucible for the new immigrants had been a European social formation distinguished by the absence of the franchise. Immigrants came to America sensitized to the power differential between rich and poor, and they received the right to vote. The threat that such a radicalized mass posed to the security of the plutocracy could be neutralized by a political machine headed by a man who knew how to appeal to the tastes of the immigrant voter—provided, of course, that this one man would not seek to take advantage of his position to chart an independent political course. Compared to the native artisan, the semiskilled immigrant had greater material and social needs, which Wood, as mayor in a growing economy, could skillfully parlay into immense local power. The massive immigration of the late 1840s and the 1850s provided Wood his electoral base. His strength at the ward level accounted in large measure for the effective challenge that he mounted to Tammany Hall, as well as to his Republican opposition. Wood forged a political organization freer of the controls of the traditional Democratic mercantile elite than that of any previous New York City Democratic leader. His independence was nourished by the divisions within the national Democratic Party.

Wood tapped into the racism of both Rynders and Walsh. Through the *Daily News*, controlled by Wood's brother Benjamin, Mozart Hall blasted Tammany as a collection of "black Republican spies and Democratic traitors." Appropriately enough, another brother, Henry, became a partner in the Christy and Wood minstrel company, confirming Alexander Saxton's observation that blackface minstrelsy was a cultural by-product of pro-slavery Democrats.[6]

The Democratic field, divided between Tammany and Mozart Halls, allowed Republicans to elect the comptroller, corporation attorney, and several aldermen in the December 1857 municipal elections. An irate President Buchanan thereupon summoned key city Democrats to the White House, where he made them personally sign a pledge to divert all customs house revenues to Tammany Hall.

A brief respite from the Panic of 1857 had occurred, appropriately enough, at election time; it soon dissipated, so that 1859 dawned gloomy. Industry was paralyzed by low production and high unemployment. African slaves were flagrantly transported into Georgia in Southern slave ships. New York City Tammany leader Augustus Belmont bankrolled Louisiana Senator John Slidell, who provoked acrimonious floor debate with his introduction of a Senate bill to annex Cuba and transform it into two slave states.

The chief literary spokesman for American democracy, Walt Whitman, failed to condemn slavery in his masterwork, *Leaves of Grass*. In fact, Whitman romanticized plantation life, as the following 1860 section, "Our Old Feuillage," confirms:

> There are the negroes at work in good health
> . . . the planter's son returning after a long absence,
> joyfully welcom'd and kiss'd by the aged mulatto nurse.

New York City had the country's second largest urban black population and three African-American newspapers that could have provided Whitman with ample opportunity to question the stereotypes of blacks he employed in his writings. Even so, his views should not come as a surprise given his affection for the New York Democracy and his need to appeal to a public steeped in democratic republican racism. This tolerance of slaveholding prompted staunch Republicans like Strong to object:

> This generation is certainly overshadowed by a superstition not yet quite exploded, that slaveholding rights possess peculiar sanctity and inviolability, that everybody who doubts their justice is an Abolitionist, and that an Abolitionist is a social pariah, a reprobate and caitiff, a leper whom all decent people are bound to avoid and denounce.[7]

Widespread antipathy to abolitionists served Wood's political purposes. In 1859, his "shoulder-hitters" took over the New York Democratic state convention auditorium from Tammany and established a new state committee to include Wood. After Wood's ticket had been endorsed and the meeting adjourned, the Softs returned and, fearing a split ticket, replaced the shoulder-hitter state committee with its predecessor, thereby excluding Wood.

Soon afterward, customs house cost cutting reduced party patronage by nearly three hundred men, and wealthy Democrats formed the Fifth Avenue Association in revulsion at both Tammany and Mozart Halls. Once again, in 1859, Havemeyer, whose mercantile ties with the South remained strong, became their mayoral candidate, while lawyer and future Democratic presidential candidate Samuel J. Tilden was nominated for corporation counsel. The *Daily News* lambasted this slate as "a kid-glove, scented, silk stocking, poodle-headed degenerate aristocracy."[8]

Then John Brown's momentous 1859 raid against the federal arsenal at Harper's Ferry to secure arms to free slaves, swiftly followed by his execution and martyrdom, galvanized all sides in the slavery debate. Tammany Hall Grand Sachem Isaac V. Fowler characterized Brown's raid as "riot, treason and murder." Merchant Tailer reported with grim satisfaction to his diary that the "traitor and murderer" had died, and that "they ought to hang all those who interfere with the rights of Southern slaveholders." He fretted that Brown's actions had jeopardized North-South trade, and he feared that the South would withdraw from the Union if Lincoln were elected.[9]

Brown's crusade contributed to a New York City voter backlash. Wood, the most openly racist of the three candidates for mayor, won for a third time in December 1859, with a record 88 percent of the eligible electorate participating. His 38.2 percent vote tally was enough, since Havemeyer and Opdyke split the majority with 34.6 and 27.4 percent respectively. Tailer voted the straight Tammany ticket. On Wood's success he observed, "It serves the *respectable portion* of the community right for *putting up two candidates*, and for permitting such an unprincipled man as Fernando Wood to become Mayor of this great City." Mozart Hall relied on the German vote but commanded greatest support from the poorest class.[10]

Immediately following Wood's inauguration, charges surfaced that he had sold the office of city inspector to Samuel Downes for $20,000 but had refused him the position after receiving the cash payment, thereby violating normal city business practice. Wood was also charged with misappropriating $420,000 and receiving tens of thousands in kickbacks while laborers under these contracts had their pay reduced from $1.25 to 95 cents per day.[11]

In the meantime, Tammany was doing even less to inspire public confidence. Its grand sachem, college graduate and postmaster Isaac V. Fowler, got away with embezzling $155,000 when U.S. Marshal and New York Democratic Party stalwart Isaiah Rynders allowed him to escape arrest in May 1860. Fowler's brother, appointed clerk to a surrogate judge upon unanimous recommendation of all seven sachems, then absconded with more than $30,000 in funds earmarked for orphans. The *Herald* echoed other conservative sentiment when it called for the formation of an independent party to deal with Tammany's and Mozart's sale of public offices; "the candidates pay them for making up the ticket," the *Herald* charged, "and the people vote it because it is 'republican.' "[12]

A cocky Mayor Wood went to the Charleston Democratic National

Convention in April as head of the pro-slavery, anti-Tammany delegation supporting John Breckinridge. In spite of the recent scandals, he left New York confident that the 1860 referendum on removing property qualifications for African-American voters would be defeated. He was right. The measure was overwhelmingly rejected by a margin of 37,471 to 1,640 in New York City.[13] A similar vote in 1846 had been tallied at 29,948 against and 5,137 in favor.

Clearly the vast majority of whites persisted in their hatred of blacks. Labor segmentation had deepened the cultural chasms between skilled Anglo-Dutch artisans, proletarianized Irish, and Germans, and between all of them and African Americans. The multiclass character of the wards in the 1840s, reflected in both neighborhood and Democratic Party, was being replaced by more class-pure neighborhoods that manifested even less toleration of the African American. At a Democratic rally on October 8, 1860, called to ratify the nomination of Stephen Douglas for president, speakers made the case before a predominantly European-American immigrant audience that freeing the slaves would mean fewer jobs for white New Yorkers.[14]

Land reformers were now more likely to favor the party of Lincoln, while the bulk of New York City's laboring classes in 1861 paraded their opposition to the war in a huge march replete with racist banners and slogans. In light of Northern support for slavery, Strong could not fathom why the South was so afraid of the Republican Party; African suffrage had, after all, been defeated by a majority of one hundred thousand in a Republican state. Still, as Tailer noted, "If Lincoln is defeated, confidence will be restored, and prosperity will return."[15]

Lincoln's election aggravated the city's persistent racial tensions. He received only 33,290 out of 95,772 votes cast in New York City, proof that democratic republicanism remained the dominant ideology. He had become president with 39 percent of the national electorate, and without a single Republican vote recorded in ten Southern states. In 1864, Lincoln would do even worse in New York City, garnering but 36,681 out of 110,390 ballots cast.

For the first time in history, a United States president was publicly committed to limiting the slaveholders' equal opportunity in the marketplace by denying them the right to extend their plantations to new territories. For the first time also, Paine's "first useful class of citizens"—the farmers, including Southern slaveholders—could no longer count on the party in the White House to place their needs first. Southern planters felt they had little choice but to secede from a North that was, according to Strong, "discordant, corrupt, deeply diseased, unable to govern themselves, and in most unfit condition for a war on others."[16] Secession also provided the South with the opportunity to renege on the enormous debt that Southerners owed Northern banks.[17]

Prior to secession, the South supported the Crittenden Compromise, which demanded both the annexation of Cuba and Mexico as slave states and an amendment to the Constitution that would guarantee slavery. If this compromise had succeeded, the fundamental instability that Strong decried would have been transferred to U.S. foreign policy, especially in Latin America. The United States would have been at a decided disadvantage in competition with European industrial powers, because to carry the threat of enslavement to other nations along with U.S. commodities would have damaged commercial relations with these countries. A growing national consensus of business leaders had come to appreciate this important point.[18] They were grimly resigned to keeping Southern slavery confined to the states in which it already flourished. Northern bankers also wanted Southern planters to repay the huge debts that they had incurred. Their tolerance of Wood receded correspondingly.

Fortunately, the mayor played into their political hands. Wood accepted a five-year 279,000 dollar street-cleaning contract underbid by twenty-three other contractors, so that brother Ben could receive one-quarter of the proceeds. Then he arranged through intermediaries to have city revenues deposited in the Artisans' Bank, which subsequently defaulted because it unlawfully lent large, unsecured amounts to Mozart Hall.[19] The day following Wood's departure on a Christmas honeymoon with his sixteen-year-old bride, the acting mayor and city council president, with the approval of the aldermen, removed Wood's chamberlain and replaced him with a Broadway Bank director. Immediately upon his return, Wood challenged this move. A friend, Judge George C. Barnard, ruled in Wood's favor, but an appeals judge, friendly with new Tammany boss William Tweed, overruled Barnard. Two more months of lucrative wrangling took place between legal counsel at public expense before the state legislature passed a bill that gave the governor sole power to remove the chamberlain. In response, on January 6, 1861, Mayor Wood formally recommended to the Common Council in his state of the city address, that the city and Long Island secede from the Union to form the republic of Tri-Insula.

This last official political gasp of Loco Focoism jeopardized Wood's appeal in the Kleindeutschland wards that had provided him with the margin of victory in 1859. Wood had captured the support of German voters because he had led the opposition against banning liquor on Sundays and was on the right side during the metropolitan police riot, which appeared to be directed against Germans. When Tammany Hall ran a largely Irish ticket in 1858 to win back the Irish vote, Wood became almost entirely dependent on the German vote the following year. Thus in 1860, while Lincoln won the German vote in the Midwest, he lost two to one in New York City's German wards.[20]

Wood's support of the South had not lost him many German or Irish votes, but it did bring him into a different sort of class conflict with Strong. The diarist observed regarding a dinner held by William Astor that

his [Wood's] invitation was a tribute by his millionaire host to the dangerous democracy. . . . Our Fernando has just married a "genteel" wife . . . has his opera box, and is trying for a "social position." But I do not think I should invite him to this house were I twenty William B. Astors, or had he married twenty Miss Drake Millses.

Two months later Strong recorded, "It's a pity we ever renounced our allegiance to the British navy."[21] When war broke out in April, Postmaster General Montgomery Blair denied Benjamin Wood's *Daily News* the right to be carried in the mails because of its pro-Southern views. The paper was forced to suspend publication in mid-September.

In the fall 1861 mayoral election, the Republicans won with 34 percent of the popular vote, because Tammany fielded its own candidate, Godfrey Gunther, the son of German immigrants, while Wood persisted in running, determined to be the only mayor in New York City history to win a fourth term. He had to settle for the U.S. Congress in November 1862.

Earlier, in the summer of 1862, pressure mounted for emancipation as a military measure to defeat the South and as a means of placating European-American workers, who feared a continued exodus of slaves escaping north to secure freedom and employment. Irish longshoremen, coopers, and iron and shipbuilding men, among others, assaulted African Americans in Brooklyn and New York City. The longshoremen persisted in their attacks until the 1863 draft riots. Generally, strikes and clashes between workers and the authorities were provoked when the merchants slashed wages and hired black substitutes to haul cotton bales. Troops were also employed to do the unloading. Only a 21 percent decline in New York City's black population from 1860 to 1865 satisfied European Americans that African-American labor posed no threat to their livelihoods[22] (see Table 1).

The Civil War gave soldiering jobs to many out-of-work men through the Federal Conscription Act of March 3, 1863. The law's most objectionable clause stipulated payment of three hundred dollars in lieu of military service. This provision allowed wealthy New Yorkers to buy their way out of the draft. To Strong, "the draft will be the *experimentum crucis* to decide whether we have a government among us."[23]

Ironically, racism aided those blacks not wanting to join the war effort, for the act automatically exempted them from military service. Many ultimately did serve, of course, once the Republican Party altered its enlistment policies in order to strike fear into the hearts of white Southerners.[24] Strong observed as follows:

> Black regiments are (or soon will be) adopted into the national army with as little objection to their color as would be made to the use of a corral of black horses captured from the rebels, and our consent to let niggers enlist and fight is a heavier blow to the rebels than the annihilation of General Lee's army would be.

He then presciently added,

> there could be no stable equilibrium and permanent peace till the peculiar institutions of the South have been broken up and ground to powder, and to do this requires at least two more years of war, and perhaps a period of Southern success and invasion of northern territory, stimulating the North to begin fighting in earnest, which it has not yet begun to do.[25]

The enlistment of black troops was generally disparaged by democratic republicans. The *Herald* alternately ridiculed and gave prominent coverage to African-American enlistment, thereby feeding racist frenzy in New York City.[26]

The Civil War substituted Republican order for Democratic disorder. It caused stocks to boom and multiplied the opportunities for a few men to make a lot of money. Republican Mayor George Opdyke's factory supplied the military with uniforms at inflated cost. A Common Council special session convened on August 21, 1861, to assist the families of poor volunteers resulted in the misappropriation of 250,000 dollars. John Washington, George's closest living descendent, sold Mount Vernon for 200,000 dollars and planned to take Washington's bones from their resting place in protest against the Northern attempt to impose its will upon the South.[27]

But the most significant financial measure was the one that made greenbacks legal tender in 1862, followed two years later by a tax on state bank notes that reduced their number by 85 percent in six years. Lincoln's Republican supporters had issued 450 million dollars in green paper backed by nothing more than the authority of the federal government. The National Banking Act of 1863, modeled after New York State's 1838 safety-fund law, then taxed the state bank notes out of existence. For the first time in U.S. history, the nation possessed a single currency. Treasury Secretary Salmon P. Chase remarked that this feat was "of perhaps equal value with the abolition of slavery, produced also by the war."[28]

The National Banking Act of 1863 represented the biggest triumph to that date for bankers. A financial revolution had been effected through the agency of civil war. Up to this time only gold and silver had been legal tender. Now paper issued by the government had to be accepted in any state. The Loco Focos had lost on both counts—slavery and hard money.

Lincoln appealed to the immigrants' sense of loyalty to their new homeland, banking on a trait they had exhibited during the Mexican-American War. Great fanfare attended the raising of Irish and German regiments in their respective neighborhoods. Germans favored the war more than the Irish. They were also more skilled, better paid, and therefore less personally violent;[29] in other words, they were less desperate. They had been steeped in German socialist republicanism and proved less bloodthirsty during the draft riots than the Irish-American unskilled, whose political education in New York City came mainly within the Democratic Party.

From among the Irish, noteworthy was the 69th Regiment of Meagher's Irish Brigade, which suffered the worst casualties of any New York State regiment. Its charismatic leader, Michael Corcoran, was suspended from duty to await court-martial for refusing to participate in a ceremony honoring the Prince of Wales, because the prince symbolized British oppression of Ireland. When Corcoran's regiment was called to active duty, many of his men threatened not to go unless he were freed. Corcoran then penned an open letter in which he "earnestly hoped and entreated" that "duty and patriotism" would lead them "to arrive at such a conclusion as will be creditable to you alike as soldiers and as Irish adopted citizens." He promised to "throw myself into the ranks for the maintenance and protection of the Stars and Stripes as soon as the decision in my case may be announced, no matter what that may result in." Thereupon, Corcoran's regiment unanimously voted to serve. The War Department was so impressed they dismissed the charges against Corcoran and restored him to command. Had Corcoran possessed the authority, he could have raised a brigade, because more than six thousand Irishmen volunteered to serve under him. Corcoran was subsequently captured by the Confederacy, and Lincoln won his freedom in a prisoner exchange. He was killed in combat on December 22, 1863.[30]

The lesson of the Irish producing fierce fighting men was not lost upon the elite. In New York City, the Democratic troublemakers were the Irish, so much so that Irish community leaders had their mail opened by the police and Secret Service. But during the Civil War, Irishmen gloriously served the political purposes of the nationalistic Republican Party by dying for the stars and stripes on the battlefield.

In an attempt to coordinate Republican control of the war effort the Union League was inaugurated on May 12, 1863. This organization of almost a thousand influential New Yorkers desired, in Strong's words,

> to sustain government against Southern rebellion and Northern sectionalism, and strengthen Northern loyalty to the nation, and stimulate property-holders and educated men to assert their right to a voice in the conduct of public affairs, national, state, and municipal, and do a little something toward suppressing the filthy horde of professed politicians that is living on us and draining our national life by parasitical suction.[31]

Strong's chairmanship of the United States Sanitary Commission placed him in a unique position to shape the Union League, since the executive committee of the Sanitary Commission became the Union League's nominating committee. A publicly visible united front on behalf of the Union was sorely needed in the major Northern cities to combat diminishing political support for Lincoln's war effort. It was a public unity that would be severely tested by the 1863 draft riots.

The Democratic Party stood firmly against General David Hunter's order freeing slaves under his command, while the Republican Party split, forcing Lincoln to rescind the order. On Independence Day 1862, Democrats were again united against granting slaves their freedom and independence. During Tammany's July 4th celebration, Grand Sachem Nelson J. Waterbury called upon the president "to set his foot firmly upon abolitionism and crush it to pieces." The next month, Secretary of War Edwin Stanton federalized the city's police by designating them a provost marshal's guard. In September, two more Democratic newspapers, the *World* and the *Express*, came out in favor of a pardon for the South, which led to their being unconstitutionally banned by the head of the Union Army, Joe Hooker.[32]

As it was for Strong, the Civil War was at center stage for both Melville and Mark Twain. But unlike Strong, whose peers were about to extend their dominion over the South, the two giants of American literature viewed the war as confirming their gloomy prognosis for the United States and the human race. These views were reinforced by the bloodiest "insurrection" in U.S. history, the New York City draft riots of 1863. The riots began as a mass protest by the immigrant population,[33] a population imbued with Democratic Party ideology. Fed by rage at the Emancipation Proclamation, the outburst swiftly degenerated into an orgy of murderous violence directed against African Americans.

Lincoln's Emancipation Proclamation freed the slaves reluctantly, and selectively, in the Confederate states not under his control, but not in the border states. It was a military measure, not a moral imperative. Had the Union struggle not been transformed into a struggle for emancipation of the slaves, the draft would not have engendered the violence it did. Before the Civil War, Republicans argued, as exemplified by the editors of the *Atlantic Monthly*, that Lincoln had as much chance of abolishing slavery as the Democratic candidates for president—Bell, Breckinridge, and Douglas—had of eliminating human nature.[34]

A month before the draft riots, Wood had sponsored the largest and most bitter anti-administration rally to that point in U.S. history—the thirty-thousand-strong peace "convention" held in and around Cooper Union on June 3. Wood and Rynders were among the featured speakers, and even though Tammany's leaders were absent, rank-and-file laborers and longshoremen voiced their opposition to the continued military pursuit of the South. Wood decried the use of the military, which he characterized as "a new and dangerous power which already overrides the courts and the constitution . . . creating a stupendous money debt which must bear down labor." The *Herald* reported that Wood had "outgeneralled all the political leaders of Tammany Hall." His speech "was the best he ever made in his life. . . . It is as statesmanlike as it is bold."[35]

The Cooper Union rally set the tone for the unparalleled urban violence in July, as did Gettysburg, a week before the riots. New York City's Southern supporters grew desperate in their desire for revenge at this crucial Southern loss. Therefore, to characterize these riots, as Iver Bernstein has done, as an "audacious . . . lost opportunity" to "solve, all at once, the problems of an industrializing city and a divided nation"[36] is to impart advanced political calculation to an essentially reactive, undisciplined, racist segment of the population. Fulfillment of this "opportunity" led to more than one hundred deaths, thousands of injuries, blocks upon blocks of burned-out residences, and a discredited Democratic Party.[37]

One need only compare the choreography of this carnage to that of the Paris Commune eight years later to appreciate how much Parisian workers differed in their aims and behavior from their New York City counterparts. Parisian artisans led a distinguished defense of the French Republic against foreign invaders and domestic turncoats. In New York City, although arrayed against state power, workers behaved like racist murderers rather than communards.[38]

Memories of 1848 in Europe and 1849 in New York City were frighteningly fresh in the minds of New York City's rich, who feared the city's July days would cause suspension of supplies to a beleaguered Union army that could not afford to divert any troops to quell the rebellion. Just after the Paris Commune, contemporary Joel Headley wrote of the draft riots:

> With the great banking-houses and moneyed institutions of New York sacked and destroyed, the financial credit of the country would have broken down entirely. . . . Had the rioters got possession of the city for a single day, their first dash would have been for the treasures piled up in its moneyed institutions.[39]

The placement of the lottery in the city's poorest European-American ward was the immediate provocation for the draft riots, because the poor did not want to serve. The Irish were underrepresented in the Union army and, despite the fame of Michael Corcoran's fighting 69th, wished to remain that way. They directed their democratic republican wrath against the industrial targets from which the Republic of the Republicans drew strength—such as the Union Steam Works owned by George Farlee, the Republican mayor's son-in-law—and against those who benefited from Farlee's charity—orphaned slave children. Rioters were encouraged in their racial bestiality by the newspapers the *Herald*, the *World*, and the *News*, which tagged the riot as a "popular insurrection"; by a Democratic Party business triumvirate of August Belmont, Joel Barlow, and Samuel J. Tilden; and by Archbishop Hughes, a staunch supporter of slavery who wrote Horace Greeley on the second day of the riots to urge that the North suspend its war effort.[40]

Herman Melville was living in New York City during the riots. He remained uncomfortably awake through a night of death and destruction:

(July, 1863.)

No sleep. The sultriness pervades the air
And binds the brain—a dense oppression, such
As tawny tigers feel in matted shades,
Vexing their blood and making apt for ravage.
Beneath the stars the roofy desert spreads
Vacant as Libya. All is hushed near by
Yet fitfully from far breaks a mixed surf
Of muffled sound, the Atheist roar of riot.
Yonder, where parching Sirius set in drought,
Balefully flares red Arson—there—and there.
The Town is taken by its rats—ship-rats
And rats of the wharves. All civil charms
And priestly spells which late held hearts in awe—
Fear-bound, subjected to a better sway
Than sway of self; these like a dream dissolve,
And man rebounds whole aeons back in nature.
Hail to the low dull rumble, dull and dead,
And ponderous drag that shakes the wall.
Wise Draco comes, deep in the midnight late;
Of black artillery; he comes, though late;
In code corroborating Calvin's creed
And cynic tyrannies of honest kings;
He comes, nor parlies; and the Town, redeemed,
Gives thanks devout; nor, being thankful, heeds
The grimy slur on the Republic's faith implied,
Which holds that Man is naturally good,
And—more—is Nature's Roman, never to be scourged.[41]

Iver Bernstein has dismissed Melville's firsthand appraisal on the grounds that we should "put aside the disillusioned Herman Melville of the sixties," and "cultivate instead the vision of the democratic Melville of the early fifties, the Melville of *Moby-Dick*, who was willing to entertain, as few of his contemporaries were, the multiple claims to authority in this era."[42] But the authority in *Moby-Dick* is Captain Ahab. There is nothing democratic about his rule; the same could be said for Lincoln, who skillfully used the war to nationally legitimize the Republican Party through the suspension of various provisions of the Constitution.

Realistically, for the working class during this era there were but two "claims to authority," neither of which arose spontaneously from the working class itself. To be on the more moral and progressive, but not democratic, side meant supporting forcible suppression of the racist draft rioters, as Melville fatalistically observed in his poem.

Bernstein has attributed the bloodletters' behavior to "watch[ing] a centralizing national government become increasingly identified with the prerogatives of a local elite . . . associated with exploitative and interventionist authority, [so that] rioters of all persuasions sought to reclaim the polity in the name of the community." Here he defines community in a manner consistent with the professed aims of democratic republicanism. Rioters were not "the most proletarianized and degraded workers," but rather "wage earners accustomed to considerable control over their jobs."[43]

It is not the case, however, that "the draft rioters' rage against the Republican Party had its origins in workers' efforts to intervene in politics on their own terms in the 1850s."[44] As already pointed out, the rioters' political home was the Democratic Party. These workers had absorbed its racist ideology and had been materially assisted in this process by being structurally integrated into party ranks by the 1840s. Sociologically, it was Democrats who possessed a near monopoly on the rioters. This is not surprising, because their ideological godfathers—Jefferson, Madison, and Jackson—were all slaveholders.

From the beginning of the century, the Democratic Party had inculcated European immigrants to accept slavery for African Americans. Racist behavior ought not, therefore, be ascribed to "social perceptions . . . shaped in the context of the neighborhood." Dominant party politics, not working-class culture, was responsible for the racism whose active agent, in Strong's words, was an "Irish anti-conscription Nigger-murdering mob."[45] The European-American longshoremen's attacks were provoked by merchants hiring African Americans at lower wages than Irish Americans, not merely by values emanating from a sense of neighborhood. When, in the spring of 1863, the national government moved to protect African-American strikebreakers on the docks, hostility was then extended to the Republican-controlled federal government.

Abraham Lincoln aggravated the ruptures within the working class. At the historical moment for national implementation of a new liberal capitalist order to serve the large private industrial corporation, Lincoln took political advantage of the little man's desire to expand his own economic horizons. In a speech to Congress on December 3, 1861, the president pictured a lost world that never was, where "the prudent, penniless beginner in the world, labors for wages awhile, saves a surplus with which to buy tools or land for himself; then labors on his own account another while, and at length hires another new beginner to help him." Portraying the self-made man as entitled to exploit another man's labor for a wage, this characterization excluded slaveowners. At the same time, it held the potential to corrupt the working class. The political hostility that Northern workingmen harbored against Northern monopoly capitalists was deflected to the Southern slaveholders. Similarly, agrarian radicalism, which had climaxed in the years 1857 to 1860,[46] was absorbed by the Civil War.

Deflection and absorption were facilitated by a print media dependent on the paid advertising of the commerce and industry that greatly profited from government war orders. The media's mass man clashed with Thoreau's self-made soul designed to replace Emerson's self-made man, who had become a machine of war.[47] Self-made men prompted Melville to spurn a career in public speaking, for "trying to scratch my brains for a Lecture," he wrote, led inevitably to thoughts of the "Daily Progress of man towards a state of intellectual and moral perfection, as evidenced in the history of 5th Avenue and 5 Points."[48]

Ahab as Puritan had triumphed. Whereas in the beginning a likeminded Manichaean, John Winthrop, had captained the *Arbella* across the Atlantic toward America, now, on the eve of the Civil War, Ahab relentlessly pursued westward his demon to conquer or be doomed. Melville had tapped into the strain of Armageddon that runs strongest at the frontiers of the American soul. With Hawthorne and Poe, he pioneered American modernism, which in Alfred Kazin's words, "expressed the greatest single fact about our modern American writing—our writers' absorption in every last detail of their American world together with their deep and subtle alienation from it . . . our alienation *on* native grounds."[49]

The political variable that accelerated the artists' alienation from society was the machine men's political reincarnation as Lincoln's Republican Party. Thoreau recognized that "the mass of men serve the state thus, not as men mainly, but as machines, with their bodies." Men were being trained to serve as cogs in a mechanistic system that would blossom as the Northern army of "Bloody" Grant. Thoreau would have none of it. He was very clear on that point: "How does it become a man to behave toward this American government to-day? I answer that he cannot without disgrace be associated with it. I cannot for an instant recognize that political organization as *my* government which is the *slave's* government also."[50] Still, Thoreau did not find Southern slavery to be the worst social system then operating in the United States: ". . . there are so many keen and subtle masters that enslave both north and south. It is hard to have a southern overseer; it is worse to have a northern one; but worst of all when you are the slave-driver of yourself."[51]

Thoreau realized how deeply the industrial organization of society had permeated man's psyche, and how viciously defensive democratic republican stalwarts had become. In contrast, the new Republicans directed the self to serve a national identity from which there was no escape, except through monetary means, as the Civil War draft exemptions demonstrated. Perversely, the collective outrage at this discriminatory policy was monstrously misdirected against "colored orphans." Their home on Fifth Avenue, the Colored Orphan Asylum, was attacked late in the afternoon of July 13. Shrubbery and fences were torn up, furniture smashed, and the building finally set afire. Strong exclaimed to his diary, "how this infernal slavery system has corrupted our blood, North as well as South!"[52]

The new Republicans personalized the principles of national identity so as to direct attention to a United States destined to become a world power through factory expansion while promising farmers a global market for their produce. Republicans were strategically concerned with foreign policy as the means to secure raw materials and markets. Or as Seward so grandly expressed it, "the nation that draws the most materials and provisions from the earth, and fabricates the most, and sells the most of productions and fabrics to foreign markets, must be, and will be, the great power of the earth."[53] Such profound reliance upon global trade made Seward one with the American patrician tradition formally initiated by Alexander Hamilton. Practical opportunity to articulate this position publicly came after industry had successfully taken root in the 1820s. By 1834, when Clay's National Republicans became the Whigs, a commercial elite, dependent on industry as well as agricultural surplus, actively sought national state hegemony through promotion of a vision of community based on consumer goods.[54]

The Democrats were placed on the defensive, not popularly, but in terms of national policy-making decisions. In the 1844 election, the party had purged itself of its anti-slavery wing led by the Van Burens, father and son, and opted to guarantee the addition of the slave state Texas through the Mexican-American War. To fight against Mexico on behalf of slavery was more than the most sensitive, like Thoreau, could tolerate, and it angered Dickens. Hawthorne and Melville grew more despondent.[55]

The Lincoln Republicans were now in a moral position to undermine the foundation of American agriculture and appear as saints through Civil War. The Republicans fought for freedom while depicting the Democrats as defenders of slavery, especially with New York City's rioters hoping to turn the war to the Confederacy's advantage.[56] So long as the Democrats defined the political agenda, racism would infect the city's working class.

Merely because "draft rioters focused on one obnoxious political party,"[57] the Republicans, does not mean that they were politically autonomous. Violent rampages in which women cut off the genitals of lynched African Americans[58] are not evidence for an independent working-class identity.[59] To suggest so expresses a position that plays down the role of local Democratic leaders who assiduously defended slavery. Put another way, if the draft rioters had identified with the Republican Party, there would have been no draft riots. Such anti-African pogroms were the consequence of Tammany and Mozart's political schooling. The rage of the Irish was very real. It was bad enough that an Irish man could hardly eke out a living in the aftermath of the 1857 Panic. Now he, his family's main means of support, could be sacrificed to the profitable Northern Republican war machine that forcibly fused workers under the banner of the national state.

The kind of cultural evidence that E. P. Thompson introduced has so dazzled some historians that they have tended to regard any working-class behavior that is distinct from that of other classes as an expression of "autonomy." Such a view disregards the political context of the social formation.[60]

The Lincoln Republicans socially cemented the Union with the blood of hundreds of thousands of men. The financial cement was provided by the National Banking Act of 1863. No wonder most public sympathy for the African American came from rich Republican Union League Club members. They also called for the most draconian reprisal against the white racist mobs who roamed the city that fateful week in July 1863. Bernstein treated the Protestantism that rich Republicans shared with the black poor as the set of beliefs most responsible for "uniting" the two classes.[61] A more historically plausible causation can be attributed to political conditioning by a coalition in the Federalist-Whig-Republican tradition that reduced black and white labor to cash equivalence; blacks saw in this tradition their only salvation against the violent racism of European-American workers. This white-black hierarchically organized alliance posed a direct threat to democratic republican normative standards of customary virtue, which arose from pride in work done by free white hands, either on farms or in workshops, and which consigned the black to economic and social ruination.

The paradox dramatized by the Civil War consisted of Northern entrepreneurs and free-soilers posing as defenders of the *Republic* against the divisive Democratic *republicans* of the rural South and urban North, who were fighting to maintain traditional racial divisions. With the exception of slaves running away of their own volition, slavery was abolished by executive order, not by a popular groundswell. It was abolished for military, not moral, reasons.

The working class and ruling class were both badly fractured before the war, except that unlike the working class, which controlled no political party, competing ruling classes were in command of both dominant parties. Northern bankers and industrialists dominated the leadership of the Republican Party, while planters held their Democratic Party allies— urban merchants and workers—in a gentlemanly vise. This political context explains why the Civil War was a sectional and not a class war, and where black troops were involved, a race war. Whitman's democratic chants were swiftly and terrifyingly harnessed to the engine of war and bled into the disillusionment of his *Democratic Vistas*.[62] The Civil War sobered Whitman, and "radical democrat" hoopla was replaced by what he now regarded as the "almost complete failure" of American democracy.

The war's end brought effective control of the entire nation to the Northern capitalist for the first time. Since the capitalist continues to exercise this prerogative today, at the helm, as the all-seeing eye at the top of the pyramid on our dollar bills, no further change has taken place in the fundamental character of the two dominant parties. Man is made to cower before Mammon.

ᴥ APPENDIX 1 ᴥ
Evolution of Dominant Party Systems

1794	1834	1854
Federalist (a)	National Republican (a)	Whig (a) Republican (p)
		Free Soil (c) Know Nothing (c)
Republican (p)	Democratic Republican (p)	Democrat (p → a)
	Anti-Mason (c)	

p = protagonist   a = antagonist   c = catalyst

❧ APPENDIX 2 ❧

Municipal Government, 1626–1863

IN THE BEGINNING, RESPONSIBILITY FOR RUNNING FORT NEW
AMSTERDAM RESTED WITH THE DUTCH WEST INDIA COMPANY'S
board of directors. In 1653, the settler-employees were granted the right
to participate in the selection of the colony's first municipal government.
They nominated eighteen men, from whom the company's director-general, Peter Stuyvesant, and the board of directors chose nine: two burgomasters, five *schepens* (aldermen), a *schout* (sheriff), and a clerk.

Four years later, the Dutch government formally created the Corporation of the City of New Amsterdam. The freemanship or "freedom of the
city," that is the right to pursue one's occupation, was granted by the
authorities to all men who paid a fee and fulfilled a seven-year apprenticeship. The threat the English posed to Dutch control of city trade soon
prompted the Dutch to restrict municipal office to the minority of the
populace who could afford to pay a steep "great" burgher fee.

The English conquest of 1664 led to a mayor and aldermen replacing
the Dutch representatives a year later, and to civil juries replacing military
tribunals. In 1676, a growing municipal debt spurred the Common Council, the city's legislative body, into taxing the city's 290 families. Through
the Dongan Charter of 1683, the town was divided into five wards in the
extreme southern section of the island and one "out" ward that included
all other settlements, like Harlem.

The Dongan Charter of 1683 conferred more rights than any other
"plantation" in the British Empire enjoyed and permitted the mayor and
several other political appointees to confer freemanship upon European
newcomers. New York City became the first city in the British Empire to
become formally incorporated. The old form of government consisting of
seven magistrates and a *schout*, or constable, was replaced by a sheriff
appointed by the governor; six aldermen elected by the freemen now
represented the six wards as the board of aldermen; while another six
became the board of assistant aldermen.

Three years later, the king ordered Governor Dongan to seek formal approval from the royal Commission on Plantations for the removal of judges, sheriffs, and other officials. In 1689, inspired by the Glorious Revolution in England, oppressed New Yorkers staged a rebellion that led to New York City's only popularly elected mayor before 1834. English forces put down the revolt, and Mayor Jacob Leisler was executed.

In 1691, an elected colonial assembly was established. Based in Albany, this assembly became a countervailing political force to the royal governor and his council, who appointed New York City's mayor, recorder, town clerk, sheriff, and clerk of the market. The colonial assembly possessed the authority to enforce city laws enacted by the city's Common Council, which consisted of the mayor, recorder, and elected aldermen and assistant aldermen.

In 1730, the Montgomerie Charter superseded Dongan's. At least four aldermen and assistant aldermen, plus the mayor and recorder, were charged with passing laws, and a civil and criminal court were established. The mayor, normally a merchant, was appointed annually on September 29, along with other city officials, by the governor and his council from among the freemen; fifteen days later they all assumed office. Until 1830 the Common Council was comprised of aldermen and assistant aldermen who sat as one body.

From 1777 to 1800, New York City was overrepresented in the state legislature. Before and after that time, it was underrepresented.

During the War of Independence, Common Council duties were routinely conducted by nineteen British appointees. There was no trial by jury, but there were no taxes either. In December 1783, elections resumed in the city's seven wards. The mayor, now most likely a lawyer or politician, was chosen by the Council of Appointment and formally nominated by the governor. The mayor had no voting powers on the Common Council, except in the case of a tie. He held judicial powers, granted licenses, and made numerous appointments. His salary was drawn from license fees for taverns, slaughterhouses, and other enterprises.

The practice was lucrative. Mayor James Duane collected 4300 pounds for the five years (1784–1789) he was in office. Only in 1813 was a regular salary substituted for fees. In 1800, elections were scheduled for the third Tuesday in November, with successful candidates assuming office the following month. Aldermen were required to be residents of the wards from which they were chosen. Assemblymen were elected at large. Merchants and lawyers made up the majority of the Common Council from

1783 to 1801, with merchants holding the edge. There were few city ordinances—fifteen in 1776, only twenty-two in 1800.

Until the war, the bar of the Mayor's Court had been highly exclusive, but afterward it gained control over civil cases, while the court of general sessions was reserved for council matters. The mayor and aldermen lost some of their important judicial functions to the recorder, the chief legal advisor of the corporation, who became a voting member of the Common Council. By 1800, market and tavern fees provided the recorder with a five hundred dollar salary. In 1806, a general court was established. The state created a special clerk for the Common Council the following year.

The charter revision of 1830 established regular executive departments under the jurisdiction of the council. It also granted the mayor the right to veto legislation, and charter revisions in 1849 and 1857 strengthened his powers. Not until the 1870 "Tweed Charter" did the mayor achieve a position of actual administrative dominance.

Administrating services and enforcing bylaws—including activities such as regulating the price of flour, superintending the new almshouse, and maintaining streetlamps—were the duties of various routine committees of the council as well as special committees. All city officials not named by the Council of Appointment or the mayor—like the chamberlain (treasurer), commissioner(s) of streets, and superintendent of scavengers—were selected by the Common Council and subject to its control. Plural officeholding was allowed.

The state franchise was more liberal than the city's; in the seven years beginning in 1784, 524 new freemen were created, of whom 385 were cartmen and laborers. From 1791 through 1800, only 50 new freemen joined the ranks of voters, and not one was a cartman; most were merchants. Until 1804, a citizen was eligible to vote in any ward where he held at least twenty-five dollars of property. This regulation did not apply to state elections. A year earlier, Democratic-Republicans created nominating, corresponding, ward, and vigilance committees to generate candidates and shepherd voters to the polls.

The property requirement and oral voting in local elections kept participation below 20 percent. Intimidation and corruption flourished, including the transfer of property before elections. In 1811, African Americans were compelled to submit proof of their freedom in order to vote.

In 1821, the Council of Appointment did away with elections for sheriff and county clerk while granting the Common Council the right to appoint the mayor. Justices of the peace and judges of the county courts were now chosen by county boards of supervisors. The property qualifications for whites were abolished, while blacks were required to possess at least 250 dollars in property in order to vote.

In 1830, the city charter was amended to separate the mayor, still not yet popularly elected, from the city council, now divided into two distinct legislative bodies consisting of the board of aldermen and the assistant aldermen. Each body had veto power over the other, and the mayor had veto power over both. Regular departments, each providing distinct city services, were created. However, real power over these services rested with the committees created by the boards of aldermen.

During the 1830s, the Common Council contracted street cleaning to party benefactors, while sewage and street repairs remained the responsibility of the private property owners who directly fronted the thoroughfares.

In addition to an alderman and assistant alderman, each ward also elected a tax collector, two assessors, and two constables. Groups of wards constituted the four congressional districts, while one senator and thirteen assemblymen represented the city in the state legislature. In 1840, election districts containing approximately five hundred voters were created within each of the twelve wards.

The 1849 charter revision reduced the powers of the Common Council, not by transferring duties to the mayor, but by leaving the choice of department heads, elected for three-year terms, up to the voters. Nine departments were formally separated from the control of the Common Council: almshouse, police, law, city inspector, street and wharves, repairs and supplies, streets and lamps, finance, and the Croton Aqueduct board. No longer would city officials be allowed to directly profit from city business. Tammany Hall dramatically increased its membership.

The mayor would be elected every two years instead of one; the November election date was synchronized with the state and national contests.

In 1852, bond issues became the source of funding for municipal projects. Contractors would now be paid in advance and local assessments levied to pay them. A year later, with the prevention of corruption as the pretext, the state legislature replaced the Board of Assistant Aldermen with a sixty-man board of councilmen chosen annually. The aldermen continued to be elected every two years.

The 1857 charter revision constituted a renewed effort by the state to control city affairs. It differed from the 1849 and 1853 revisions in that it was not submitted for formal public approval, owing to a justifiable fear that it would be rejected. The new charter created a state police force for New York City and replaced the wards with seventeen aldermanic districts and a twenty-four-man city council elected from the four senatorial districts. Five departments were condensed to three: Croton Aqueduct, streets, and city inspector. The mayor appointed the heads, subject to aldermanic approval. Grand jury members were selected by the mayor, the first judge of common pleas, and the chief justice of the superior court. Two-thirds of the aldermen could override a mayoral veto. Comptroller, corporation counsel, recorder, register, surrogate, and eighteen judges of different courts would be popularly elected. The mayor no longer controlled the board of education, almshouse, or fire and health departments. The Common Council was placed in charge of city contracts.

The mayoral election was set for December 1, 1857, thereby separating it from all other contests. Municipal projects were taken over by the state. The governor appointed state commissions to oversee the construction of Central Park, a new city hall, and Harlem Bridge and to control piers, wharves, and harbor pilots. The mayor's control over city patronage was reduced to only 29 out of 4,644 city jobs.

The "reforms" of the 1850s weakened democracy by reducing the power of the wards, which had more closely reflected neighborhood and the public interest than any other political unit of administration.

⊰ TABLE 1 ⊱

New York City African-American Population, 1737–1865

(IN THOUSANDS)

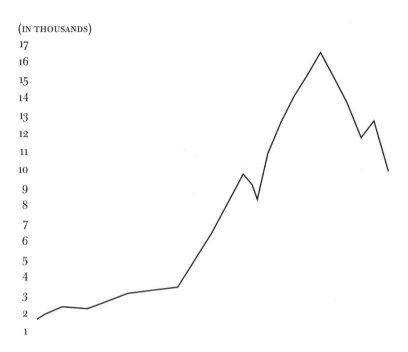

1740 | 50 | 60 | 70 | 80 | 90 | 1800 | 10 | 20 | 30 | 40 | 50 | 60 | 70

SELECTED YEARS

1737	1.7	1790	3.4	1820	10.9	1840	16.4
1741	2.0	1800	6.4	1825	12.6	1850	13.8
1746	2.4	1810	9.7	1830	14.0	1855	11.8
1756	2.3	1814	9.1	1835	15.1	1860	12.6
1771	3.1	1816	8.3	1837	16.0	1865	9.9

⊰ TABLE 2 ⊱

1844 Democratic Party Organizations

First Rank

Tammany Society
Democratic Republican General Committee
Democratic Republican Young Men's General Committee

Second Rank

The ward committees

Third Rank

Young Men's Central Hickory Association
Young Men's Hickory Club (Association)
Central convention of Van Buren Associations
Democratic Republican electors
Tammany Hall sponsors
Democratic Associations
Democratic Empire Club
Young Men's Junior Empire Club
Independent Polk Club

Fourth Rank

Young Hickory Pioneers
8th ward, 8th district Young Hickory Association
Young Hickory associations from each of the wards
Polk and Dallas associations from some of the wards
Van Buren Associations
Ironsides Club
Jefferson Associations
Democratic Committee of Arrests

Democratic Republican Committee to arrest illegal voters
Butt-End Coon Hunters
School districts
Central Democratic Republican reading room
Polk-Wright Association
People's Club
Silas Wright Club
Wright End Coon Hunters
Polk and Dallas Volunteers
New York State Tyler Democratic Committee
Johnson Association
Democratic ex-lamplighters
Democratic-Republican watchmen and lamplighters
Democratic-Republican butchers
Democratic cabinetmakers
Democratic grocers
Franklin Typographical Association
General meeting of journeymen printers
Mechanics and workingmen Polk and Dallas Association of
11th and 17th wards
Irish Emigration Society
German Democratic-Republican Association
German Democrats
German Democratic-Republican electors of 16th ward
United Irish Repeal Association
United Naturalization Society
Watch department general committee
1st district Franklin Association of Watchmen
1st district watch
3rd district watch
Morris Watch Association
Ex-sixth district watch
Young Hickory Association of proscribed watchmen
White Eagle Club of New York
White Eagle Club of 14th ward
X.W.T.H. 5,9,8,17
10th ward Owl Club
Fearnot Club
Democracy Mounted Minute Men
Old men's general committee

⊰ TABLE 3 ⊱
1844 Democratic Party Events

First Rank

District electors
Delegates from state of New York to Democratic National Convention
Delegates selected to Syracuse convention

Second Rank

Delegates to county convention for selection of delegates to
Syracuse state convention
Delegates to nominating convention: senatorial convention
(3 from each ward)
Delegates to nominating convention: congressional convention
(7 from each ward)
Delegates to nominating convention: assembly convention
(3 from each ward)

Third Rank

Each ward's district electors to mayoralty convention
and inspectors of election
Mayoralty convention
General convention of wards
Democratic Republican county convention
Great county meeting at Tammany Hall
to confirm nominations
"Spontaneous meeting" of the Democracy of New York
Democratic electors to assemble en masse to hear report of
delegates to Baltimore convention
Castle Garden rally of 20,000
Meeting of patriotic citizens
6th Congressional District Friends of Polk and Dallas meet

"A confidential circular" attacking Van Buren's rejection
over Polk and Dallas
General procession of Empire Club
Grand Democratic procession of Empire Club
Committee for Election of Polk cruise
Tammany mass rally to ratify Wright and Gardiner nominations
One large and nine smaller rallies for Polk and Dallas
Committee from various ward committees and Empire Club to make
arrangements for Albany meeting
Mass meeting of the young men of the city and county of New York
Ward delegate meeting from 4th Congressional District
Butchers' rally
4th Congressional District electors "response to Democratic
nominations"
6th Congressional District's Democratic electors meet
3rd Congressional District's "ratification" of Tammany's nominees
Ex-Democrats rejoining party from the American Republicans
Mechanics and workingmen's Tammany Hall meeting
Great county meeting of Empire Club
Old Tammany Tremendous Re-Union of the Democracy of New York
(9 separate meetings)
Central convention of Democratic associations (grand torch-light
procession, November 1 at Tammany Hall)
Tammany meeting to respond to county nominations
Complimentary ball in honor of Captain Rynders of Empire Club—
sponsors listed

FOURTH RANK

Tammany Society grand ball
5th district Watch Association—first annual ball
Young Men's Van Buren Association 11th ward fancy dress
and civic ball
10th ward third annual ball
United Irish Repeal Association ball
Meeting of citizens opposed to Sailor's Home monopoly
Morris Association first annual ball
5th ward Democratic ball
14th ward report

Grand jubilee on Jackson's birth night
Opening of the presidential campaign of 1844 at the
Broadway Tabernacle
Municipal reform—Great Movement of the People
Friends of Abraham G. Crasto meeting
Mechanics jubilee
Meeting of citizens born in France
"Great meeting" of the Democratic portion of the Native American Party
Democratic house carpenter's meeting
17th ward municipal reform meeting
8th ward municipal reform meeting

❧ TABLE 4 ❧

Rank Ordering of Positions Within Organizations and Events
of 1844 Democratic Party

I (TOP)

Gubernatorial candidate
U.S. Senate candidate
Mayoral candidate
Chairman or called meeting to order
Chief of staff or captain, leader, or commander
Chairman pro tem
Grand sachem
Grand marshal or chief marshal
President or president pro tem
"Prominent" or "leading" member
Central committee member
Executive committee member
Member of executive committee of General Committee
General Committee or ward committee member

II (MIDDLE)

U.S. House candidate
Alderman candidate
Assistant alderman candidate
Attorney general candidate
Delegate or representative
Director or leader
Manager
Electors
Letter of regret reader
Marshal or captain
Motion maker

On the platform or stage
Resolution maker
Sachem
Scribe
Sponsor or pledge
Vice president or first vice president
Vice president (second)
Wiskinskie
Citizens' committee member
Constitution and bylaws committee member
District or district leaders' committee member
General Committee member
Investigation or 14th ward report committee member
Legislation committee member
Municipal reform committee member
Nominating committee member
Organization or permanent organization committee member
Resolutions committee member
Speaker procurement committee member
Ward committee to nominate charter officers or
ward nominating committee member
Young Men's general committee member

III (WORKHORSE)

State assembly candidate
State senate candidate
Judge candidate
Assessor candidate
Constable candidate
Coroner candidate
Deputy coroner candidate
District attorney candidate
Assistant district attorney candidate
Addresser or speaker
Aide (including assistant, chief, and special)
All members of equal standing
Assistant marshal or assistant to marshal
Clerk

Corresponding secretary
Inspector of election
Mayoral convention delegates
Recording secretary
Secretary or secretary pro tem
Signer
Treasurer or teller
Treasurer pro tem
Member of arrangements or joint committee
Campaign committee member
Member of committee to certify, count, or ratify voters
Member of committee to get representation from each district
Conference committee member
Member conferring with other associations and clubs
Finance committee member
Naturalization committee member
Safety or vigilance committee member
Ward district committee member
School district trustee

IV (BODY)

Attender
Constable or watch
Member or participant
Sergeant at arms
Member of committee of 2, 3, 5, 7, 10, or 24 or organizing committee of 9
Member of committee to notify candidate of nominations or reception
Conference subcommittee member
Legislation subcommittee member
Ticket or transportation and hotel accommodations or
floor committee or managers of ball

⊰ TABLE 5 ⊱

1844 Democratic Party Elective and Appointive Officials

I (Top)

Governor
U.S. Senator
U.S. Representative
State congressman (assemblyman)
State senator
Mayor
Alderman
Assistant alderman
Attorney general
Assistant attorney general
District attorney (U.S.)
U.S. loan commissioner

II (Middle)

Judge
Corporation counsel
Commissioner
Aqueduct commissioner
Charities and corrections commissioner
Deputy commissioner
Deeds commissioner
Dock commissioner
Fire commissioner
Parks commissioner
Police commissioner
Public works commissioner
Streets commissioner
Tax commissioner
Controller

District attorney (city)
Supreme court judge
Deputy sheriff
Lamps and gas superintendent
Paving superintendent
Sawmill superintendent
Streets superintendent
Ports and customs supervisor
Post office supervisor
Master warden of port
Other county official
Other city official
Other state official
Other government official

III (LOWER MIDDLE)

Arsenal yard clerk
City directory clerk
Common Council clerk
Court of commercial pleas clerk
Clinton Market clerk
Customs house clerk
Dock clerk
1845 mayor's clerk
Deputy coroner
Judge advocate
Assistant judge
Court of common pleas judge
Marine court judge
Police judge
Keeper
Deputy keeper
Politician
Recorder
Register
Deputy register
Board of assistant aldermen clerk
Marine court clerk

IV (Low)

Constable
Local school board official
Collector
City revenue collector
County court house collector
Customs house deputy collector
Assistant district attorney
General inspector of beef and pork
Customs inspector
Docks inspector
Flour inspector
Leather inspector
Lumber inspector
Pot and pear lashes inspector
Spirits inspector
Stage inspector
Deputy stage inspector
Streets inspector
Tobacco inspector
Marshal
City court marshal
Marine court marshal
Measurer (U.S.)
School committee member
Sergeant at arms
Watch captain
Weigher (U.S.)
Weigher (city)

⊰ TABLE 6 ⊱
1844 Democratic Party Personnel Occupations

I. BANKERS, CAPITALISTS, OWNERS, MANAGERS, PREFERRED PROFESSIONS, AND TRADES

Bank president (2)

Banker (1)

Blind factory (1)

Bone setter (5)

Chinaware (1)

Clothier (7)

Commissary general (1)

Company (own) (1)

Dockbuilder (2)

Forwarding (1)

Garrick House (1)

Glue & iron (1)

Hardware merchant (7)

Insurance president (1)

Ladies' shoes (2)

Lawyer (155)

Lawyer (own co.) (1)

Leather (4)

Liquors (18)

Master in chancery (2)

Merchant (38)

Merchant (commercial) (11)

Music publisher (2)

Oil (1)

Proprietor of Castle Garden (1)

Provisions (5)

Publisher (4)

Shipbuilder (3)

Shipyard (1)

Spices & coffee (1)

Tobacco merchant (2)

Wine merchant (2)

II. WHITE-COLLAR, PROFESSIONALS, LESS PREFERRED PROFESSIONALS

Accountant (4)

Agent (15)

Agent, railway (1)

Agent, navy (1)

Almshouse shoe department (1)

Almshouse superintendent (2)

Almshouse visitor (4)

Appraiser (1)

Architect (1)

Artist (1)

Assessor (1)

Auctioneer (9)

Bankrupt assignee (1)

Baths (1)

Birdcages (1)

Boardinghouse (11)

Boards (4)

Bookkeeper (3)

Books (2)
Boots (4)
Brewer (4)
Broker (10)
Brush manufacturer (3)
Brushes (1)
Builder (8)
Building material (1)
Butter & lard (1)
Capitol Exchange (1)
Cedarware (1)
Chronometers (1)
Civil engineer (1)
Clerk (32)
Clocks (1)
Coffeehouse (2)
Confectionary (1)
Constable (8)
Contractor (5)
Crockery (1)
Democratic Hall (1)
Dockmaster (1)
Druggist (6)
Drugs (4)
Dry goods (18)
Dutch Hall (1)
Eatinghouse or restaurant (1)
Editor (6)
Exchange office, Prince Hall (1)
Fancy store (1)
Feed (1)
Findings (1)
Fishing tackle (1)
Fish (5)
Flour (5)
Founder (2)
Fringe & tassels (1)
Fruit (3)
Fruit store (3)

Furniture (3)
Furs (1)
Glassware (1)
Grain measurer (4)
Grates & stoves (1)
Grocer (120)
Harbormaster (1)
Hats, caps, & millinery (1)
Hats & caps (2)
Health warden (1)
Hoist wheels (1)
Hotel (11)
Ice (3)
Inks (1)
Inspector (5)
Jeweler (5)
Junk (1)
Leather findings (1)
Lime (2)
Looking glass (3)
Lumber (6)
Mahogany (1)
Major (1)
Manufacturer (2)
Maps (1)
Marshal (2)
Morocco (1)
Musical instruments (1)
Musician (1)
Mustard (1)
Naval officer (1)
Naval officer of port (1)
Negotiator (1)
Notary (2)
Oil (1)
Organmaster (1)
Ornamental composition (1)
Oysters (2)
Paints (6)

Pawnbroker (1)
Public house (1)
Purveyor (1)
Refectory (6)
Refreshments (1)
Reporter (1)
Saddlery hardware (1)
Safes (1)
Saloon (1)
Sandpaper (1)
Sausages (1)
Segars (4)
Sexton (1)
"The Shades" (1)
Ship captain (3)

Shoes (4)
Shoe store (4)
Speculator (2)
Stables, livery (5)
Stage inspector deputy (1)
Stages (1)
Superintendent, sawmill (1)
Tavern (12)
Teacher (5)
Teacher of singing (1)
Trunks (1)
Undertaker (3)
Water purveyor (1)
Wood inspector (1)
Wool (2)

III. SKILLED CRAFTSMAN OR WORKER

Baker (15)
Basketmaker (1)
Blacksmith (14)
Block & pump maker (1)
Bookbinder (3)
Bookmaker (2)
Bootmaker (5)
Bricklayer (1)
Brushmaker (1)
Butcher (55)
Cabinetmaker (11)
Carpenter (45)
Carpetweaver (2)
Carriagemaker (1)
Carver (2)
Caulker (3)
Chairmaker (4)
Coachmaker (2)
Coachtrimmer (2)
Combmaker (2)
Confectioner (2)

Cooper (9)
Cordwainer (2)
Costumer (1)
Doormaker (1)
Dyer (1)
Engineer (1)
Framemaker (2)
Gilder (2)
Glazier (1)
Goldbeater (1)
Gratemaker (1)
Gunsmith (1)
Harnessmaker (2)
Hat finisher (1)
Hatter (10)
Hosemaker (2)
Instrumentmaker (1)
Iron railing maker (1)
Keymaker (1)
Lastmaker (1)
Lockmaker (2)

Locksmith (4)
Machinist (9)
Marblecutter (1)
Marble turner (1)
Mason (12)
Molder (1)
Nailcutter (1)
Organ builder (1)
Painter (8)
Patternmaker (1)
Pencilmaker (1)
Rigger (1)
Saddler (7)
Sailmaker (4)
Sashmaker (5)

Sawyer (4)
Segarmaker (4)
Ship carpenter (6)
Ship carver (1)
Ship chandler (3)
Ship joiner (6)
Shipwright (5)
Shoemaker (35)
Shoe manufacturer (1)
Silversmith (2)
Smith (4)
Staircase (1)
Steam sawyer (1)
Steel pen maker (1)

IV. UNSKILLED OR LOW SKILLS

Banner painter (1)
Barber (4)
Barkeeper (1)
Bell hanger (1)
Blockman (1)
Boatman (1)
Bonnet presser (1)
Carman or cartman (46)
Fisherman (1)
Gardener (1)

Hairdresser (2)
Laborer (15)
Lamplighter (4)
Mariner (2)
Seaman (1)
Stonecutter (6)
Waiter (1)
Watercart (1)
Whitewasher (1)

❧ NOTES ☙

PREFACE

1. I found that in 1844, 39 percent of Democratic Party activists were working class; in 1884 that figure had dropped to 2 percent. In 1844, though the Irish made up less than one-quarter of New York City's population, their share of party activists stood at 31 percent; by 1884, when more than 40 percent of the city's population was Irish, only 30 percent of Democratic activists were Irish. Clearly, the structural impact on the party of the working class and of the Irish was significantly less in the later period. These results were presented in my "Labor's Decline Within New York City's Democratic Party From 1844 to 1884," in *Immigration to New York*, ed. William Pencak, Randall Miller, and Selma Berrol (London: Associated University Presses, 1991), 7–24.

2. It is Edmund Morgan who first explored the term *paradox* in this context. "Slavery and Freedom: The American Paradox," *Journal of American History* 59, no. 1 (June 1972): 5–29.

3. Amy Bridges, *A City in the Republic, Antebellum New York and the Origins of Machine Politics* (New York: Cambridge University Press, 1984); Sean Wilentz, *Chants Democratic: New York City and the Rise of the Working Class, 1788–1850* (New York: Oxford University Press, 1984). Both Bridges and Wilentz can be seen as responding to David Montgomery's directive concerning Herbert Gutman's pioneering scholarship, namely "that much work remains to be done on the local operation of political life, as it interacted with the workers, and on the precise meaning of 'power' in this social context." David Montgomery, "Gutman's Nineteenth-Century America," *Labor History* 19, no. 3 (summer 1978): 429. Bridges and Wilentz's assessments are similar to those of Gustavus Myers, who wrote in his classic study of Tammany Hall that "since the passing of the Equal Rights party, the mechanics and laborers had taken no concerted part in politics, not even as a faction," until the labor strikes of 1850. Gustavus Myers, *The History of Tammany Hall* (1917; reprint, New York: Dover Publications, 1971), 156.

4. Bridges, *A City in the Republic*, 110, 113, 147. Amy Bridges, "Rethinking the

Origins of Machine Politics," in *Power, Culture, and Place: Essays on New York City*, ed. John Hull Mollenkopf (New York: Russell Sage, 1988), 57.

5. Carl Degler, "Labor in the Economy and Politics of New York City, 1850–1860, A Study of the Impact of Early Industrialization" (Ph.D. diss., Columbia University, 1952), 331. This doctoral dissertation provided local evidence in support of a lonely 1886 scholarly assessment made by Richard T. Ely that "the Democratic Party from 1829 to 1841 was more truly a workingmen's party than has been the case with any other great party in our history"; *The Labor Movement in America* (New York: Thomas Y. Crowell & Co., 1886), 43. More than a half century later, in what remains the most popularly assigned account of the period, Arthur Schlesinger, Jr., in his New Deal interpretation, contended that Jacksonian Democracy embodied the aspirations of eastern labor; *The Age of Jackson* (1945; reprint, Boston: Little, Brown, 1953).

6. Wilentz, *Chants Democratic*, 7, 8. See Richard Hofstadter, *The American Political Tradition and the Men Who Made It* (1948; reprint, New York: Vintage, 1974); and Lee Benson, *The Concept of Jacksonian Democracy, New York As a Test Case* (Princeton: Princeton University Press, 1963). Wilentz attacked the Progressives for "narrowing their understanding" by taking "the politicians' most fiery 'class' rhetoric at face value" (p. 7). Yet Wilentz accepts the "chants democratic" of men like Mike Walsh, or even Walt Whitman, at face value. By ending his story in 1850 at a high point of labor organizing, he leaves the impression that labor organizations were ideologically independent of the dominant parties, when it can be established that they were not.

7. Wilentz, *Chants Democratic*, 306–314, 182–189, 191–195, 198–203, 205–206, 212, 214, 227, 240, 341.

8. Jean H. Baker, *Affairs of Party: The Political Culture of Northern Democrats in the Mid-Nineteenth Century* (Ithaca, N.Y.: Cornell University Press, 1983), 269.

9. Property is at the root of both republican and liberal thought—at the root of James Harrington's vision of the independent freeholder commonwealth and John Locke's vision of freely associating individuals acting in concert with like-minded men. John L. Brooke, *The Heart of the Commonwealth: Society and Political Culture in Worcester County, Massachusetts 1713–1861* (Cambridge: Cambridge University Press, 1989), xiv.

10. Leo Marx's *The Machine in the Garden, Technology and the Pastoral Ideal in America* (New York: Oxford University Press, 1964), highlights the pastoral when explaining the social and cultural contradictions inherent in the

American experience. Marx's work was inspired by his teacher, Henry Nash Smith, whose masterwork is *Virgin Land: The American West as Symbol and Myth* (Cambridge: Cambridge University Press, 1950). The link between white male domination over blacks and women is divinely revealed in the Civil War eve sermons of the Reverend Frederick A. Ross and his cohorts. *Slavery Ordained of God* (1859; reprint, New York: Greenwood, 1969), 20, 57, 99, 124–125, 166.

11. James Harrington, *The Commonwealth of Oceana* (1656; reprint, London: George Routledge and Sons, 1887), 19. For an important study of the historical origins of early American republicanism, see J. G. A. Pocock, *The Machiavellian Moment: Florentine Political Thought and the Atlantic Republican Tradition* (Princeton: Princeton University Press, 1975). For a summary of Pocock's argument, see Judith Barry Wish, "From Yeoman to Industrious Producer: The Relationship Between Classical Republicanism and the Development of Manufacturing in America from the Revolution to 1850" (Ph.D. diss., Washington University, 1976), 3–13.

12. A convincing historical analysis of this progressive ideology is Eric Foner's, *Free Soil, Free Labor, Free Men, the Ideology of the Republican Party Before the Civil War* (New York: Oxford University Press, 1970).

13. See the *American Citizen,* October 26, 27, 1801, for early recognition of the theoretical importance of Locke to the development of American politics.

14. John Locke, "Of the Ends of Political Society and Government," in *The Second Treatise of Government,* Chap. 9, Sec. 123. Elsewhere, he writes of "lives, liberties, and possessions"; "Of Paternal, Political, and Despotical Power Considered Together," ibid., Chap. 15, Sec. 171. Charles Dickens, *American Notes for General Circulation* (1842; reprint, Middlesex, England: Penguin, 1975), 128, 284. Herman Melville alluded to "Republican slaves" in *Moby-Dick* (1850; reprint, Middlesex, England: Penguin, 1972), 507.

15. Frank Bourgin, *The Great Challenge, the Myth of Laissez-Faire in the Early Republic* (New York: Braziller, 1989). James Henretta, *The Evolution of American Society, 1700–1815: An Interdisciplinary Analysis* (Lexington, Mass.: Heath, 1973), 180–182. Beatrice G. Reubens is useful for the early national phase; see her "State Financing of Private Enterprise in Early New York" (Ph.D. diss., Columbia University, 1960). Nathaniel Hawthorne's classic short story "Celestial Railroad" provides an ironic perspective on the machine's impact on people. *United States Magazine and Democratic Review,* May 1843, 515–523.

16. James Fenimore Cooper attributed "the principal distinctions" between the American people to "slavery, and . . . the greater or less support that is

given to the common schools." *Notions of the Americans, Picked by a Travelling Bachelor* (1828; reprint, New York: Ungar, 1963), 1:283.

17. Richard Slotkin finds the "myth of regeneration through violence" to be "the structuring metaphor of the American experience"; see his *Regeneration Through Violence: The Mythology of the American Frontier, 1600–1860* (Middletown, Conn.: Wesleyan University Press, 1973), 5. I find useful the notion that the century beginning in 1760 stood for "a unique process of capitalist national liberation involving . . . a multi-phase struggle against the constraints imposed by a globally hegemonic British capital on the growth of native bourgeois society," Mike Davis, *Prisoners of the American Dream: Politics and Economy in the History of the US Working Class* (London: Verso, 1986), 12.

18. Eric Foner finds that "anti-slavery was one of the few policies which united all Republican factions." *Free Soil, Free Labor, Free Men,* 304.

19. *American Citizen,* April 15, 1809.

20. It was widely believed in prerevolutionary America that a man could not be "HAPPY without being free, without being secure in our property." *New-York Journal,* February 25, 1768. An account of the ideological antecedents of this association can be found in C. B. Macpherson, *The Political Theory of Possessive Individualism: Hobbes to Locke* (New York: Oxford University Press, 1964).

21. Literary dissent peaked in the 1840s. David S. Reynolds found that "subversive literature," which he characterized as "bizarre, nightmarish, and often politically radical," with "roots in eighteenth-century British criminal and Gothic fiction," accounted for 55 percent of the volumes produced during this decade. The remainder were made up of what Reynolds classified as "Conventional" and "Romantic Adventure" stories. David S. Reynolds, *Beneath the American Renaissance, the Subversive Imagination in the Age of Emerson and Melville* (New York: Knopf, 1988), 8.

22. Samuel McRoberts to the Members of the General Assembly of Illinois (n.p., n.d.), 7, as quoted in John Ashworth, *"Agrarians" and "Aristocrats": Party Ideology in the United States, 1837–1846* (1983; reprint, Cambridge: Cambridge University Press, 1987), 8. During the first party system, less extravagant claims were made for American exceptionalism. See Polybius in the *American Citizen,* September 16, 1806; and see the *Evening Post,* June 15, 1821. The best contemporary analysis remains Alexis de Tocqueville's *Democracy in America,* lauded in 1837 in the inaugural issue of an important Democratic Party journal as "decidedly the most remarkable and really valuable book that has yet appeared in this country from the hands of a for-

eigner." *United States Magazine and Democratic Review,* October 1837, 91. Also see the *Evening Post,* September 16, 1839.

23. Colonel Diver, editor of the *New York Rowdy Journal* in Charles Dickens, *Martin Chuzzlewit* (1843; reprint, New York: Oxford University Press, 1975), 257.

24. Paul W. Gates, *The Farmer's Age: 1815–1860* (New York: Holt, 1960), 183.

25. See David Roediger, *The Wages of Whiteness: Race and the Making of the American Working Class* (London: Verso, 1991), 71–87. Recent research on twentieth-century American workers continues to find their political behavior different from European workers; see Robert H. Zieger, *American Workers, American Unions, 1920–1985* (Baltimore: Johns Hopkins University Press, 1986). My own experience at an NEH Summer Seminar, The Historical Sociology of European and American Labor, held in 1987 at the University of Michigan, Ann Arbor, under the direction of William Sewell, Jr., has strengthened my conviction on this point.

26. Iver Bernstein attributes the draft riots to an independent working-class politics; see his *The New York City Draft Riots: Their Significance for American Society and Politics in the Age of the Civil War* (New York: Oxford University Press, 1990). His work is considered in Chapter 8 herein.

I will examine the significance of the antebellum labor experience to aborting the New York City labor movement of the 1870s and 1880s in a subsequent volume that carries the story forward from the draft riots through the First World War.

27. For William Appleman Williams, international trade is the critical factor in shaping the course of American economic development; see his "The Age of Mercantilism: An Interpretation of the American Political Economy, 1763 to 1828," *William and Mary Quarterly* 15 (October 1958): 419–437.

28. As defined by Jerzy Topolski, a social formation is "the totality of productive forces, relations of production, and superstructure," or "a social macrosystem analysed from the point of view of development," *Methodology of History* (Boston: Reidel, 1976), 295–296, 301.

29. Diane Lindstrom, "Economic Structure, Demographic Change and Income Inequality in Antebellum New York," in *Power, Culture, and Place: Essays on New York City,* 11.

30. The impact that slavery had on the labor movement is variously discussed in Eric Foner, "Abolitionism and the Labor Movement in Ante-bellum America," in *Politics and Ideology in the Age of the Civil War* (New York: Oxford University Press, 1980); Michael Bernstein, "Northern Labor Finds a Southern Champion: A Note on the Radical Democracy, 1833–1849," in

New York and the Rise of American Capitalism: Economic Development and the Social and Political History of an American State, 1780–1870, ed. William Pencak and Conrad Wright (New York: New-York Historical Society, 1989), 271–302; and Iver Bernstein, "What Did the New York City Draft Rioters Think They Were Doing?" in ibid., 147–167.

31. See Charles Beard, *American Government and Politics* (New York: Macmillan, 1911), *The Economic Basis of Politics* (New York: Knopf, 1945), *An Economic Interpretation of the Constitution of the United States* (New York: Macmillan, 1913), and *The Economic Origins of Jeffersonian Democracy* (New York: Macmillan, 1915), in which Beard states, ". . . the conflict over the new system of government was chiefly between the capitalistic and agrarian classes," 3–4. See also Carl Becker, *The History of Political Parties in the Province of New York* (1909; reprint, Madison: University of Wisconsin Press, 1960); and Vernon Parrington, *Main Currents in American Thought, an Interpretation of American Literature from the Beginnings to 1920*, 3 vols. (1927–1930; reprint, Norman: University of Oklahoma Press, 1987).

CHAPTER 1

1. Henry Cabot Lodge, *A Short History of the English Colonies in America* (New York: Harper & Bros., 1881), 285. Also see Robert G. Albion, *The Rise of New York Port 1815–1860* (New York: Scribner, 1939), 2; Adam Smith, *The Wealth of Nations* (1776), Bk. 4, Chap. 7; Thomas J. Condon, *New York Beginnings—The Commercial Origins of New Netherland* (New York: New York University Press, 1968), 8; *New York Times*, August 23, 1984.

2. For a panoramic account of this perspective, see Arthur Lovejoy, *The Great Chain of Being, A Study of the History of an Idea* (1933; reprint, Cambridge, Mass.: Harvard University Press, 1964); Winthrop D. Jordan, *White Over Black: American Attitudes Toward the Negro, 1550–1812* (1968; reprint, New York: Norton, 1977), 17–20.

3. Edgar J. McManus, *A History of Negro Slavery in New York* (Syracuse: Syracuse University Press, 1966), 12. Nan A. Rothschild has concluded that slaves "had more rights than Jews"; see her *New York City Neighborhoods: The Eighteenth Century* (New York: Academic Press, 1991), 88.

4. Eric Homberger, *The Historical Atlas of New York City, a Visual Collection of Nearly 400 Years of New York City's History* (New York: Holt, 1994), 23.

5. The best succinct survey of the seventeenth-century historical context of

Dutch and English relations is Eric Hobsbawm, "The General Crisis of the European Economy in the 17th c," *Past and Present* 5 & 6 (1954), 33–65.

6. Edmund Morgan, "The Labor Problem at Jamestown, 1607–1618," *American Historical Review* 76 (June 1971): 602, 606–607. Marx, *The Machine in the Garden*, especially Chapter 3.

7. Thomas J. Archdeacon, *Becoming American: An Ethnic History* (London: Collier Macmillan, 1983), 6. Condon, *New York Beginnings*, 105.

8. Eric Williams, *Capitalism and Slavery* (1944; reprint, New York: Capricorn, 1966), 19; David Galenson, *White Servitude in Colonial America, an Economic Analysis* (Cambridge: Cambridge University Press, 1981), 177. Thomas Archdeacon, *New York City, 1664–1710: Conquest and Change* (Ithaca, N.Y.: Cornell University Press, 1976), 145. Henretta, *The Evolution of American Society 1700–1815*, 90. Edmund Morgan has chronicled the evolution of a racial politics for late-seventeenth-century Virginia that in general outline resembles what transpired in New York City; see his *American Slavery, American Freedom: The Ordeal of Colonial Virginia* (New York: Norton, 1975), 71–130. Edmund B. O'Callaghan, ed., *Documents Relative to the Colonial History of the State of New York* (Albany: Weed, Parsons, Printers, 1855), 1:246.

9. *Collections of the New-York Historical Society for the year 1885* (New York: New-York Historical Society, 1936), 1.

10. See Appendix 2 herein for a capsule history of municipal government, 1626–1863.

11. Peter Arundle of Virginia in 1622, *Virginia Company Records* 3:589, as quoted in Richard B. Morris, *Government and Labor in Early America* (1946; reprint, Boston: Northeastern University Press, 1981), 45.

12. Graham Russell Hodges, *New York City Cartmen 1667–1850* (New York: New York University Press, 1986), 3, 26; and by the same author, "Legal Bonds of Attachment: The Freemanship Law of New York City, 1648–1801" (Ph.D. diss., New York University, 1982), 44–46.

13. Leonard W. Levy, *The Establishment Clause and the First Amendment* (New York: Macmillan, 1986), 10. The quotation is from McManus, *A History of Negro Slavery*, 23. Joyce D. Goodfriend, *Before the Melting Pot: Society and Culture in New York City 1664–1730* (Princeton: Princeton University Press, 1992), 130, citing Morgan Dix, ed., *A History of the Parish of Trinity Church in the City of New York* (New York, 1898), 1:113.

14. John M. Murrin, "English Rights as Ethnic Aggression: The English Conquest, the Charter of Liberties of 1683, and Leisler's Rebellion in New York," in *Authority and Resistance in Early New York*, ed. William Pencak

and Conrad Edick Wright (New York: New-York Historical Society, 1988), 62–63. Murrin found that those who supported the more liberal Dongan Charter opposed Leisler and his followers because the latter sought to curtail "traditional English rights," 57.

15. Thomas J. Archdeacon, "The Age of Leisler in New York City, 1689–1710: A Social and Demographic Interpretation" (Ph.D. diss., Columbia University, 1971), 68. Hendrik Hartog, *Public Property and Private Power: The Corporation of the City of New York in American Law, 1730–1830* (Chapel Hill: University of North Carolina Press, 1983), 21, 63.

16. Bruce M. Wilkenfeld, "New York City Neighborhoods, 1730," *New York History* 57 (April 1976): 172. Similar political lines were drawn that same year in Boston, indicating a shared political economy; see G. B. Warden, *Boston 1689–1776* (Boston: Little, Brown, 1970), 169. Morris, *Government and Labor in Early America*, 148–149.

17. David W. Galenson, *Traders, Planters, and Slaves: Market Behavior in Early English America* (New York: Cambridge University Press, 1986), 153, 159.

18. Malachy Postlethwayt, *The African Trade and the Great Pillar and Support of the British Plantation Trade in America* . . . (London: J. Robinson, 1745), 14.

19. Morris, *Government and Labor in Early America*, 182–183; McManus, *A History of Negro Slavery in New York*, 48–49; Jordan, *White Over Black*, 128; Thomas J. Davis, *A Rumor of Revolt: The "Great Negro Plot" in Colonial New York* (New York: Free Press, 1983), 32; Goodfriend, *Before the Melting Pot*, 118–119. Hodges, *New York City Cartmen*, 25. *Minutes of the Common Council of the City of New York 1625–1776* (New York, 1905), 1:179; Arthur Peterson and George W. Edwards, *New York as an Eighteenth Century Municipality* (New York: Columbia University, 1917), 1:70; William Dunlap, *History of the New Netherlands, Province of New York and State of New York to the Adoption of the Federal Constitution* (New York: Carter & Thorp, 1839, 1840), 2:Miscellaneous Matter, CLXVI. Staughton Lynd, "The Mechanics in New York Politics, 1774–1785," in *Class Conflict, Slavery and the United States Constitution* (Indianapolis: Bobbs-Merrill, 1967), 79–108. McManus, *A History of Negro Slavery*, 11. Shane White, " 'We Dwell in Safety and Pursue Our Honest Callings': Free Blacks in New York City, 1783–1810," *Journal of American History* 75, no. 2 (September 1988): 448.

20. John R. Brodhead, ed., *Documents Relative to the Colonial History of the State of New York* (Albany: Weed, Parsons and Company, 1853), 3:357–359, 371.

21. Charles Howard McCormick, *Leisler's Rebellion* (New York: Garland Publishers, 1989), 234, 277. Murrin, "English Rights as Ethnic Aggression," 79.

22. Carl Becker, *The History of Political Parties*, 7–8.

23. Michael Kammen, *Colonial New York* (New York: Scribner, 1975), 80. Archdeacon, *New York City 1664–1710*, 137.

24. Archdeacon, *New York City 1664–1710*, 39, 41, 43, 50. Goodfriend, *Before the Melting Pot*, 61. Quoted in Lawrence H. Leder, "The Politics of Upheaval in New York, 1689–1709," *New-York Historical Society Quarterly* 44 (October 1960): 426.

25. Donald R. Wright, *African Americans in the Colonial Era, From African Origins Through the American Revolution* (Arlington Heights, Ill.: Harlan Davidson, 1990), 72. James Weldon Johnson, *Black Manhattan* (New York: Knopf, 1930), 5. *Book of Trade of the Sloop Rhode Island, 1748–1749,* Manuscripts Division, New-York Historical Society. McManus, *A History of Negro Slavery*, 23, 29. Charles W. Baird, *History of Rye* (New York, 1871), 182, 393.

26. Kenneth Scott, "The Slave Insurrection in New York in 1712," *New-York Historical Society Quarterly* 45 (January 1961): 43–74. Goodfriend, *Before the Melting Pot*, 120–121. Samuel McKee, *Labor in Colonial New York, 1660–1776* (New York: Columbia University Press, 1938), 139.

27. *Minutes of the Common Council 1665–1776*, 3:27, 28, 30, 31. Scott, "The Slave Insurrection in New York in 1712," 73. James F. Richardson, *The New York Police, Colonial Times to 1901* (New York: Oxford University Press, 1970), 5.

28. Locke, *Second Treatise*, Chap. 5, "Of Property," Secs. 37, 85, 23. Locke conceives of man as "the Maker's" property, Sec. 6. Jack P. Greene stresses the prevailing spirit of law and order with which the early colonial leaders were imbued in *Pursuits of Happiness: The Social Development of Early Modern British Colonies and the Foundation of American Culture* (Chapel Hill: University of North Carolina Press, 1988), 21–22. John Keegan attributes the global success England had in conquering other peoples to excessive ruthlessness; see his *A History of Warfare* (New York: Knopf, 1993). David Brion Davis, *The Problem of Slavery in Western Culture* (Ithaca, N.Y.: Cornell University Press, 1969), 120.

29. Robert A. Dahl, *Democracy and Its Critics* (New Haven: Yale University Press, 1989), 4. Morgan, *American Slavery, American Freedom*, 381.

30. Thomas J. Davis, *A Rumor of Revolt*, 38. Although Davis provides the most complete account to date, see also the diary of Daniel Horsmanden, *The*

New York Conspiracy (1741; reprint, Boston: Beacon Press, 1971); and Joel Tyler Headley, *The Great Riots of New York, 1712–1873* (New York: E. B. Treat, 1873), 24–45.

31. Davis, *A Rumor of Revolt,* 260.

32. Hartog, *Public Power and Private Property,* 40.

33. Carl Becker, *The History of Political Parties,* 16. William Smith, *The History of the Late Province of New York, from Its Discovery to the Appointment of Governor Colden in 1762* (New York: New-York Historical Society, 1830), 1:367.

34. *New-York Journal,* February 20, March 3, 1768.

35. Carl Becker, "Nominations in Colonial New York," *American Historical Review* 6 (January 1901): 262. In the 1860s Boss Tweed remarked that so long as he controlled the nominations, he didn't care who else was involved in the selection process. Edward K. Spann, *The New Metropolis: New York City, 1840–1857* (New York: Columbia University Press, 1981), 327. Becker, *The History of Political Parties,* 7–8, 18–19.

36. Jack P. Greene, "An Uneasy Connection: An Analysis of the Preconditions of the American Revolution," in *Essays on the American Revolution,* ed. Stephen G. Kurtz and James H. Hutson (Chapel Hill: University of North Carolina Press, 1973), 36. Bernard Bailyn, "Political Experience and Enlightenment in Eighteenth-Century America," *American Historical Review* 67, no. 2 (January 1962): 342; Gordon S. Wood, *The Creation of The American Republic 1776–1789* (1969; reprint, New York: Norton, 1972), 167–168.

37. Becker, "Nominations in Colonial New York," 273, 274. David Brion Davis has concluded that "Given the lack of an alternative labor supply, it is difficult to see how European nations could have settled America and exploited its resources without the aid of African slaves . . . the availability of Negro slaves limited the need to exploit a large mass of unskilled white labor." Davis, *The Problem of Slavery in Western Culture,* 10, 304. Likewise, a century of formal racial segregation after the Civil War made employment opportunities more attractive to European immigrants.

38. Edmund Morgan, *The Challenge of the American Revolution* (1967; reprint, New York: Norton, 1978), 166.

39. Quoted in Wood, *The Creation of the American Republic,* 230. George Rude, *The Crowd in History 1730–1848, a Study of Popular Disturbances in France and England* (New York: Wiley, 1964), 197. A discussion on the difficulties of defining and ranking the factors responsible for the shift in values from feudal to capitalist can be found in Paul Sweezy, Maurice Dobb, H. K. Takahashi, Rodney Hilton, and Christopher Hill, *The Transi-*

tion *From Feudalism to Capitalism, A Symposium* (1950, 1952, 1953; reprint, New York: Science & Society, 1967). See also Steve J. Stern, "Feudalism, Capitalism, and the World System in the Perspective of Latin America and the Carribean," *American Historical Review* 93, no. 4 (October 1988): 838.

40. Hartog, *Public Property and Private Power*, 42.

41. The quotation is from Dickens, *American Notes*, 287. Hartog, *Public Power and Private Property*, 65.

42. Sidney Pomerantz, *New York: An American City, 1783–1803, a Study of Urban Life* (New York: Columbia University Press, 1938), 36. Wood, *The Creation of the American Republic*, 12–13.

43. Bruce M. Wilkenfeld, *The Social and Economic Structure of the City of New York, 1695–1796* (New York: Arno, 1975), 23, 160, 193. By way of comparison, the richest 10 percent of Americans owned 68 percent of all national assets in 1992. Paul Conklin, *American Historical Perspectives* (April 1992): 11. One percent owned 40 percent in 1989. *New York Times*, April 17, 1995.

44. Beard, *American Government and Politics*, 1–2.

45. *New-York Journal*, February 6, 1768.

46. Hodges, *New York City Cartmen*, 62. James and John Montresor, *The Montresor Journals* (New York: New-York Historical Society, 1881), 336–371, 382–384. Little was made of those incidents in the city's newspapers. Stanley Katz, "Between Scylla and Charybdis: James Delancey and Anglo-American Politics in Early Eighteenth Century New York" in *Colonial America, Essays in Politics and Social Development*, ed. Stanley N. Katz and John M. Murrin (New York: Knopf, 1983), 401. Patricia U. Bonomi also names Delancey as a leader; see her *A Factious People*, 240–241. See also Morris, *Government and Labor in Early America*, 189; and the *New-York Journal*, December 16, 1773. Edward Countryman, *A People in Revolution: The American Revolution and Political Society in New York, 1760–1790* (Baltimore: Johns Hopkins University Press, 1981), 112.

47. Oscar Barck, *New York City During the War for Independence* (New York: Columbia University Press, 1931), 54. Arthur Schlesinger, Sr., *The Colonial Merchants and the American Revolution, 1763–1776* (1918; reprint, New York: Facsimile Library, 1939), 255. More recently, see Stuart M. Blumin, *The Emergence of the Middle Class, Social Experience in the American City, 1760–1900* (New York: Cambridge University Press, 1989), 64–65.

48. Hodges, *New York City Cartmen*, 64.

49. Albert Soboul, *The Sans-Culottes* (New York: Vintage, 1972), 252. Bernard Bailyn, *The Ideological Origins of the American Revolution* (Cambridge,

Mass.: Belknap Press of Harvard University Press, 1967), 283. Roger Champagne, "New York and the Intolerable Acts, 1774," *New-York Historical Society Quarterly* 44 (1961): 204. Eric Foner finds a similar pattern of artisan apathy in Philadelphia, *Tom Paine and Revolutionary America* (New York: Oxford University Press, 1976), 52; while in Boston, "laboring people" were "conspicuously inactive as a separate group . . . [making] virtually no demands for their role in the political process," Gary Nash, *Race, Class and Politics* (Urbana: University of Illinois Press, 1986), 359 (quote), 369–370. Bonwick also reaches that conclusion for England with ". . . artisan, let alone working class, radicalism . . . still in the future," Colin, *English Radicals and the American Revolution* (Chapel Hill: University of North Carolina Press, 1977), 132. Blumin, *The Emergence of the Middle Class,* 64.

50. Although Ronald Schultz notes that 40 percent of Philadelphia artisans held slaves in 1720, and that this number declined to 10 percent by 1770, this comparison is the sole reference to blacks in his account; see his *The Republic of Labor: Philadelphia Artisans and the Politics of Class, 1720–1830* (New York: Oxford University Press, 1993), 40.

51. Sharon Salinger, "Artisans, Journeymen and the Transformation of Labor in Late Eighteenth Century Philadelphia," *William and Mary Quarterly* 40 (January 1983): 65. According to Elizabeth Blackmar, in the antebellum period, "among modestly 'independent' artisans or professional households that shared a house with one or two other families . . . to hire (or share) a servant could signal recognition of the new code of domestic respectability. Elizabeth Blackmar, *Manhattan for Rent, 1785–1850* (Ithaca: Cornell University Press, 1988), 121.

52. Iowerth Prothero, "Artisans and Politics in Pre-Reform England," paper delivered at the annual meeting of the American Historical Association, 1990, 5. The traditional paternal right to juvenile exploitation was co-opted by early capitalists. Seth Luther noted that of the fifty-seven thousand persons engaged in cotton and woolen mills in twelve cities in the United States in 1834, over thirty-one thousand were under sixteen years of age. Seth Luther, *An Address to the Origin of Progress and its Deleterious Effects on Human Happiness* (Boston, 1834), 32, as quoted in Wish, "From Yeoman to Industrious Producer," 164.

53. Alexander Hamilton, *Federalist* No. 35.

54. Hodges, *New York City Cartmen,* 62. Schlesinger, *Colonial Merchants,* 255. Nash finds the same to be true of Philadelphia; see his "Artisans and Poli-

tics in Eighteenth Century Philadelphia," in Nash, *Race, Class and Politics*, 253.

55. This was also true of Philadelphia. See Gary B. Nash, *Forging Freedom: The Formation of Philadelphia's Black Community, 1720–1840* (Cambridge, Mass.: Harvard University Press, 1988), 48–49.

56. Graham Russell Hodges, "Black Revolt in New York City and the Neutral Zone, 1775–1783," in *New York in the Age of the Constitution, 1775–1800*, ed. Paul A. Gilje and William Pencak (Rutherford, N.J.: Associated University Presses, 1992), 21–23, 31. Sylvia Frey finds that in the South, the Revolutionary War was transformed into a war over slavery, with the majority of the slaves supporting the British cause. Sylvia R. Frey, *Water from the Rock, Black Resistance in a Revolutionary Age* (Princeton, N.J.: Princeton University Press, 1991), 58, 132.

57. Benjamin Quarles, *The Negro in the American Revolution* (Chapel Hill: University of North Carolina Press, 1961), 171.

58. Shane White, *Somewhat More Independent: The End of Slavery in New York City, 1770–1810* (Athens, Georgia: University of Georgia Press, 1991), 6. White, " 'We Dwell in Safety,' " 448, 455.

59. Death rates for slaves rose after 1820. Robert William Fogel, *Without Consent or Contract, The Rise and Fall of American Slavery* (New York: Norton, 1989), 129.

60. Thomas Paine, "African Slavery in America" (originally written for *Pennsylvania Magazine*, March 8, 1775), in *The Complete Writings of Thomas Paine*, ed. Philip Foner (New York: Citadel University Press, 1945), 2:15–19. Paine wrote that

> The first useful class of citizens are the farmers and cultivators. These may be called citizens of the first necessity because everything comes originally from the earth. After these follow the various orders of manufacturers and mechanics of every kind . . . they contribute to the accommodation rather than to the first necessities of life. Next follow those called merchants and shopkeepers. They are occasionally convenient but not important. They produce nothing themselves as the first two classes do, but employ their time in exchanging one thing for another and living by the profits. [*Public Advertiser*, May 30, 1807]

61. *American Citizen*, January 5, 1804. In toasting "Agriculture, manufacturers, and a free commerce," the General Society of Mechanics and Tradesmen looked forward to an idealized harmony of interests that never came to pass. *American Citizen*, January 9, 1806. In their 1808 July 4th celebration, the Tammany Society's first toast was to "Agriculture, the basis of natural wealth; commerce & manufacturing, valuable as assistants." *Public Adver-*

tiser, July 15, 1808. See also Paine, "African Slavery in America." However, in his major essays, *Common Sense, The American Crisis, Rights of Man, The Age of Reason,* and *Agrarian Justice,* the subject is ignored, most likely because these tracts were aimed at a wider American audience, which tolerated slavery.

62. See Cooper, *Notions of the Americans,* 286.

63. Ninety-three percent of all artisans were native born with 86 percent of these originating from New York City, New York State, and New Jersey. Howard B. Rock, *Artisans of the New Republic: The Tradesmen of New York in the Age of Jefferson* (New York: New York University Press, 1979), 12, 243. White, " 'We Dwell in Safety,' " 462. Phyllis Field, *The Politics of Race in New York: The Struggle for Black Suffrage in the Civil War Era* (Ithaca: Cornell University Press, 1982), 35–36.

64. See Gary Nash, "Artisans and Politics in 18th Century Philadelphia," in *The Origins of Anglo-American Radicalism,* ed. Margaret Jacob and James Jacob (Boston: Allen & Unwin, 1984), 162; and Charles Steffens, *The Mechanics of Baltimore: Workers and Politics in the Age of Revolution, 1763–1812* (Urbana: University of Illinois Press, 1984), 98–99.

65. Paul E. Johnson, *A Shopkeeper's Millennium: Society and Revivals in Rochester, New York, 1815–1837* (New York: Hill & Wang, 1978), 8; Stuart Blumin, "The Hypothesis of Middle-Class Formation in Nineteenth Century America: A Critique and Some Proposals," *American Historical Review* 90, no. 2 (April 1985): 299–338. Douglas C. North, *The Economic Growth of the United States, 1790–1860* (1961; reprint, New York: Norton, 1966), 63. Brian Danforth, "Merchants and Politics: The Influence of Socio-Economic Factors Upon Political Behavior: A Quantitative Look at New York City Merchants, 1828–1844" (Ph.D. diss., New York University, 1973), 191. See also Margaret Myers, *The New York Money Market,* vol. 1 of *Origins and Development* (1931; reprint, New York: Columbia University Press, 1971), 70.

66. Lindstrom, "Economic Structure, Demographic Change and Income Inequality," 6. The city's share of U.S. textile imports reached an all-time high of 84 percent in 1860. Albion, *The Rise of the New York Port,* 59.

67. Brian Danforth has presented conclusive quantitative evidence to substantiate Philip Foner's thesis concerning the vital importance of slavery to New York City businessmen. Danforth discovered that the 83 percent of the merchants "who traded solely with the South were overwhelmingly in favor of the Democrats. . . . As the degree of involvement in southern commerce decreased to one-third, support for the Democrats among these merchants

declined to 39 percent." Danforth, "Merchants and Politics," 163, 164. Philip Foner, *Business and Slavery: The New York Merchants and the Irrepressible Conflict* (Chapel Hill: University of North Carolina Press, 1941).

68. The relevant passage from *Federalist Paper* No. 10 reads as follows: "Extend the sphere, and you take in a greater variety of parties and interests; you make it less probable that a majority of the whole will have a common motive to invade the rights of other citizens; or if such a common motive exists, it will be more difficult for all who feel it to discover their own strength, and to act in unison with each other."

69. Pomerantz, *New York,* 54. *The Independent Gazette or the New-York Journal Revisited,* December 20, 1783; January 17, 1784; *1787 City Directory.* Four of the remaining aldermen were merchants, one a manufacturer, and the last a "gentleman."

70. *New-York Journal and Patriotic Register,* May 1, 1788. *American Citizen,* April 15, 1803. English political rights were so severely delimited that agitators made suffrage central to the defense of artisan communities besieged by machinery manned by less skilled labor. Or as Gwyn Williams aptly phrased it, "An iron curtain shut off the artisans from English political society." Gwyn Williams, *Artisans and Sans-Culottes, Popular Movements in France and Britain During the French Revolution* (New York: Norton, 1969), 96. Artisan activists grouped themselves into radical organizations outside the formal parties, and parliamentary authorities responded by undertaking brutal countermeasures. E. P. Thompson, *The Making of the English Working Class* (New York: Vintage Press, 1963), 197; *American Citizen,* April 6, 1807. Gary Nash, *Race, Class and Politics,* 169.

71. Headley, *The Great Riots of New York,* 56–65. For an account of how mob actions of the 1760s and 1770s embodied a "long-standing plebeian tradition," see Paul A. Gilje, "Republican Rioting" in Pencak and Wright, *Authority and Resistance in Early New York,* 222.

72. Hugh Henry Brackenridge, *Modern Chivalry* (1792), 128; as cited in Parrington, *Main Currents in American Thought,* 1:394.

73. Washington Irving, *Salmagundi* (1807), No. 3, 5, 7, 9, 11 (quote), 14–17. This Federalist, and later, Whig position was echoed by Grant Thorburn, *Life and Writings* (New York: Edward Walker, 1852), 194.

74. Samuel Peters, *A General History of Connecticut . . . to which is added an Appendix wherein New and True Sources of the Present Rebellion are pointed out . . . By a Gentleman of the Province* (London: J. Bew, 1781), 376.

75. Wood, *The Creation of the American Republic,* 391–425. The importance attached to a "republican" appearance is satirized in Cornelius Mathews's

play, *The Politicians*, in *The Various Writings of Cornelius Mathews* (New York: Harper & Bros., 1843), 121, 131.

76. *New-York Weekly Journal*, February 14, 1736. Over a century later, the same prediction concerning artisan virtue being made by Philip Hone, as well as by others closer to the working man. Blumin, *The Emergence of the Middle Class*, 128–129.

77. John Adams as quoted in Wood, *The Creation of the American Republic*, 574. This lament was in evidence during the revolutionary conflict itself. *American Citizen*, October 8, 1805.

78. North, *The Economic Growth of the United States*, 53. Albion, *The Rise of the New York Port*, 8. Anthony Gronowicz, "Political 'Radicalism' in New York City's Revolutionary and Constitutional Eras," in Gilje and Pencak, *New York in the Age of the Constitution*, 98–111. Rock, *Artisans of the Republic*, 281, 310–312.

79. Christine Stansell, *City of Women: Sex and Class in New York 1789–1860* (1986; reprint, New York: Knopf, 1987), 18, 20 (quote), 46, 55, 105, 130–133. See also Joan Hoff Wilson, "The Illusion of Change: Women and the American Revolution," in *The American Revolution: Explorations in the History of American Radicalism*, ed. Alfred F. Young (De Kalb: Northern Illinois University Press, 1976), 385–445; Linda K. Kerber, *Women of the Republic: Intellect and Ideology in Revolutionary America* (Chapel Hill: University of North Carolina Press, 1980); Rock, *Artisans of the Republic*, 281; David Montgomery, *Citizen Worker, the Experience of Workers in the United States and the Free Market During the Nineteenth Century* (Cambridge: Cambridge University Press, 1993), 7. Wilentz, *Chants Democratic*, 168. In the 1798 novel *Alcuin*, Charles Brockden Brown portrayed a Mrs. Carter who despairs, "What have I, as a woman, to do with politics? . . . Law-makers thought as little of comprehending us in their code of liberty, as if we were pigs, or sheep." Charles Brockden Brown, *Alcuin* (New York: T&J Swords, 1798), 51–52. Michael Kaplan has interpreted the gang raping of women in working-class taverns as a means of excluding women from "a white male republican political community." Michael Kaplan, "B'hoys will be b'hoys: Tavern Violence and the Creation of a Working-Class Male Identity in Antebellum New York City" (paper delivered at the annual meeting of the Society for the Historians of the Early Republic, 1993), 1, 20–24. Roland Berthoff, "Conventional Mentality: Free Blacks, Women, and Business Corporations as Unequal Persons, 1820–1870," *Journal of American History* 76, no. 3 (December 1989): 759–761. Blackmar, *Manhattan for Rent*, 54. Kerber, *Women of the Republic*, 120.

80. Hamilton to John Jay, March 14, 1779, *The Papers of Alexander Hamilton,* ed. Harold C. Syrett (New York: Columbia University Press, 1961), 2:18–19. White, *Somewhat More Independent,* 86.

81. Theodore Roosevelt attributed to slavery "the streak of coarse and brutal behavior which ran through the Southern character. . . ." Theodore Roosevelt, *Thomas Hart Benton* (Boston: Houghton, Mifflin, 1887), 161. In colonial times, Virginia was notorious for its violence. "In the south, stealing a horse, or committing a robbery on the highway, was punished by death, killing a negro is fine and imprisonment." Thus, a couple was executed for stealing a horse. Rhys Issac, *The Transformation of Virginia, 1740–1790* (Chapel Hill: University of North Carolina Press, 1982), 39, 98; *National Advocate,* March 3, 1820. John Hope Franklin, *From Slavery to Freedom: A History of Negro Americans* (New York: Knopf, 1980), 87–89.

82. Claudia Dale Golden, "The Economics of Emancipation," *Journal of Economic History* 33 (March 1973): 70. Ignatiev, *How the Irish Became White* (New York: Routledge, 1995), 49. *Evening Post,* December 30, 1816; January 2, 1817. *National Advocate,* July 23, 1817.

83. Morgan, "Slavery and Freedom: The American Paradox," 5–6, 24, 28–29.

CHAPTER 2

1. L. Ray Gunn has pointed out, refuting the historical myth of laissez-faire, that from 1800 until 1840, "New York engaged in large-scale pragmatic state intervention to stimulate and direct the course of economic development." This amounted to the state using "all its services to assist capital accumulation and to remove obstacles from the path of private enterprise . . . the proliferation and privatization of corporations drained the concept of 'public interest' of any communal meaning." L. Ray Gunn, "The Crisis of Distributive Politics: The Debate Over State Debts and Development Policy in New York, 1837–1842," in Pencak and Wright, *New York and the Rise of Capitalism,* 170, 175, 176. Bray Hammond, *Banks and Politics in America from the Revolution to the Civil War* (Princeton, N.J.: Princeton University Press, 1957), 68–69, 104.

2. *New York Gazette & Weekly Mercury,* June 11, 1781. Paine, *Common Sense,* 102. Hamilton to Robert Morris, April 30, 1781, *The Papers of Alexander Hamilton,* 2:635. The historical flaw in Paine's logic is captured by an anonymous ironist who observed, "The history of the country gives no instance of a defaulter ever being tried, or committed. A public defaulter, is a true republican, an advocate and supporter of the people's rights, who

scorn to be controlled by laws, not of their own choosing." *A Week in Wall Street By One Who Knows* (New York: Frederick Jackson, 1841), 107.

3. J. G. A. Pocock, "Review Article, "*The Machiavellian Moment* Revisited: A Study in History & Ideology," *Journal of Modern History* 53 (March 1981): 64. The quotations are from the *American Citizen,* April 17, 1807; October 8, 1805.

4. Carl Kaestle, *The Evolution of an Urban School System: New York City, 1750–1850* (Cambridge, Mass.: Harvard University Press, 1973), 31. *American Citizen,* April 4, 1804 (quote). Thomas Jefferson, "Opinion on the Constitutionality of a National Bank," February 15, 1791, *The Papers of Thomas Jefferson,* ed. Julian P. Boyd (Princeton: Princeton University Press, 1974), 19: 275–280.

5. *Evening Post,* April 17, 1805; *American Citizen,* August 14, 1805. John R. Commons et al., *History of Labor in the United States* (1918; reprint, New York: Augustus M. Kelley, 1966), 81–82. *New-York Journal and Patriotic Register,* August 13, 1790.

6. Hammond, *Banks and Politics in America,* 56. Janet A. Riesman, "Republican Revisions: Political Economy in New York After the Panic of 1819," in Pencak and Wright, *New York and the Rise of Capitalism,* 2.

7. Edmund P. Willis, "Social Origins and Political Leadership in New York City from the Revolution to 1815" (Ph.D. diss., University of California, 1967), 164, 169–170. *American Citizen,* October 8, 1805 (quote).

8. Alfred Young, "The Mechanics and the Jeffersonians: New York, 1789–1801," in *Past Imperfect: Alternative Essays in American History: From Colonial Times to the Civil War,* ed. Blanche Wiesen Cook, Alice Kessler Harris, and Ronald Radosh (New York: Knopf, 1972), 166–170. The significance of this switch is difficult to trace because just 43 percent of the city's residents in 1789 remained to be counted as voters seven years later. Dominick De Lorenzo, "The New York Federalists: Forces of Order," 2 vols. (Ph.D. diss., Columbia University, 1979), 1:195.

9. *American Citizen,* October 17, 1806; *Public Advertiser,* April 29, 1812. "Leonidas," *New-York Journal and Patriotic Register,* February 22, 1792; April 20, 1786.

10. Young, "The Mechanics and the Jeffersonians," 171; Myers, *The History of Tammany Hall,* 9. Written in 1901, Myers's work was unable to find a publisher for sixteen years owing to Tammany pressure. Rock, *Artisans of the New Republic,* 128. *Columbian Gazeteer,* May 15, June 9, 1794; *American Citizen,* October 21, 1805. *Public Advertiser,* July 7, 1807 (quote); *New-York*

Journal and Patriotic Register, July 9, 1794; August 25, 1798; December 15, 1798. *Evening Post,* April 22, 1795.

11. *American Citizen,* July 1, 1808.

12. Alfred F. Young, *The Democratic Republicans of New York, The Origins, 1763–1797* (published for the Institute of Early American History and Culture at Williamsburg, Virginia, by Chapel Hill: University of North Carolina Press, 1967), 33, 56–57, 203.

13. *Minutes of the Common Council,* February 15, 1786; February 15, 1808; June 6, 1808; November 28, 1808; January 31, 1809; May 8, 1809; "Report of the Committee on the Accounts of William Mooney," October 30, 1809. Edward C. Smith, "Sketch," June 8, 1807, Box 21, Kilroe Collection, Columbia University.

14. Blackmar, *Manhattan for Rent,* 71. Edwin P. Kilroe, *Saint Tammany and the Origin of the Society of Tammany or Columbian Order in the City of New York* (New York: Columbia University Press, 1913), 12–13. Jerome Mushkat, *Tammany, the Evolution of a Political Machine, 1789–1865* (Syracuse: Syracuse University Press, 1971), 25.

15. Hartog, *Public Property and Private Power,* 40. *Public Advertiser,* July 6, 1807. Foner, *Tom Paine,* 40. Susan E. Hirsch, "From Artisan to Manufacturer: Industrialization and the Small Producer in Newark, 1830–1860," in *Small Business in American Life,* ed. Stuart Bruchey (New York: Columbia University Press, 1980), 81.

16. *Public Advertiser,* August 22, 1807.

17. *New-York Journal and Patriotic Advertiser,* April 9, 1791.

18. *Evening Post,* April 25, 1803; April 5, 1816. Hostility to foreigners grew, especially after the War of 1812 when immigration increased.

19. Alvin F. Harlow, *Old Bowery Days, the Chronicles of a Famous Street* (New York: D. Appleton, 1931), 155–156. Walter J. Walsh, "Religion, Ethnicity, and History: Clues to the Cultural Construction of Law," in *The New York Irish,* ed. Ronald H. Bayor and Timothy J. Meagher (Baltimore: The Johns Hopkins Press, 1996), 51–52. *Evening Post,* April 11, 1807; *Public Advertiser,* April 24, 1807. *Morning Chronicle,* April 28, 1807, as noted in the *American Citizen,* April 29, 1807. The *Commercial Advertiser* had reported that "The Democratic ticket for the Assembly has gained its election by the votes of that class who had no fixed place of residence . . . together with *foreign fugitives, Irish rebels . . .* this wretched *rabble . . . ,*" April 29, 1803, as quoted in the *American Citizen,* April 25, 1806; April 30, 1807. See the *Evening Post,* April 27, 1807; and *Public Advertiser,* August 19, 1811, for additional evidence of Federalist antipathy toward the Irish.

20. *Public Advertiser,* April 24, 1807. Irving, *Salmagundi,* No. 14.

21. *American Citizen,* April 29, 1807. *Evening Post,* April 20, 1808. As far back as the 1790s, the Irish were linked to Jefferson Republicans. Parrington recorded that, "A New England gentleman, traveling in the nineties, wrote home: 'I have seen many, very many Irishmen, and with a few exceptions, they are . . . the most God-provoking Democrats on this side of Hell,' " as quoted in Parrington, *Main Currents,* 1:359.

22. *American Citizen,* March 19, 1808. *National Advocate,* November 29, 1819. E. P. Thompson recorded "a clear consecutive alliance between Irish nationalism and English Radicalism between 1790 and 1850 . . . ," *The Making of the English Working Class,* 441.

23. As quoted in Richard Stott, "The Worker in the Metropolis: New York City, 1820–1860" (Ph.D. diss., Cornell University, 1983), 71. See also Herbert Gutman, "Work, Culture and Society in Industrializing America 1815–1919," *American Historical Review* 78, no. 3 (June 1973): 553–554; and *Public Advertiser,* September 31, 1808. *American Citizen,* September 1–4, 1801; April 28, 1806; April 23, 1807; April 25, 1808. Young, *The Democratic Republicans of New York,* 476–480.

24. *American Citizen,* May 17, 1804; April 4, 1807; May 6, 1808; *Public Advertiser,* August 19, 1811; July 9, 1812. Kerby Miller, *Emigrants and Exiles: Ireland and the Irish Exodus to North America* (New York: Oxford University Press, 1985), 193.

25. Michael MacDonagh, *Daniel O'Connell and the Story of Catholic Emancipation* (Dublin: Talbot Press, 1929), 128–134; Raymond Moley, *Daniel O'Connell, Nationalism Without Violence* (New York: Fordham University Press, 1974), 85–96. Sean O'Faolain, *King of the Beggars: A Life of Daniel O'Connell, the Irish Liberator, in a Study of the Rise of the Modern Irish Democracy (1775–1847)* (New York: Viking Press, 1938), 220–224. Sister M. F. Cusack, *Life of Daniel O'Connell, the Liberator. His Times—Political, Social, and Religious* (New York: D. & J. Sadlier, 1872), 492–512.

26. *American Citizen,* April 6, 1807; April 25, 1808. *Evening Post,* April 17, 1807; April 7, 1817. *Public Advertiser,* April 12, 1810. On July 4, 1805, the twelfth toast of the Tammany Society was to "The Republicans of foreign countries, who have made America their asylum—Welcome to this land of Liberty." *American Citizen,* July 9, 1805.

27. *American Citizen,* June 17, 1808. "United Irishmen" designates the men who initiated the 1798 Rebellion.

28. Myers, *History of Tammany Hall,* 30. See Miller, *Emigrants and Exiles,* 329–330. His account squares with earlier ones, notably Robert Ernst, *Im-*

migrant Life in New York City, 1825–1863 (1949; reprint, Port Washington, N.Y.: 1965), 166; and Oscar Handlin, *Boston's Immigrants, a Study in Acculturation, 1790–1880* (1941; reprint, New York: 1941, 1975). Handlin wrongly asserts of the Irish: ". . . every phase of their experience in America heightened the disparity between their heritage and that of their neighbors" (p. 125). Steven P. Erie glosses over the early impact of the prefamine Irish on New York City politics and instead emphasizes the "mature urban machine" of the 1870s and 1880s; see his *Rainbow's End: Irish-Americans and the Dilemmas of Urban Machine Politics, 1840–1985* (Berkeley: University of California Press, 1988), 2. Because Mike Davis relies on these interpretations, he does not appreciate the degree to which the Democratic Party had co-opted immigrant labor by the 1840s; see his *Prisoners of the American Dream,* 25.

29. *American Citizen,* April 22, 1809; April 2, 20, 23, 25, 1810. *Public Advertiser,* March 6, 1810; July 10, 1812. *National Advocate,* October 8, 1816.

30. *Liberator,* January 1, 1831.

31. *Public Advertiser,* June 11, 1812; White, " 'We Dwell in Safety,' " 460, 453–454, 469. *American Citizen,* April 28, 1808. A similar decline can be found in Philadelphia, although White places the timing a generation later. Nash, *Forging Freedom,* 251.

32. John J. Zuille, *Historical Sketch of the New York African Society for Mutual Relief* (New York: John Zuille, 1892), 5. At the turn of the nineteenth century, New York City's newspapers began to carry reports of slaves who had escaped to Northern territory being kidnapped for return to Southern plantations. See the *American Citizen,* August 16, 1800. For a more general treatment of the subject that correlates an increase in kidnapping of Northern free blacks with higher slave prices, see Carol Wilson, *Freedom At Risk, the Kidnappings of Free Blacks in America, 1780–1865* (Lexington: University Press of Kentucky, 1994), especially 17–18, 38.

33. Jordan, *White Over Black,* 115. *New-York Journal and Patriotic Register,* October 5, 1791. Michael Zuckerman, "The Power of Blackness," in *Almost Chosen People: Oblique Biographies in the American Grain* (Berkeley: University of California Press, 1993), 181, 182–183. For Eugene Genovese, this rebellion "constituted a turning point in the history of slave revolts and indeed of the human spirit . . . from attempts to secure freedom from slavery to attempts to overthrow it as a social system. . . . For the first time . . . a slave revolt had become a great national revolution and a vital point of the historical process that irrevocably remade the entire world." Eugene Genovese, *From Rebellion to Revolution, Afro-American Slave Revolts in the*

Making of the Modern World (Baton Rouge: Louisiana State University Press, 1979), xix, 3, 88–97, 123–125, 90. For the classic account of this heroic struggle see C. L. R. James, *Black Jacobins: Toussaint L'Ouverture and the San Domingo Revolution* (1938; reprint, New York: Vintage, 1963). Earlier, the slave revolt in Surinam had provoked considerable alarm. *New-York Journal,* October 22, 1772. For parallels to Philadelphia see Nash, *Forging Freedom,* 174–176.

34. *The Weekly Museum* (1792), as cited in Harlow, *Old Bowery Days,* 125.

35. Robert J. Swan, "John Teasman: African-American Educator and the Emergence of Community in Early Black New York City, 1787–1815," *Journal of the Early Republic* 12 (Fall 1992): 343–344. Paul Gilje, *The Road to Mobocracy: Popular Disorder in New York City, 1763–1834* (Chapel Hill: University of North Carolina Press, 1987), 147–149; White, *Somewhat More Independent,* 144–145. *National Advocate,* July 25, 1817; *Evening Post,* August 15, 1829.

36. Charles C. Andrews, *The History of the New York African Free Schools* (New York: M. Day, 1830), 8–9, 31. *Laws of the State of New-York,* 31st sess., ch. 96. Also see Ignatiev, *How the Irish Became White,* 140–141.

37. *Commercial Advertiser,* July 20, 1821.

38. *American Citizen,* May 9, 1804.

39. *New-York Journal and Patriotic Register,* March 16, 1799. Michael Zuckerman evaluates Jefferson's race hatred in "The Power of Blackness," 185, 191–218.

40. *Public Advertiser,* September 14, April 26, April 27, 1810.

41. *American Citizen,* May 2, 1807.

42. *Evening Post,* April 19, 1813.

43. *Daily Advertiser,* January 3, 1791. No indication of this early concentration is given in Gilbert Osofoksy, *Harlem: The Making of a Ghetto, New York, 1890–1930* (1963; reprint, New York: Harper, 1971). *American Advertiser,* May 4, 1807. *American Citizen,* December 8, 1807. Michael D'Innocenzo, "The Popularization of Politics in Irving's New York," in *The Knickerbocker Tradition: Washington Irving's New York,* ed. Andrew Myers (Tarrytown, N.Y.: Sleepy Hollow Restorations, 1974), 16. *Evening Post,* April 16, 1811; March 25, April 18, April 22, 1815; March 30, 1816; *National Advocate,* June 29, 1821.

44. *Evening Post,* March 19, April 25, 1803. *American Citizen,* April 12, 1803; March 30, 1801. For the next half century, mechanics directed their verbal protests against prison labor competition. *Evening Post,* November 7, 1833; June 6, 1834; October 8, 1834; December 12, 1834; January 17, 1835; May

15, 1835; August 10, 1835; October 26, 1837; *Tribune,* September 25, 1850. In 1834, stonecutters briefly rioted when Sing Sing inmates were used to build New York University. Timothy J. Gilfoyle, *City of Eros: New York City, Prostitution, and the Commercialization of Sex, 1790–1920* (New York: Norton, 1992), 43–45, 49.

45. *American Citizen,* December 14, 1801. *Evening Post,* December 16, 1801. See Rock, *Artisans of the Republic,* Chap. 7, "The Specter of Monopoly," for a summary of anti-monopoly activity in the Jefferson era.

46. *American Citizen,* March 28, 1801. Hammond, *Banks and Politics in America,* 39.

47. *American Citizen,* March 28, 1801.

48. Hammond, *Banks and Politics in America,* 145.

49. Riesman, "Republican Revisions," 2. *American Citizen,* December 14, 1801; *Public Advertiser,* May 1, 1812. *National Advocate for the Country,* July 10, 1818. The influx of British capital contributed to monopolization: ". . . the more wealthy booksellers have *combined,* in order to exclude men of small capital from the business. . . . Nor is this *combination* confined to the city of Philadelphia. It extends from Georgia to Maine, and from the Atlantic Ocean to our western frontiers." *Public Advertiser,* November 9, 1810.

50. *National Advocate,* August 19, 1820. Myers, *The History of Tammany Hall,* 14.

51. *American Citizen,* December 11, 1801. *Evening Post,* December 11, 1801.

52. *American Citizen,* February 3, 1804; December 7, 1807; *Public Advertiser,* April 26, 1810; *Evening Post,* April 26, 1816.

53. *Evening Post,* March 21, 1803.

54. *National Advocate,* February 3, 1818. *American Citizen,* November 25, 1803. *Evening Post,* March 30, 1811. Myers, *The History of Tammany Hall,* 19.

55. Dixon Ryan Fox, *The Decline of Aristocracy in New York* (New York: Columbia University Press, 1919), 69.

56. Gregory Hunter, "The Manhattan Company: Managing a Multi-unit Corporation in New York, 1799–1842," in Pencak and Wright, *New York and the Rise of American Capitalism,* 125–127, 133, 138, 141. *Evening Post,* January 26, 1808. The corruption by banks of the "republican farmer" is decried in the *American Citizen,* October 8, 1805.

57. *American Citizen,* October 8, 1805. *Public Advertiser,* February 26, 1807.

58. *Evening Post,* April 9, 1804. *Public Advertiser,* June 29, 1808; May 1, 1812.

59. *National Advocate,* April 23, 1818; Riesman, "Republican Revisions," 21.

60. *American Citizen,* March 18, 1803.

61. Gilfoyle, *City of Eros,* 45. *American Citizen,* March 18, 1803.

62. Gilje, *The Road to Mobocracy*, 116–117. *Public Advertiser*, March 18, 1811.

63. *Public Advertiser*, March 18, 1811.

64. *Public Advertiser*, July 21, August 18, November 18, November 24, 1812. Seven years later, Clinton was accused of fostering a personality cult. "All [issues] have been subservient to purposes wholly *individual*. . . . If a citizen of claims and qualifications requires an office . . . he must first avow himself a *Clintonian*." *National Advocate*, April 27, 1819. See also the *National Advocate for the Country*, April 20, 1819.

65. The rich cultural context of native American rituals as interpreted by Tammany Hall can be gleaned from a "Grand Anniversary Festival," *Public Advertiser*, May 11, 1807; December 21, 1812.

CHAPTER 3

1. *American Citizen*, May 12, 1804; *Public Advertiser*, May 1, 1812. *New York Review*, May 14, 1804, in *The Complete Works of Washington Irving, Miscellaneous Writings, 1803–1859*, ed. Wayne P. Kline (Boston: Twayne, 1981), 1.

2. Stephen Watts, *The Republic Reborn: War and the Making of Liberal America, 1790–1820* (Baltimore: Johns Hopkins University Press, 1987), 102, 276. As a subscriber to Joyce Appleby's interpretation that Jefferson was a liberal republican, a concept that progressive Vernon Parrington popularized in the 1920s, Watts does not come to terms with slavery's role in the evolution of American liberalism. However, he does acknowledge the violent character of nineteenth-century American republicanism.

3. *Evening Post*, October 30, 1818; April 24, 1821. *National Advocate*, December 2, December 7, December 30, 1816; June 13, 1817; December 18, 1818; January 19, January 21, 1819.

4. Gates, *The Farmer's Age*, 22.

5. Willis, "Social Origins of Political Leadership," 110. The number of persons without real property substantially grew between 1703 and 1789, p. 174. As late as the 1830s, the bulk of poor relief was supplied by rich citizens, not by municipal authorities. *The Diary of Philip Hone*, ed. Allan Nevins (New York: Dodd, Mead, 1936), 35. *Evening Post*, February 17, February 18, February 21, February 24, March 12, 1817; January 18, 1821. Gilfoyle, *City of Eros*, 63. *Commercial Advertiser*, January 9, 1821.

6. *National Advocate*, November 20, 1813. *Evening Post*, April 27, 1818; April 20, 1820 (quote). Myers, *The History of Tammany Hall*, 44. *National Advocate for the Country*, March 27, 1818.

7. Myers, *The History of Tammany Hall,* 50–51. *Evening Post,* February 24, 1819.

8. *National Advocate,* March 29, 1819; January 25, 1819. Abraham Martling owned a tavern on a lot at Nassau and Spruce Streets where Tammany erected its first building; he subsequently became a sachem.

9. Hendrik Hartog, "Pigs and Positivism: Do the Streets Belong to the People? An Essay on Pigs and the Customs of New York City" (paper delivered at the New-York Historical Society Conference on "The Law in America, 1607–1861," New York, May 17, 1985), 19.

10. Richardson, *The New York Police,* 14–16, 25–26. *Evening Post,* February 28, March 5, March 8, March 11, 1817. *National Advocate,* July 29, 1820. Perhaps in recognition of this fact, executions in the 1830s ceased being public spectacles, and instead became private affairs. Louis P. Masur, *Rites of Execution, Capital Punishment and the Transformation of American Culture, 1776–1865* (New York: Oxford University Press, 1989), 94–99.

11. *Evening Post,* May 3, 1820. *National Advocate,* July 29, 1820.

12. Charles Wesley, "The Negroes of New York in the Emancipation Movement," *Journal of Negro History* 24 (January 1939): 91. According to *The Annual Register,* of almost 40,000 African Americans in New York State in 1825, only 298 were eligible to vote in state and county elections. Bella Gross, "Freedom's Journal and the Rights of All," *Journal of Negro History* 17, no. 3 (July 1932): 29 n, 252–253. In 1850, there were only 71 black property owners in New York City. Ten years later, the number was 85. Roy Rosenzweig and Elizabeth Blackmar, *The Park and the People: A History of Central Park* (Ithaca: Cornell University Press, 1992), 70. Jabez D. Hammond, *The History of Political Parties in the State of New York* (Albany: C. Van Benthuysen, 1842), 2:21.

13. Field, *The Politics of Race,* 60.

14. *Commercial Advertiser,* February 5, May 12, 1824.

15. Richard B. Stott, *Workers in the Metropolis: Class, Ethnicity, and Youth in Antebellum New York City* (Ithaca: Cornell University Press, 1990), 10. Diane Lindstrom, "The Economy of Antebellum New York City" (unpublished paper, Social Science Research Council), 8. Hone wrote that "the staple commodity of the country [cotton] has enriched all through whose hands it has passed, the merchant, mechanic, and proprietor of land all rejoice in the result. . . ." Hone, *Diary,* April 8, 1835.

16. Matthew Carey, February 16, 1839, George Folsom Papers, New-York Historical Society.

17. *American Citizen,* June 2, June 5, 1810. In 1832, journeyman carpenters

staged a strike demanding one dollar and fifty cents per day while their employers insisted upon paying thirteen cents less. The journeymen's city-wide parade from shop to shop angered Philip Hone. Hone, *Diary,* May 17, 1832. *Evening Post,* April 9, 1821. Stott, *Workers in the Metropolis,* 35.

18. *National Advocate for the Country,* April 21, 1818; May 21, 1819. *National Advocate,* April 19, 1819; July 31, 1817.

19. *Evening Post,* August 24, 1821.

20. Peter Way, "Evil Humors and Ardent Spirits: The Rough Culture of Canal Construction Laborers," *Journal of American History* (March 1993): 1419–1422. Gilje, *The Road to Mobocracy,* 133.

21. Paul Goodman described how Anti-Masonic energies were harnessed by the two-party political system in *Towards a Christian Republic: Anti-Masonry and the Great Transition in New England, 1826–1836* (New York: Oxford University Press, 1988), 235.

22. *Evening Post,* October 28, 1823; January 2, 1824. Steven E. Siry, *De Witt Clinton and the American Political Economy: Sectionalism, Politics, and Republican Ideology, 1787–1828* (New York: P. Lang, 1990), 314–315.

23. *National Advocate,* March 29, 1819. A generation later, the same charges would be leveled in connection with the selection of Democratic Party congressional candidates. *Evening Post,* September 21, 1842.

24. *New York Public Advertiser,* April 13, 1809.

25. *National Advocate for the Country,* February 13, 1821.

26. The actual vote tally was: Andrew Jackson, 153,544 popular votes, 99 electoral votes; John Quincy Adams, 108,740 popular votes, 84 electoral votes; Henry Clay, 47,136 popular votes, 37 electoral votes; William Crawford, 46,136 popular votes, 41 electoral votes. *Evening Post,* September 30, 1828. The importance of Jackson as a political symbol cannot be overemphasized. The contemporary Whig historian R. McKinley Ormsby marveled: "We all remember the enthusiasm that pervaded the Democracy of those days—styled Jacksonian Democracy." R. McKinley Ormsby, *A History of the Whig Party* (Boston: Crosby, Nichols & Company, 1859), 190–191; see also page 282.

27. Fitzwilliam Byrdsall, *The History of the Loco-Foco or Equal Rights Party* (New York: Clement & Packard, 1842), 13–14. In 1844, Byrdsall formed the Calhoun Central Committee of New York to boost the presidential candidacy of South Carolina Senator John C. Calhoun, the chief spokesman for U.S. slave interests. Bernstein, "Northern Labor Finds a Southern Champion," 156.

28. The very first issue of the *Workingmen's Advocate,* the party organ, was truly

radical. The masthead on that occasion read, "All children are entitled to equal education; all adults to equal property; and all mankind to equal privileges." By the fourth issue, democratic republican values had triumphed, for the inscription had been changed to read only, "All children are entitled to equal education; all adults to equal privileges." Other than Walter Hugins, Edward Pessen has done the most to place these fringe political movements in sociological perspective. Walter Hugins, *Jacksonian Democracy and the Working Class: A Study of the New York Workingmen's Movement, 1829–1837* (Stanford: Stanford University Press, 1960); Edward Pessen, *Most Uncommon Jacksonians: Radical Leaders of the Early Labor Movement* (Albany: State University of New York Press, 1967). See also Frank Carleton, "The Workingmen's Party of New York City: 1829–1831," *Political Science Quarterly* 22 (September 1907): 413.

29. Craig Calhoun, *The Question of Class Struggle: Social Foundations of Popular Radicalism During the Industrial Revolution* (Chicago: University of Chicago Press, 1982), and Gutman's "Work, Culture and Society in Industrializing America," both make this important point.

30. Thompson, *The Making of the English Working Class*, 681–691.

31. Dickens, *American Notes*, 134.

32. *Workingmen's Advocate*, October 19, 1829. "The Question of Prices," *United States Magazine and Democratic Review*, October 1840, 348.

33. Byrdsall, *The History of the Loco-Foco or Equal Rights Party*, 20.

34. The *Boston Statesman* as quoted in the *New York City Commercial Advertiser*, October 24, 1822.

35. Wilentz, *Chants Democratic*, 172–216.

36. Hugins, *Jacksonian Democracy and the Working Class*, 220.

37. Wilentz, *Chants Democratic*, 197.

38. Samuel Savetsky, "The New York Workingmen's Party" (M.A. thesis, Columbia University, 1948). Lee Benson, *The Concept of Jacksonian Democracy: New York As a Test Case* (Princeton, N.J.: Princeton University Press, 1961). Hugins, *Jacksonian Democracy and the Working Class*, 222. See also Jonathan Glickstein, *Concepts of Free Labor in Antebellum America* (New Haven: Yale University Press, 1991), 68.

Amy Bridges's attempt to situate the Workingmen within America's radical tradition is misleading on a number of points. Aside from ignoring the race issue as well as Hugins's solid research efforts, she fails to point out that the Equal Rights Party of 1835 represented a continuation of the Workingmen's efforts. Both parties opposed the power of wealth from the perspective of small-scale entrepreneurs, not from a worker viewpoint as she maintains. Her claims that the Democratic Party did not ". . . welcome the political assertiveness of common men," or "succeed in winning the allegiance of the labor movement," are offered without evidence. In general, she relies on secondary sources. Amy Bridges, "Becoming American: The Working Classes in The United States before the Civil War," in *Working-Class Formation: Nineteenth-Century Patterns in Western Europe and the United States,* ed. Ira Katznelson and Aristide R. Zolberg (Princeton, N.J.: Princeton University Press, 1986), 163, 165.

39. Hirsch, "From Artisan to Manufacturer," 81.

40. Hugins, *Jacksonian Democracy and the Working Class,* table 16, 209; Wilentz, *Chants Democratic,* table 17, 408.

41. *Evening Post,* November 10, 1828; December 27, 1828; November 8, 1828.

42. Commons et al., *History of American Labor,* 1:170. Dickens, *American Notes,* 128, 130.

43. Edgar A. Poe, *Doings of Gotham, Poe's Contributions to the Columbian Spy,* ed. Jacob Spannuth (Pottsville: Jacob E. Spannuth, publisher, 1929), 40–41.

44. *National Advocate,* March 28, 1821. *Evening Post,* November 2, 1832; February 26, 1829; January 25, March 11, 1831; July 17, 1832; March 31, 1835; February 8, 1836. For an account of the values artisans idealized, but did not necessarily practice, see E. P. Thompson, "The Moral Economy of the English Crowd," *Past and Present* 51 (1971): 76–136. L. Ray Gunn, *The Decline of Authority, Public Economic Policy and Political Development in New York, 1800–1860* (Ithaca, N.Y.: Cornell University Press, 1988), 92.

45. *Evening Post,* September 30, 1828; June 21, 1832.

46. Hone, *Diary,* June 13, 1832. *Evening Post,* November 17, 1832.

47. Alexander Saxton, *The Rise and Fall of the White Republic: Class Politics and Mass Culture in Nineteenth-Century America* (London: Verso, 1990), 61.

48. *American Citizen,* August 26, 1806; Myers, *The History of Tammany Hall,* 68. Blackmar, *Manhattan for Rent,* 7.

49. Hone, *Diary,* May 9, 1831.

50. Ibid., August 17, 1841. Bray Hammond summarizes the role that this bank played in shaping political discourse in the early republic. Hammond, *Banks and Politics in America,* 47, 114, 115, 118, 128. *National Advocate,* April 16, 1821; March 29, 1820.

51. See Chapter 6 herein. Meyers covers the Tammany side of this corruption in *The History of Tammany Hall,* 22–24. The Whigs have yet to be adequately analyzed, although no one ought to doubt their complicity.

52. *American Citizen,* December 13, 20, 1806; January 15, 1807; *Public Advertiser,* February 26, 1807. Hartog, *Public Property and Private Power,* 4.

53. A. J. Hamilton to George Folsom, May 7, 1845; O. Mauran to George Folsom, May 6, 1845; Stephen Allen to George Folsom, September 3, 1846; William A. Osabb to George Folsom, March 28, 1845. Osabb remarked how "never before witnessed" was the lobbying on behalf of the Erie Rail Road bill. See also A. J. Hamilton to George Folsom, March 27, 1845. Herman W. F. Childs protested the closing of 33rd Street (as it is today) to accommodate the Harlem Rail Road, "in every respect, very objectionable . . . being merely for the private benefit of the Rail Road Company, and the heirs of John R. Murray [of the Murray Hill district] . . . a very dangerous and mischievous precedent . . . you would render a service to all real estate owners, and to the public at large, by opposing the proposed measure." Herman W. F. Childs to George Folsom, March 27, 1845. See also John R. Murray to George Folsom, March 11, 1845. This was not the only instance of collusion against the public interest that I uncovered. The president of the Long Island Rail Road personally lobbied Folsom (George B. Fisk to Folsom, March 12, 1846), while J. H. Van Alen wrote to Folsom concerning the Erie (March 10, 1847). George Folsom Papers. Gunn, *The Decline of Authority,* 49.

54. Riesman, "Republican Revisions," 20-21. Myers, *The History of Tammany Hall,* 70-71. There is the incredible account of how one rich man escaped the gallows by arranging to have a fire set in the cupola of the Tombs while a body resembling the escapee, with a knife through its heart, was placed in his cell to make it appear as if he had committed suicide. John McGinn, *Ten Days in the Tombs: Or, a Key to the Modern Bastille* (New York: P. F. Harris, 1855), 47-48.

55. *Evening Post,* April 3, 1833.

56. Johnson, *A Shopkeeper's Millennium,* 8; Blumin, "The Hypothesis of Middle-Class Formation in Nineteenth Century America," 312-317.

57. Stanley Nadel, *Little Germany: Ethnicity, Religion, and Class in New York City, 1845-1880* (Urbana: University of Illinois Press, 1990), 63-64. Bruce Levine, *The Spirit of 1848: German Immigrants, Labor Conflict, and the Coming of the Civil War* (Urbana: University of Illinois Press, 1992), 62-64.

58. *Evening Post,* October 11, October 25, 1828; March 26, 1830; July 7, 1832.

59. *Evening Post,* May 9, 1833.

60. Poe, *Doings of Gotham,* 25, 26. According to Dickens, in company housing in Lowell, Massachusetts, no girl was ever denied a room owing to inability to pay the rent. *American Notes,* 116.

61. *Evening Post,* May 13, 1833.
62. Richardson, *The New York Police,* 31, 57–58, 62, 69, 74, 76.
63. *Philadelphia National Gazette,* as reported in the *Evening Post,* September 6, 1828; October 10, 1837.
64. Ernst, *Immigrant Life in New York City,* 48. *Evening Post,* February 19, 1829.
65. Nash, *Forging Freedom,* 185, 86–87. George Walker, "The African-American in New York City 1827–1860" (Ph.D. diss., Columbia University, 1975), 275. Lewis Tappan, *The Life of Arthur Tappan* (New York: Hurd & Houghton, 1870), 135–136, 164.
66. Gross, "Freedom's Journal and the Rights of All," 242–243. Jonathan Sarna, *Jacksonian Jew: The Two Worlds of Mordecai Noah* (New York: Holmes and Meier, 1981), 112. Charles H. Wesley, "The Negroes of New York in the Emancipation Movement," *Journal of Negro History* (January 1939), 80.
67. Hodges, *New York City Cartmen,* 152. Kaplan, "B'hoys will be B'hoys," 9, 15–19. Leonard L. Richards, *"Gentlemen of Property and Standing:" Anti-Abolitionist Mobs in Jacksonian America* (New York: Oxford University Press, 1970), 26–27. Rhoda G. Freeman, "The Free Negro in New York City in the Era Before the Civil War" (Ph.D. diss., Columbia University, 1966), 292.
68. Fogel, *Without Consent or Contract,* 82. Dickens, *American Notes,* 76. See also Walt Whitman, *Franklin Evans or the Inebriate, A Tale of the Times* (1842; reprint, New York: Random House, 1929), 104–105.

CHAPTER 4

1. Hone, *Diary,* June 14, 1834.
2. *The First Annual Report of the New York Committee of Vigilance for the year 1837* (New York: Piercy & Reed, 1837), 3.
3. Walt Whitman, *The Gathering of the Forces,* ed. Cleveland Rogers and John Black, 2 vols. (New York: G. P. Putnam's Sons, 1920), 1:266.
4. Edward Neufville Tailer, *Diary,* December 17, 1850, New-York Historical Society.
5. Dickens, *American Notes,* 76, 284, 112–113. Philip Hone characterized such devastation as "a via infernale." *Diary,* July 10, 1847. More recently, Paul Gates has summarized the dire ecological consequences of these "wasteful farm practices" in *The Farmer's Age: 1815–1860,* 3–7. He writes of "a general weakness of American agriculture" being the tendency to "skim the cream

off the land" and a lack of willingness "to maintain it by better farm practices" (p. 10) that in some cases led to malnutrition and hookworm and
therefrom to that perennial stereotype, "poor white trash" (p. 14).

6. In this respect, the Germans were no different from the Irish. Levine, *The
   Spirit of 1848*, 150.

7. Cooper, *Notions of the Americans*, 1:266.

8. Barbara Fields reminds us that "Race is a product of history, not of nature."
   Borrowing from Christopher Lasch, she affirms that it is only when the
   morality of slavery came to be questioned that "the idea of race came into
   its own." Barbara Fields, "Ideology and Race in American History," in
   Region, Race, and Reconstruction, Essays in Honor of C. Vann Woodward,
   ed. J. Morgan Kousser and James M. McPherson (New York: Oxford University Press, 1982), 152. Gilfoyle, *City of Eros*, 41.

9. Davis, *The Problem of Slavery in Western Culture*, 317–318. Tappan, *The Life
   of Arthur Tappan*, 126.

10. This pro-bank Jacksonian newspaper became a Whig journal. Editor Webb
    was responsible for its political odyssey. Tappan, *The Life of Arthur Tap-
    pan*, 173. Hone, *Diary*, October 3, 1833. *The Emancipator and Journal of
    Public Morals*, August 6, 1834, New-York Historical Society. The paper
    was formerly called the *Genius of Temperance*. Richards, "*Gentlemen of
    Property and Standing*," 28–29.

11. *Proceedings of a Meeting of the Whig Young Men of the City of New York held
    August 5, 1834, together with the address of the General Committee of Whig
    Young Men to the Young Men of the State* (New York: T. Snowden, 1834),
    19, Kilroe Collection, Columbia University Library. Hone, *Diary*, January
    1, 1834. McGinn, *Ten Days in the Tombs*, 6. Dickens, *American Notes*, 131.
    The Tombs was also within a two-minute walk of Broadway. "Thus the
    'Tombs' is hemmed in on both sides by wealth and wretchedness—Fashion
    and Famine—Beauty and Brutality." McGinn, *Ten Days in the Tombs*, 8.

12. Byrdsall, *The History of the Loco-Foco or Equal Rights Party*, 14. *The Man*,
    March 24, 31, 1834.

13. *The Man*, March 21, February 18, 1834.

14. It was during this period that the cult of "separate spheres" reached its peak.
    Glickstein, *Concepts of Free Labor in Antebellum America*, 371 n. 58.

15. Bribing voters and sponsoring ineligible or repeat voters became a minor
    cottage industry during this period. Philadelphia Whigs were offered thirty
    dollars each in 1838 to come to New York City and illegally vote. The
    following year they were caught doing so. James B. Glentworth, *A State-*

ment of the Frauds on the Elective Franchise in the City of New York (New York: n.p., 1841).

16. *The Man,* April 12, 1834, reprinted from the *Standard.* Hone, *Diary,* April 9–11, 1834. Paul O. Weinbaum, *Mobs and Demagogues: The New York Response to Collective Violence in the Early Nineteenth Century* (Ann Arbor: University of Michigan Press, 1979), 4–10. Headley places the blame for the disorders squarely on the Irish, while Gilje contends that the guilt must be shared. Headley, *The Great Riots of New York,* 70–76; Gilje, *The Road to Mobocracy,* 138–141.

17. *The Man,* March 24, April 12, 1834.

18. Weinbaum, *Mobs and Demagogues,* 21–33, 35. Gilje, *The Road to Mobocracy,* 162–170. Linda K. Kerber, "Abolitionists and Amalgamators: The New York City Race Riots of 1834," *New York History* 48, no. 1 (January 1967): 28–39. See the *Evening Post,* July 8, 10, 12, 1834; and August 6, August 26, September 4, 1835, for additional anti-abolitionist statements. Tappan, *The Life of Arthur Tappan,* 203–219. Headley, *The Great Riots of New York,* 79–95. The first quote is taken from Samuel Ringgold Ward, *Autobiography of a Fugitive Negro, His Anti-Slavery Labors in the United States, Canada, and England* (1855; reprint, Chicago: Johnson Publishing Company, 1970), 35–37.

19. *The Emancipator,* July 15, 1834. Richards, *"Gentlemen of Property and Standing,"* 118. Gilje, *The Road to Mobocracy,* 166.

20. Bruce Laurie, *Working People of Philadelphia* (Philadelphia: Temple University Press, 1980), 62–65. Ignatiev has also found that "What was true of New York was true of Philadelphia"; see his *How the Irish Became White,* 204 n. 20.

21. Tappan, *The Life of Arthur Tappan,* 222–223.

22. *Evening Post,* April 3, May 6, 1834.

23. Blumin presents evidence drawn from contemporary sources that artisans formed the original nucleus of the middle class. *The Emergence of the Middle Class,* 246–249. A closer reading of John Jentz's abolitionist petition data for the 1830s demonstrates the contrary of his claim that New York City merchants were more partial to slavery than artisans were. John Jentz, "The Antislavery Constituency in Jacksonian New York City," *Civil War History* 27, no. 2 (June 1981): 101–122. See also the *Emancipator,* October 10, 1835.

24. *Evening Post,* May 14, March 29, 1834. *The Softs, the True Democracy of the State of New-York* (New York, 1856), 36–37. Kilroe Collection, Columbia University Library.

25. See Alan Dawley, *Class and Community, the Industrial Revolution, in Lynn* (Cambridge, Mass.: Harvard University Press, 1976).

26. The political significance of the reactionary Loco Focos is recognized by Thomas R. Hietala, *Manifest Design, Anxious Aggrandizement in Late Jacksonian America* (Ithaca, N.Y.: Cornell University Press, 1985), 105.

27. Byrdsall, *The History of the Loco-Foco or Equal Rights Party*, 140. "Thoughts on the Times," *United States Magazine and Democratic Review*, December 1839, 462.

28. See Jefferson's "Opinion on the Constitutionality of a National Bank," for the classic attack on the National Bank as a corporation that would own land and therefore threaten the farmer's independence from the banks. Jeffrey Williamson, "American Prices and Urban Inequality Since 1820," *Journal of Economic History* 36 (June 1976): 313.

29. "The Credit System Definition of Terms," *United States Magazine and Democratic Review*, February 1839, 151.

30. *Evening Post*, June 21, 1836; see also August 21, 1834; August 26, 1837.

31. "Thoughts on the Times," *United States Magazine and Democratic Review*, December 1839, 456.

32. *Evening Post*, April 4, 1834.

33. "American Aristocracy," *United States Magazine and Democratic Review*, December 1840, 128–129. See also the *Evening Post*, October 31, 1837, which condemned "The policy of fastening upon the community, through the aid of extensive monied corporations a bloated paper currency, by which prices are exorbitantly raised . . . ruinous and extreme."

34. Myers, *The New York Money Market*, 1:229–230. Hone, *Diary*, 199. Soon after, Hone marveled at the high cost of food: "What is to become of the laboring classes?" he asked. Ibid., February 18, 1837. *Evening Post*, August 11, 1836; December 15, 1841.

35. Nelson M. Blake, *Water for the Cities: A History of the Urban Water Supply in the United States* (Syracuse: Syracuse University Press, 1956), 105.

36. Ibid., 138, 161, 142. Hone, *Diary*, October 12, 1842.

37. Hone, *Diary*, December 17, 1835.

38. Hammond, *Banks and Politics in America*, 419. As chief justice of the Supreme Court, Taney drafted the 1857 Dred Scott decision that strengthened slavery. Hunter, "The Manhattan Company," 135. Hone, *Diary*, March 25, 1834.

39. *Evening Post*, March 20, 1835.

40. *Democrat*, July 7, 1834.

41. *Evening Post*, October 29, 1835; August 29, 1836.

42. Byrdsall, *The History of the Loco-Foco or Equal Rights Party*, 29–31. Fox, *The Decline of Aristocracy in New York*, 383–386; *Evening Post*, October 30, 1835.

43. *Democrat*, October 19, 1836. *Evening Post*, April 28, 1837.

44. *Evening Post*, October 7, 1836. Generally, though, Strong disparaged Democrats for relying on "dock loafers and scavengers to whom bankbills are a rarity and whose circulating medium consists of coppers and sixpences and 'such small beer.' " Strong, *Diary*, April 13, 1837; see also May 3, 1837. Hone condemned Loco Focos for being "the destructives of the city." Hone, *Diary*, November 6, 1837.

45. *Evening Post*, November 11, 1835. Byrdsall, *The History of the Loco-Foco or Equal Rights Party*, 19.

46. *Evening Post*, October 26, 1836; November 25, 1835.

47. Richards, *"Gentlemen of Property and Standing,"* 16.

48. *Emancipator*, November 1835, January 1836. Wesley, "Negroes of New York in the Emancipation Movement," 86. *The First Annual Report of the New York Committee of Vigilance for the year 1837*, 3, 7.

49. Byrdsall, *The History of the Loco-Foco or Equal Rights Party*, 39.

50. Hone, *Diary*, February 24, 1836. *Herald*, February 25, 1836.

51. Byrdsall, *The History of the Loco-Foco or Equal Rights Party*, 49, 61, 52, 74. *Proceedings of the Convention of Mechanics, Farmers, and Working Men of the State of New-York, held at the City of Utica, in the County of Oneida on the 15th, 16th, and 17th September 1836; with the Address of the Convention to the People of the State of New-York*, Kilroe Collection. For an account of how "monopoly" was construed as "part and parcel of the principles of Monarchy and Aristocracy," see the *Report and Organization or Plan of Organization of the Democratic Party in favor of Equal Rights, and opposed to all monopolies by legislation, as submitted by the general convention, and adopted by the general county meeting in the City of New-York*. (New York: Windt & Conrad, 1836). Kilroe Collection.

52. *Evening Post*, May 13, 1837.

53. Byrdsall, *The History of the Loco-Foco or Equal Rights Party*, 75.

54. Ibid., 76.

55. Ibid., 164. The ideological linkages between the Levelers and Paine, the English revolution and American republicanism, are cited in Christopher Hill, *Puritanism and Revolution: Studies in Interpretation of the English Revolution of the Seventeenth Century* (New York: Schocken Books, 1958), 75, 78–80, 99–104. See also Young, *The Democratic Republicans of New York*, 580.

56. *Evening Post,* July 23, 1836. On at least one other occasion, Equal Rights men and Tammany Democrats rallied together; *Evening Post,* March 3, 1837. On October 17, 1842, at an all-ward meeting of mechanics and workingmen, Levi Slamm, soon to be founder and editor of the Loco Foco *Daily Plebeian,* denounced capital for bringing about "white slavery"; *Evening Post,* October 19, 1842.

57. Byrdsall, *The History of the Loco-Foco or Equal Rights Party,* vi, 2, 41, 168.

58. Jefferson, "Opinion on the Constitutionality of a National Bank." "Philadelphia Banking," *United States Magazine and Democratic Review,* July 1839, 10.

59. Dirk Hoerder has found that mechanics' journals stressing an alliance between agriculture and labor were likely to be Democratic. Dirk Hoerder, "Some Connections Between Craft Consciousness and Political Thought Among Mechanics, 1820 to 1840s," *Amerikastudien* 30, no. 3 (1985): 331.

60. *Evening Post,* September 30, 1836.

61. Byrdsall, *The History of the Loco-Foco or Equal Rights Party,* 187. Sellers, *The Market Revolution,* 354.

62. Byrdsall, *The History of the Loco-Foco or Equal Rights Party,* 104.

63. Reynolds, *Beneath the American Renaissance,* 198. Samuel P. Rezneck, "The Social History of an American Depression, 1837–1843," *American Historical Review* 40 (1935): 664. Stott, *Workers in the Metropolis,* 156–157.

64. "The Business Man," *Broadway Journal,* August 2, 1845.

65. *Evening Post,* November 3, 1837.

66. "Notes of the Month," *United States Magazine and Democratic Review,* December 1839.

67. *New-York Democrat,* April 10, 1841.

68. "Further Extracts from the Private Diary of a Certain Bank Director," *United States Magazine and Democratic Review,* December 1838, 360, 361. "Thoughts on the Times," *United States Magazine and Democratic Review,* December 1839, 461.

69. Joel H. Silbey, *The Shrine of Party: Congressional Voting Behavior, 1841–1852* (Pittsburgh: University of Pittsburgh Press, 1967), 67, 51, 55. *Evening Post,* November 9, 1837.

70. *Evening Post,* October 4, 5, 6, 1837.

71. "European Visions of American Democracy," *United States Magazine and Democratic Review,* July 1838, 345. For evidence of anti-bank rhetoric leading Whigs to disparagingly define the Democrats as the Loco Foco Party, see *The Diary of an Apprentice Cabinetmaker: Edward Jenner Carpenter's "Journal," 1844–1845,* ed. Christopher Clark, with the assistance of Donald

M. Scott (reprinted from the *Proceedings of the American Antiquarian Society* Worcester, Mass., 1988, 98:part 2), 336. Also see the *Tribune,* May 31, 1850; Hone, *Diary,* October 13, October 15, December 7, December 15, December 27, 1838; January 24, April 12, July 3, August 7, August 22, 1839; January 27, 1840; Tailer, *Diary,* November 8, 1848; April 9, 1849; November 2, 1852; George Templeton Strong, *Diary,* ed. Allan Nevins and Milton Henry Thomas (New York: Macmillan, 1952), May 8, 1840. Republican Strong later became head of the North's Sanitary Commission. It is primarily through his efforts that the Republican Party's Union League was established.

The degree to which Arcadian Republican rhetoric permeated political dialogue is discussed in Rowland Berthoff, "Independence and Attachment, Virtue and Interest: From Republican Citizen to Free Enterpriser, 1787–1837," in *Uprooted Americans; Essays to Honor Oscar Handlin,* ed. Richard L. Bushman, Neil Harris, David Rothman, Barbara Miller Solomon, and Stephan Thernstrom (Boston: Little, Brown, 1979).

72. *Evening Post,* December 2, 1837. *American Whig Review* 1, no. 2 (1845): 115.

73. Dickens, *American Notes,* 141.

74. Hone, *Diary,* March 9, 1836. Blackmar, *Manhattan for Rent,* 87.

75. James Fenimore Cooper, "Autobiography of a Pocket-Handkerchief," *Graham's Magazine,* February 1843, 94.

76. Hone, *Diary,* December 31, 1839.

77. Strong, *Diary,* January 29, 1840. See also Dickens, *American Notes,* 140.

78. Cooper to George Palmer Putnam, July 23, 1851, *The Letters and Journals of James Fenimore Cooper,* ed. James Franklin Beard (Cambridge, Mass: The Belknap Press of Harvard University Press, 1968), 6:279–281. See also Tailer, *Diary,* May 4, 1849; May 5, 1855.

79. Robert Benjamin Winthrop, "Old New York," New-York Historical Society Address, February 4, 1862.

80. *Evening Post,* April 7, 1838; April 7, 1843; March 5, 1840; July 7, 1843; January 24, 1834.

81. Hone, *Diary,* March 16, March 21, 1836.

82. *Evening Post,* May 31, June 11, June 14, 1836. Hone, *Diary,* June 6, 1836. Cooper, "Autobiography of a Pocket-Handkerchief," *Graham's Magazine,* January 1843, 8; February 1843, 97.

83. Stott, *Workers in the Metropolis,* 145.

84. Freeman, *The Free Negro in New York City,* 98. Wesley, "The Negroes of New York in the Emancipation Movement," 73, 79, 92–93. In 1845, only ninety-one African-American New Yorkers were deemed eligible to vote out

of a total black population of some thirteen thousand. On the eve of the Civil War, that number remained under one hundred. Rosenzweig and Blackmar, *The Park and the People*, 72. William M. Brewer, "John Russwurm," *The Journal of Negro History* 13, no. 4 (October 1928): 415.

85. Wilson, *Freedom at Risk*, 112. *The First Annual Report of the New York Committee of Vigilance for the year 1837*, 13, 14, 19. Tappan, *The Life of Arthur Tappan*, 178–180. Davis, *The Problem of Slavery in Western Culture*, 47. Also see David Eltis, "Europeans and the Rise and Fall of African Slavery in the Americas: An Interpretation," *American Historical Review* 98, no. 5 (December 1993): 1417.

86. Freeman, "The Free Negro in New York City," 67–68, 72–81. *The First Annual Report of the New York Committee of Vigilance for the year 1837*, 20–30.

87. *The First Annual Report of the New York Committee of Vigilance for the year 1837*, 31, 34–35. *Laws of New York State*, 40th sess., ch. 137, March 31, 1817. *Laws of New York State*, 42nd sess., ch. 141, April 19, 1819.

88. *Evening Post*, November 3, 1837. Bray Hammond, "Free Banks and Corporations: The New York Banking Act of 1838," *Journal of Political Economy* 44 (1936): 184–209. Hammond judged the act to have been "drawn in very careless form"; see his *Banks and Politics in America*, 352, 337.

89. "The Credit System," *United States Magazine and Democratic Review*, November 1838, 199. The article went on to point out that this new credit system had the

> direct tendency to subvert the equality of rights which is the foundation of our forms of Government—to sacrifice . . . upon the altar of Mammon for the advantage of the few—to bestow inordinate power upon the mere shadow of wealth at the expense of permanent general prosperity—to invest combinations of irresponsible individuals with the monopoly of an artificial measure of value, by which arbitrary control over the subsistence of all other classes is conferred upon them, and they are enabled to modify, pervert, and break down, with impunity, all laws which interfere with their cupidity. By means of secret and concerted arrangements, these soulless combinations are able to practice acts of injustice, vitally affecting the most important interests of those who are unable to resist their power, which no individual could venture to perpetuate without becoming obnoxious to the penal laws. Hence the manifold advantages of capital loaned upon credit for the encouragement of industry and enterprise are diminished by the increase of risk. (p. 196)

From the vantage of the 1990s, this analysis also helps to explain the reasons for the current half-trillion dollar savings and loan peculations and the 5 trillion dollar national debt—none of which could have occurred without the precedent-breaking nature of the 1838 Free Banking Act. "Freedom" was ensured for the banks, at the long-term expense of the people.

90. *The Man,* March 27, 1834. "The Credit System," *United States Magazine and Democratic Review,* November 1838, 196.

91. Hone, *Diary,* July 23, 1839; January 5, 1838.

92. *Evening Post,* November 6, 1837. See also October 4, 5, 6, 1837.

93. Byrdsall, *The History of the Loco-Foco or Equal Rights Party,* 103–104. For accounts that blame the rioters for their plight, see Headley, *The Great Riots of New York,* 103–104; and Hone, *Diary,* February 13, 1837. *Evening Post,* February 14, 1837. Headley, *The Great Riots of New York,* 97–110.

94. Irving to Catherine Paris, March 22, 1838, *Letters of Washington Irving,* vol. 2 of *Complete Works,* ed. Richard Dilworth Rust (Boston: Twayne, 1979), 925.

95. *Evening Post,* April 6, 1840. Myers, *The History of Tammany Hall,* 118, 126.

96. "The Credit System," *United States Magazine and Democratic Review,* February 1839, 152. *Evening Post,* September 22, 1843.

97. *Evening Post,* November 4, 1837.

98. Laurie, *Working People of Philadelphia,* 226.

99. Herbert Gutman with Ira Berlin, "Class Composition and the Development of the American Working Class, 1840–1890," in Herbert Gutman, *Power and Culture, Essays on the American Working Class,* ed. Ira Berlin (New York: Pantheon, 1987), 382; originally published in German in *Historical Review* 26 (1983): 224–236.

100. Mike Walsh, "Speech at County Meeting of Tammany Hall," in *Sketches of the Speeches and Writings of Mike Walsh* (New York: Thomas McSpedon, 1843), 27. *Evening Post,* December 17, 1836. Cooper, "Autobiography of a Pocket-Handkerchief," *Graham's Magazine,* February 1843, 91. For a discussion of the republican substitution of boss for master, see Roediger, *The Wages of Whiteness,* 50–54.

101. Richardson, *The New York Police,* 65.

102. *Impartial Citizen,* March 14, 1849.

103. F. O. Matthiessen has termed this concentration of literary genius an "American Renaissance," which he defined as "an organic union between labor and culture," with "no split between art and the other functions of the community." Matthiessen, *American Renaissance: Art and Expression in the Age of Emerson and Whitman* (New York: Oxford University Press, 1941), xiv–xv. See also Perry Miller, *The Raven and the Whale: The War of Words and Wits in the Era of Poe and Melville* (New York: Oxford University Press, 1956), 110.

CHAPTER 5

1. The term "artifical wants" is taken from Grant Thorburn, *Fifty Years of Reminiscences of New York* (New York: n.p., 1845), 208. Herbert Marcuse, *One-Dimensional Man: Studies in the Ideology of Advanced Industrial Society* (Boston: Beacon Press, 1964), 32.

2. The most complete discussion of the b'hoy is to be found in Peter Buckley, "To the Opera House: Culture and Society in New York City, 1820-1860" (Ph.D. diss., State University of New York at Stony Brook, 1984), Chap. 19. See also Reynolds, *Beneath the American Renaissance,* 477. Dickens, *American Notes,* 129. Walt Whitman, "The Old Bowery," in *Prose Works 1892,* ed. Floyd Stovall (New York, 1964), 2:595. Contemporaries generally blamed political violence on "sinister politicians and scheming functionaries." James Burns, *"The Beggar Boy"* (London: Hodder & Stoughton, 1882), 318. Random violence against blacks had become an accepted part of the political culture; ibid., 331-332.

3. Reynolds, *Beneath the American Renaissance,* 287. Reynolds observes that, "On the popular level, the b'hoy was usually associated with working-class politics, when assimilated by the major writers, he became a source of egalitarian sympathy but lost direct connections with political activism" (p. 466).

4. George Foster, *New-York by Gas-Light and other Urban Sketches,* ed. Stuart M. Blumin (1850; reprint, Berkeley: University of California Press, 1990), 170. See also Whitman, *Franklin Evans or the Inebriate,* 41. Wilentz's claimed "very new culture" being created by "plebeian white 'insiders' " that in turn "acquired a new ideological significance as well" turns out to be not so new after all (Wilentz, *Chants Democratic,* 263). A plebeian culture was in existence prior to the second party system and politically percolated through organizations affiliated with the two-party system, such as the Butt-End Coon Hunters and Captain Rynders's Empire Club. These groups are discussed in Chapter 6 herein. What was new was "yellow" journalism, spawned by industrialization and a consequent technological revolution in printing, that sensationalized this subculture, bringing it to the attention of the nineteenth-century public and of twentieth-century historians. Wilentz has confused the image makers' newly marketable characters with a new social type. See also Chapter 8 herein, n. 61.

5. For the prototype of the b'hoy, the English plebeian dandy, see Pearce Egan, *Life in London, the Day and Night Scenes* (London: Sherwood, Neeley, & Jones, 1821).

6. *Evening Post,* January 6, 1835. Hone, *Diary,* May 14, 1842; July 4, 1838; December 31, 1839; January 1, 1840.

7. Reynolds, *Beneath the American Renaissance,* 509. Hone, *Diary,* October 17, 1831.

8. Buckley, "To the Opera House," 370–371, 373, 375, 377, 390. Hone, *Diary,* September 14, 1842. See Elliott J. Gorn, *The Manly Art: Bare-Knuckle Prize Fighting in America* (Ithaca, N.Y.: Cornell University Press, 1986); Elliott Gorn, " 'Goodbye Boys, I Die a True American': Homicide, Nativism, and Working-Class Culture in Antebellum New York City," *Journal of American History* 74, no. 2 (September 1987): 388–410.

9. Gilfoyle, *City of Eros,* 18, 19, 89–91.

10. Ibid., 119.

11. *National Advocate,* September 21, 1821.

12. The Park Theater burned shortly after the evening curtain fell on a performance of Tammany leader Mordecai Noah's play, *The Battle of Chippewa.* It reopened August 1, 1821. *The Picture of New York* (New York: A. T. Goodrich, 1828), 337. *Commercial Advertiser,* January 9, January 16, 1822. *National Advocate,* October 27, 1821. Herbert Marshall and Mildred Stock, *Ira Aldridge, the Negro Tragedian* (London: Rockcliff, 1958), 32, 37. Peter G. Buckley, "Popular Entertainment Before the Civil War," in *Encyclopedia of American Social History,* ed. Mary Kupiec Cayton, Elliott J. Gorn, Peter W. Williams, 3 vols. (New York: Scribner, 1992), 3:1620. Shane White, " 'It Was a Proud Day': African Americans, Festivals, and Parades in the North, 1741–1834," *Journal of American History* (June 1974): 49.

13. Nash, *Forging Freedom,* 254–259. Thomas Low Nichols, *Forty Years of American Life* (London: J. Maxwell & Co., 1864), 369–370. Dickens, *American Notes,* 138–139.

14. I concur with Eric Lott's observation that "the counterfeit was a means of exercising white control of subversive cultural forms as much as it was an avenue of racial derision," though to say the one is perhaps also to say the other. Eric Lott, " 'The Seeming Counterfeit': Racial Politics and Blackface Minstrelsy," *American Quarterly* 43, no. 2 (June 1991): 229. Leslie Harris, "Rulers of Five Points: Interracial Sex and Class in Antebellum New York City" (paper delivered in New York City at the annual meeting of the American Historical Association, 1997).

15. *Broadway Journal,* July 12, 1845.

16. Harris, "Rulers of Five Points." White, " 'It Was a Proud Day,' " 32.

17. Davis refers to "cheerful and willing-minded laborers," in *The Problem of Slavery in Western Culture,* 306; while David Grimsted has discovered that

"the one American low-comedy stereotype to retain a servant's position was the stage Negro," in his *Melodrama Unveiled, American Theater and Culture, 1800–1850* (Chicago: University of Chicago Press, 1968), 190.

18. Rosenzweig and Blackmar, *The Park and the People*, 89.

19. Hone notes its appearance in the 1830s. Hone, *Diary*, 271.

20. McGinn, *Ten Days in the Tombs*, 29–30.

21. Julia Ward Howe, "A Trip to Cuba," *Atlantic Monthly*, May 1859, 604.

22. *Evening Post*, August 16, September 29, 1841. The uniform hostility American authors evinced toward this new yellow journalism is discussed in Reynolds, *Beneath the American Renaissance*, 171–173.

23. Richards, *"Gentlemen of Property and Standing,"* 72. See James L. Crouthamel, "The Newspaper Revolution in New York, 1830–1860," *New York History* 45 (April 1964): 91–113. Poe, "The Literati of New York City," *Essays and Reviews* (New York: Literary Classics of the United States, Distributed by Viking Press, 1984), 1214.

24. In his essay, "Evil Humors," Peter Way presents an incisive social portrait of this class of workers, who are neglected in Wilentz's *Chants Democratic*.

25. P. T. Barnum, *Struggles and Triumphs* (Hartford, Conn.: J. B. Burr & Company, 1869), 271.

26. Barnum, *Struggles and Triumphs*, 73–76. A. H. Saxon, *P. T. Barnum, the Legend and the Man* (New York: Columbia University Press, 1989), 82 (photo).

27. These were the "big bugs" for Edward Jenner Carpenter, a Massachusetts cabinetmaker. *The Diary of an Apprentice Cabinetmaker*, 336, 345.

28. Dickens, *American Notes*, 112. A more personally lucrative motive for New York City's rich was the appreciation in real estate values that preceded and accompanied the construction of Central Park. Rosenzweig and Blackmar, *The Park and the People*, 7, 17–18, 31–36, 40–42, 47–48, 54, 56, 78–81, 85–87, 188. There was also another motive. As Nathaniel P. Willis put it in 1844, "As a metropolis of wealth and fashion, New York City has one great deficiency—that of *a driving park*." Henry Hope Reed and Sophia Duckworth, *Central Park, A History and a Guide* (New York: Clarkson N. Potter, 1972), 16. Central Park took care of that objection by providing miles of curvaceous carriage roads.

29. Cooper, "Autobiography of a Pocket-Handkerchief," *Graham's Magazine*, January 1843, 9.

30. Miller, *The Raven and the Whale*, 303. See Michael Paul Rogin's, *Subversive Genealogy, the Politics and Art of Herman Melville* (New York: Knopf, 1983), for a brilliant synthesis of politics, history, and the psychology of the

age and of the family as filtered through the phantasm of Melville's literary art.

31. Henry Nash Smith, *Democracy and the Novel, Popular Resistance to Classic American Writers* (New York: Oxford University Press, 1978), 15. Smith adds that "the unstated and probably unrecognized purpose of the best-selling novels of the 1850s was to relieve the anxieties aroused by rapid upward mobility, especially the fear of failure, and to provide assurance that the universe is managed for man's benefit."

32. Thomas Bender assigns to the second party system the creation of a "literary culture," in his *New York Intellect: A History of Intellectual Life in New York City, from 1750 to the Beginning of our own Time* (New York: Knopf, 1987). This "literary culture" was frequently at odds with whom we now regard as the literary luminaries of the time, namely Cooper, Poe, Hawthorne, Melville, Thoreau, Dickinson, and Whitman.

33. Cooper to Mrs. Cooper, August 21, 1830. Cooper's children were in Germany at the time and besieged by their German counterparts, eager to see " 'of what shade of black they were?' " *The Letters and Journals*, 2:5–6.

34. Laurence W. Levine, *Highbrow/Lowbrow, the Emergence of Cultural Hierarchy in America* (Cambridge, Mass.: Harvard University Press, 1988), 13–104. George G. Foster, *New York Naked* (New York: De Witt & Davenport, 1851), 142.

35. *Evening Post*, March 13, 1840.

36. Cooper to Cornelius Mathews and Evert Augustus Duyckinck, December 6, 1841, *The Letters and Journals*, 4:202–203.

37. Irving to David Hoffman, August 22, 1839, *Letters*, 3:19.

38. Miller, *The Raven and the Whale*, 12.

39. Ralph Waldo Emerson, "The Young American," a Lecture read before the Mercantile Library Association, Boston, February 7, 1844, in *Ralph Waldo Emerson: Essays and Lectures* (New York: Library of America, 1983), 216.

40. "Introduction," *United States Magazine and Democratic Review*, October 1837, 2, 3, 13, 14.

41. *The Working Man's Advocate*, 1, no. 2, 27; 1, no. 6, 97.

42. *Walt Whitman, Complete Poetry and Prose*, ed. Justin Kaplan (New York: Literary Classics of the United States, Distributed by Viking Press, 1982), 939.

43. The popular misconception persists that Whitman was anti-science. For example, the *New York Times* obituary of one of the last of America's intellectual giants, Lewis Mumford, noted that "Because Mr. Mumford tended to be a moralist in the tradition of Emerson and Whitman, he was accused of

seeing science as evil and machinery as the Devil's handmark." *New York Times*, January 28, 1990.

44. *Broadway Journal*, August 2, 1845.

45. Whitman, in Kaplan, *Complete Poetry and Prose*, 994.

46. Henry David Thoreau, "Advantages and Disadvantages of Foreign Influence on American Literature" (1836) in *Early Essays and Miscellanies*, ed. Joseph J. Moldenauer & Edwin Moser with Alexander Kern (Princeton, N.J.: Princeton University Press, 1975), 39.

47. Of the origins of American culture, Fuller had written, "All symptoms are confined to the African race . . . the Caucasian race have yet their rail-roads to make. . . ." Margaret Fuller, "The Entertainments of the Past Winter," *The Dial*, 1842, 52. Strong, *Diary*, December 20, 1858.

48. William Gienapp, *The Origins of the Republican Party, 1852–1856* (New York: Oxford University Press, 1987), 372.

49. Dickens, *Martin Chuzzlewit*, 283.

50. Hone, *Diary*, February 28, 1840.

51. Stott, "The Worker in the Metropolis," 173. Edgar A. Poe, "The Philosophy of Furniture," *Collected Works of Edgar Allan Poe, Tales and Sketches, 1843–1849*, ed. Thomas Ollive Mabbot (Cambridge, Mass.: Belknap Press of Harvard University Press, 1978), 2:495–504.

52. Stott, *Workers in the Metropolis*, 172, 176, 195. Dickens, *American Notes*, 130.

53. John Bunyan, *The Pilgrim's Progress* (1678; reprint, New York: 1965), 91, 94. Machiavelli, "The Prince," trans. Russell Price, and Quentin Skinner ed. (Cambridge: Cambridge University Press, 1988), 63. *Putnam's Monthly Magazine*, 1857, 335, 448.

54. Cooper, *The Letters and Journals*, 4:146–147. Cooper to Thomas Baldwin, November 24, 1841, ibid., 195.

55. Cooper, *The Letters and Journals*, 436. Cooper to William Branford Shubrick, May 30, 1844, ibid., 462–463.

56. Hone, *Diary*, June 6, 1840.

57. Ibid., April 10, 1840.

58. Edgar A. Poe, "The Man That Was Used Up," *Broadway Journal*, August 9, 1845.

59. Machiavelli, "The Prince," 63.

60. "Signed 'Old Whig' " in *New-York Journal*, March 3, 1768. *Evening Post*, March 13, September 7, 1840.

61. Hone claimed for himself the honor of coining the term Whig at a political meeting over which he presided at Washington Hall, the party's New York City headquarters. *Diary*, June 18, 1840. See also September 8, 1840.

62. Marcuse, *One-Dimensional Man,* 3. See also chap. 3, as well as Henryk Skolimowski, "The Role of Philosophy and Values in the Right Model of Peace," *Dialectics and Humanism* 3-4 (1985): 59-67.

63. Barnum, *Struggles and Triumphs,* 271-354.

64. The prima ballerina Fanny Ellser captivated New York audiences a decade earlier. Hone, *Diary,* May 11, 12, 14, June 9, 1840; June 9, 14, 1841. To Henry C. Watson, though, "the negro rivals Fanny Ellser." *Broadway Journal,* July 12, 1845.

65. Poe, "Philosophy of Furniture," 498, 499. *The New Yorker Staats-Zeitung,* May 10, 1854, reported that "Distinguished individuals, family connections, and to the utmost degree the 'almighty dollar' creates in this land of freedom an influence as widely extended, as ever in some monarchies. . . . The rich and distinguished stand here higher above the law than in any other country." As cited in Levine, *The Spirit of 1848,* 89.

66. Poe, "Philosophy of Furniture," 498.

67. David Reese, *Humbugs of New-York* (New York: J. S. Taylor, 1938), 17. Reynolds observes that, "On the popular level, the b'hoy was usually associated with working-class politics, when assimilated by the major writers, he became a source of egalitarian sympathy but lost direct connections with political activism." Reynolds, *Beneath the American Renaissance,* 466.

68. Edgar A. Poe, "Mellonta Tauta," *Collected Works,* 3:1293.

69. The Democrat Cooper was appropriately enough scorned by the Whig Hone. *Diary,* October 12, November 22, 1838.

70. Emerson wrote, "The true reformer is calm and mild. . . . True reform works by the law of nature, and like all nature's laws, is not to be accelerated or counterfeited. . . . The spirit of pure reform . . . [is] both conservative and progressive." *Awl,* July 17, 1844, as quoted in Dirk Hoerder, "Some Connections Between Craft Consciousness and Political Thought Among Mechanics," 333.

71. Herman Melville, *The Confidence-Man, His Masquerade* (Evanston, Ill.: Northwestern University Press and the Newberry Library, 1984), 198. Ralph Waldo Emerson, "On the Relations of Man to the Globe," in *The Early Lectures,* ed. Stephen E. Whichler and Robert E. Spiller (Cambridge: The Belknap Press of Harvard University Press, 1966), 1:48.

72. D. H. Lawrence, *Studies in Classic American Literature* (New York: Thomas Seltzer, 1923), Chap. 1.

73. Cooper to Cornelius Mathews and Augustus Duyckinck, December 6, 1841, *The Letters and Journals,* 4:202-203.

74. Dickens, *Martin Chuzzlewit,* 291.

75. *The Diary of an Apprentice Cabinetmaker,* 341, 343, 392; Dickens, *Martin Chuzzlewit,* 293, 294. Poe, *Doings of Gotham,* 48.

76. In his short story and political satire on the presidency "The Man That Was Used Up," Poe placed this phrase in the mouths of his protagonist General A. B. C. Smith's admirers, none of whom was aware of how physically decrepit, yet technologically advanced, the general really was.

CHAPTER 6

1. Allan Pred, *Urban Growth and City Systems in the United States, 1840–1860* (Cambridge: Harvard University Press, 1980), 32. Lindstrom, "Economic Structure, Demographic Change, and Income Inequality," 6.

2. Myers, *The History of Tammany Hall,* 96–98. George Curtis to George Folsom, May 7, 1846, Folsom Papers. An act to authorize banking passed April 18, 1838, in the assembly, but lost on May 13, 1846, by one vote short of the necessary two-thirds majority in the state senate. *New York Senate Journal,* 69th sess. (1846): 755. *New York State Assembly Journal,* 69th sess., doc. #31 (1846): 108–109, 116–117.

3. Myers, *The New York Money Market,* 1:32.

4. Jabez D. Hammond, *History of Political Parties,* 2:457. Rezneck, "The Social History of an American Depression," 665. *Evening Post,* July 20, 1839; July 14, 1840; December 15, 1840; February 19, 1841; May 1, 1839; May 26, April 23, 1842; June 8, 1843.

5. Gunn, "The Crisis of Distributive Politics," 192. C. F. Adams, Jr., and Henry Adams, *Chapters of Erie & Other Essays* (Boston: J. R. Osgood, 1871), 4.

   On the eve of the Civil War, with 773 miles of track laid, the Erie again failed to make interest payments. In 1861, a new company was organized, only to foreclose a year later. After a swift reorganization, the Erie Rail Road Company emerged. Revenue, which had gone up two and a half times to 5 million dollars in a generation by 1859, accelerated to 16.5 million dollars by 1865. The public never received a dime in repayment for the project.

6. *Evening Post,* March 23, 1835; January 11, February 14, February 17, March 10, March 16, 1842.

7. Edward Pessen, *Riches, Class, and Power Before the Civil War* (Lexington, Mass.: Heath, 1973), 35.

8. Hone, *Diary,* April 27, 1846; June 2, 1836. He continued to blame these immigrants for their poverty; January 29, 1847.

9. Poe, "Mellonta Tauta," 1300.

10. Michael Feldberg finds this to be the case in Philadelphia. *The Philadelphia Riots of 1844, A Study of Ethnic Conflict* (Westport, Conn.: Greenwood Press, 1975), 3.

11. Upstate New York reflected the political split between Democrats and Whigs over blacks. Field, *The Politics of Race in New York,* 51. Paul Finkelman stresses Seward's advocacy of "civil rights in his state"; see his "The Protection of Black Rights in Seward's New York," *Civil War History* 34, no. 3 (1988): 211.

12. *Evening Post,* August 20, 1839; September 9, 1841; February 23, August 24, August 26, 1842; June 24, 1839. Charles Frederick Briggs, *The Adventures of Harry Franco, a Tale of the Great Panic* (New York: F. Saunders, 1839), 120–123.

13. *Evening Post,* January 28, March 2, March 27, 1833.

14. Poe, *Doings of Gotham,* 49.

15. Jay P. Dolan, *The Immigrant Church: New York's Irish and German Catholics, 1815–1865* (Baltimore: Johns Hopkins University Press, 1975), 29. *Evening Post,* April 8, 1840. Strong, *Diary,* December 10, 1839.

16. Feldberg, *The Philadelphia Riots of 1844,* 4, passim. See Hone, *Diary,* May 8, July 11, 1844. Also David Montgomery, "The Shuttle and the Cross: Weavers and Artisans in the Kensington Riots of 1844," *Journal of Social History* 5 (1972): 411–446.

17. Mushkat, *Tammany,* 185. Hone opposed universal suffrage for large communities: "It works better in the country, where a large population of the voters are Americans, born and brought up on the spot, and where if a black sheep comes into the flock he is marked immediately." Hone, *Diary,* November 4, 1840.

18. *Evening Post,* March 30, 1842. Leonard R. Riforgiato, "Bishop John Timon, Archbishop John Hughes, and Irish Colonization: A Clash of Episcopal Views on the Future of the Irish and the Catholic Irish in America," in Pencak, Miller, and Berrol, *Immigration to New York,* 54.

19. *Mysteries of New York* (London: William Walker, 1847), 63.

20. Stott, *Workers in the Metropolis,* 168–169.

21. Richardson, *The New York Police,* 27. *Constitution and Bye-Laws of the American Republican Party,* James Harper Papers, New-York Historical Society. "Petition" (to require a law for a year's residence in the state and six months in the county after nationalization before a man is allowed to vote), November 20, 1844, American Republican Party Papers, 1843–1847, New-York Historical Society. Reform mania is a satirical target in Cornelius

Mathews's *The Career of Puffer Hopkins* (1842; reprint, New York: Garret Press, 1970), 25–26.

22. *Subterranean,* August 31, 1843. In Philadelphia, Feldberg found the same pattern of Whig crossover to the American Republicans; see his *The Philadelphia Riots of 1844,* 166, 172.

23. Richardson, *The New York Police,* 46.

24. "Declaration of Principles Comprised in the Address and Resolutions of the Native American Convention Assembled at Philadelphia, July 4, 1845," American Republican Party Papers. As the law-and-order party, the Native Americans introduced legislation on April 8, 1844, that abolished the watch department and replaced it with a 750-man police department.

25. *Harbinger,* August 2, 1845.

26. This assessment was derived from checking party rosters against city directories. Since directories tended to omit members of lower socioeconomic classes, it is likely that percentages of men belonging to the skilled and unskilled categories were even greater than I have noted. For an analysis of party morphology at this time, see Gronowicz, "Labor's Decline Within New York City's Democratic Party From 1844 to 1884, in *Immigration to New York,*" from which the quantitative portion of this chapter is adapted.

Following the lead of Lee Benson, I cose 1844 as the year to examine in depth, for it was a critical election year at the historic moment when, in Benson's words, "similarities and differences between the major New York parties . . . crystallized . . . and were reflected in the platforms and addresses adopted at national and state conventions," and Democratic-Republicans officially designated themselves as "the American Democracy." Benson, *The Concept of Jacksonian Democracy,* 219, 226.

27. Kilroe, *Saint Tammany,* 12–13. A full rank ordering of organizations, events, positions, elective or appointive officials, and occupations can be found in Tables 2–6 herein.

28. Even Karl Marx's New York emissary, Joseph Weydemeyer, organized his New York Workingmen's alliance along ward lines. Ernst, *Immigrant Life in New York City,* 118–119.

29. Since voter fraud was conducted by both major parties, voting inspectors were augmented by party stalwarts. The *Daily Plebeian,* edited by Loco Foco Levi Slamm, "warned" its readers on October 14, 1844, "The Whig leaders have no hope of electing Clay in a fair fight—the weapons they rely on are falsehood and fraud. Protect your Organization—Guard the Ballot Boxes."

30. James Bryce's observation that "Parties had been organized far more elabo-

rately in the United States than anywhere else in the world . . ." certainly holds true for the 1840s. *The American Commonwealth* (New York: Commonwealth Publishing Company, 1905), 1:6.

31. The term *organizational* has been employed to describe routine, ongoing party business, while nonroutine activity is classified as an *event*. (See Tables 2–4 herein for rank-ordering lists of organizations, events, and positions within both.)

For example, though the "committee to nominate charter officers" chosen by the ward committees was active in all wards, it is classified as an event owing to its exclusive association with a nonroutine activity—the mayoral primary elections. Since its power was directly related to the role it played in the selection of candidates, it ranks higher than clubs or associations that fulfilled more of a social function.

When classifying, it is useful to assign first-rank status to those men summoned to perform specific one-time party tasks on the broadest geographical level. These ultimately consisted of district electors and state and national convention delegates. They were first publicly mentioned in 1840. (*Evening Post,* August 24, 1840). Delegates to statewide institutions or conventions are accorded secondary importance (4 such groupings). In third place are those engaged in citywide political occurrences (30 events); in fourth place is everyone else (56 events).

Assigned third rank among 1844 political organizations are citywide organizations like the Empire and Polk clubs that were active in party functions. All other organizations—principally at ward or below ward level, as well as the more obscure least mentioned citywide organizations—are relegated to last place.

It is also necessary to rank positions within organizations and events. Four broad classifications emerge: "top," to which 17 positions like "president" are assigned; "middle," composed of 35 groups (e.g., General Committee member); "workhorse," 33 separate groups (e.g., treasurer); "body" (e.g., attender).

Also required is a hierarchy of civic officials. This category includes those holding elective or appointive positions within the authoritative political structure outside the formal party apparatus (see Table 5 for a list of all elective and appointive officials). Included are all men running for office, those merely mentioned as possible candidates, and those who formally held that office. They are divided into 4 categories related to their administrative duties and labeled top, medium, high white-collar, and low white-collar: "top" (e.g., governor) is broken down into 12 classifications; "middle" (e.g., judge) 29; "lower middle" (e.g., keeper) 22; and "low" (e.g., flour inspector) 29. Once a hierarchy of organizations and events is established, each of the 2,391 men gleaned from the 1844 party newspapers can theoretically be ranked as to his individual importance.

32. In his political satire, *The Career of Puffer Hopkins*, Cornelius Mathews depicts a vibrant working-class presence at Democratic Party meetings as seen through the eyes of a young aspiring politician. Indeed, the very first scene in the book takes place at what is most likely a ward meeting at the fanciful Fog-Fire Hall (pp. 10, 12, 18, 19).

33. *Daily Plebeian,* September 11, 24, 10, 1844.

34. In classifying the population in terms of the role played in the economy, it is useful for statistical as well as analytical purposes to divide the workforce into 4 categories. (See Table 6 for a list of all occupations found.) Bankers, capitalists, owners, managers, preferred professions, and trades make up the first category (80 classifications); less preferred professions and trades the second (225 classifications); skilled craftsmen or workers the third (124 classifications); and finally unskilled or low-skilled workers (30 classifications).

LABOR CATEGORIES (IN PERCENTAGES)	1	2	3	4
1844 population-at-large occupational structure	16	19	50	15
Democratic Party occupational structure	23	37	33	7
Total of men belonging to distinct organizations	23	38	33	6
Total of men belonging to distinct events	28	35	31	6
Party members of one political organization	52	58	68	79
Party members belonging to two or three political organizations	33	31	25	18
Party members belonging to four or more political organizations	15	11	7	3
Party members participating in one political event	55	55	67	76
Party members participating in two or three political events	29	29	24	24
Party members participating in four or more political events	16	16	8	0

The fundamental class division lies between categories 2 and 3—between those who sell their labor power versus those who are in a position to employ other labor to support themselves. In general, though, the four broad categories do not differ to any significant degree from occupation tables drawn up by Stuart Blumin, Robert Dockhorn, Clyde Griffen, Theodore Hershberg, and Michael Katz. See Stuart Blumin, "Mobility and Change in Ante-Bellum Philadelphia," in *Nineteenth-Century Cities, Essays in the New Urban History,* ed. Stephan Thernstrom and Richard Sennett

(New Haven: Yale University Press, 1969), 165–208; Clyde Griffen, "Occupational Mobility in Nineteenth-Century America: Problems and Possibilities," *Journal of Social History* 5 (Spring 1972): 310–330; Robert Dockhorn and Theodore Hershberg, "Occupational Classification," *Historical Methods Newsletter* 9 (March–June 1976): 59–98; and Michael B. Katz, "Occupational Classification in History," *Journal of Interdisciplinary History* 3 (Summer 1972): 63–88.

35. Among those involved in political events and not in organizational work, the corresponding figures were 28 percent (245), 35 percent (314), 31 percent (274), and 6 percent (54).

The correlation between number of political events and occupation was Contingency Coefficient = .16 at the .001 level of significance.

The correlation between number of political organizations and occupations was Contingency Coefficient = .16 at the .001 level of significance.

The contingency coefficient measures the strength of a relationship: 1 to 1 is the best relationship; above .3 is considered very strong; a reading below .15 is considered random. Level of significance measures the degree to which we may generalize to the population at large. Below .05 is considered significant, with 0.000, meaning that the significance is absolute. Thus, in the particular case cited here, occupation is predictive of how active a person was.

36. The correlation between position, if civic official, and occupation, was Contingency Coefficient = .34 at the .148 level of significance.

It is clear that Walt Whitman, from whom Wilentz derives his title, *Chants Democratic,* regarded the Democratic Party, at least until the 1840s, as New York City's labor party. Whitman even sought to transform the *New York Aurora,* which he edited, into the principal party organ. Betsy Erkkila, *Whitman the Political Poet* (New York: Oxford University Press, 1989), 27–28.

37. The correlation between position in secondary organizations (i.e., ward committees) and occupations was Contingency Coefficient = .10 at the .947 level of significance.

38. The party comprised 65 percent old stock, 22 percent Irish, 9 percent German, and 4 percent "others." The same groups were present in the general population with percentages of 67, 20, 11, and 2, respectively. As a group, the Germans were disproporionately skilled, compared to other groups in the general population. Nadel, *Little Germany,* 24.

The correlation between number of political organizations and ethnicity was Contingency Coefficient = .07 at the .268 level of significance. The correlation between the number of political events and ethnicity was Contingency Coefficient = .08 at the .218 level of significance.

Bridges, in "Rethinking the Origins of Machine Politics," 65, has written of "the later political ascent of the Irish," while Iver Bernstein has stated that, "The Tweed years [1860s] were the first time that one Democratic organization in the city could rely on the political support of virtually all of the Irish social and fraternal associations." Bernstein, *The New York City Draft Riots*, 198. Yet it is clear from analyzing party data that the Irish played a critical role and were united behind the Democrats by the 1840s.

39. The correlation between position in the primary organizations and ethnicity was Contingency Coefficient = .30 at the .006 level of significance. The Irish occupied 30 percent of the top positions in these primary organizations.

40. Of the 184 men involved in primary organizations, 64 percent were old stock and 27 percent were Irish, with the top-ranked officers comprising 64 percent old stock and 30 percent Irish. The correlation between position in primary organizations and ethnicity was Contingency Coefficient = .30 at the .006 level of significance.

41. In absolute terms, all three major ethnic groups were equally active. While 9 percent of the old stock participated in four or more organizations, 11 percent of the Germans and 6 percent of the Irish were so involved. Conversely two-thirds of all three groups were involved in only one party organization. While 12 percent of the old stock participated in four or more events, 7 percent of the Germans and 6 percent of the Irish were so involved. Again, roughly two-thirds of all three groups could be found in only one party event, though the Irish, at 69 percent, held a six-point spread over the old stock and Germans, respectively.

42. Among the 264 men belonging to ward committees, the figures were remarkably similar, with 62 percent and 26 percent being the respective shares. The correlation between position in secondary organizations and ethnicity was Contingency Coefficient = .13 at the .847 level of significance.

43. Among subcommittees and auxiliary organizations, the proportion of old stock rose to 71 percent, while the Irish fell to 12 percent, a fraction of a percentage point below the Germans. The correlation between position in tertiary organizations and ethnicity was Contingency Coefficient = .17 at the .554 level of significance.

The lowest-ranked organizations yielded similar results. Though only nineteen men were involved in this sample, they carried 74 percent of the positions within primary activities as contrasted with 21 percent for the

Irish. The correlation between position in these events and ethnicity was Contingency Coefficient = .25 at the .866 level of significance. Comparable percentages for secondary events were 64 and 25 (Contingency Coefficient = .12 at the .384 level of significance), and for quartenary events, 68 and 18 (Contingency Coefficient = .13 at the .092 level of significance).

The correlation between position in primary organizations and ethnicity was Contingency Coefficient = .28 at the .001 level of significance. Here old-stock men increased their presence from 63 to 66 percent, going from ward to above ward levels, while the Germans and Irish decreased their percentages 7 to 5 and 30 to 20, respectively.

Tertiary organizations yielded figures of 69 to 73, 10 to 12, and 19 to 10 respectively. The correlation between level of tertiary organizations and ethnicity was Contingency Coefficient = .11 at the .320 level of significance.

Among quartenary organizations the corresponding percentages were 66 to 58, 7 to 11, and 23 to 26. Only on the lowest levels of party organization, therefore, did new immigration increase its share. The correlation between level of quartenary organizations and ethnicity was Contingency Coefficient = .07 at the .074 level of significance.

Analagous results were obtained with events.

	OLD STOCK		GERMAN		IRISH	
EVENTS	WARD	ABOVE WARD	WARD	ABOVE WARD	WARD	ABOVE WARD
Primary	63	80	0	7	38	13
Secondary	64	83	6	0	25	17
Tertiary	66	71	9	9	24	13
Quartenary	65	69	9	10	23	18

The correlation between levels of primary, secondary, tertiary, and quartenary events—and ethnicity—was Contingency Coefficient = .29, .06, .18, .05, at the .341, .748, .000, .547 levels of significance, respectively.

44. Of the 202 officials for whom ethnic data has been obtained, 154, or 76 percent, were old stock, 14 percent Irish, and 7 percent German. A slight bias in favor of old stock was in evidence, but it was nowhere as salient as class. The correlation between position, if one was a civic official, and ethnicity was Contingency Coefficient = .16 at the .821 level of significance.

45. Edwin Percy Whipple, "The Romance of Rascality," in *One Hundred Years Ago: American Writing of 1848,* ed. James Playstead Wood (New York: Funk & Wagnalls, 1948), 484, as cited in Reynolds, *Beneath the American Renaissance,* 182.

46. Dickens, *Martin Chuzzlewit*, 255. *Evening Post*, July 21, 1843. *Subterranean*, September 30, 1843. At an early age, Dickens had become a competent observer of the British political process. Fred Kaplan, *Dickens, a Biography* (New York: Morrow, 1988), 61.

47. There are still scholars who are unaware of this point. In the *American Historical Review* 92, no. 2 (April 1987): 474, in a review of Thomas C. Leonard, *The Power of the Press: The Birth of American Political Reporting* (New York: Oxford University Press, 1986), Mark E. Neeley, Jr., observed that ". . . politics remained astonishingly underreported in the early republic, even largely unrecorded with any accuracy until . . . 1858."

48. The suborganizations ranged from the Irish Emigrant Society to the German Democrats to the various watch associations that patrolled the city's streets prior to the establishment of a uniformed police force in 1845. *Daily Plebeian*, June 5, 17, July 1, 4, 1844.

49. *Daily Plebeian*, September 18, 19, 1844. Michael Bernstein discusses "radical" Democratic support for the 1844 presidential bid of Southern slavemaster spokesman John C. Calhoun. Bernstein, "Northern Labor Finds a Southern Champion." See also Hofstadter, *The American Political Tradition and the Men Who Made It*, 113–114.

50. Tammany opposed the tariff. *Evening Post*, November 17, 1841. *Daily Plebeian*, August 22, September 11, 1844.

51. Lindstrom, "Economic Structure, Demographic Change, and Income Disparity," 6, 11. Wilentz, *Chants Democratic*, 118. Henretta, *The Evolution of American Society*, 201.

52. Danforth, *Merchants and Politics*, 191. Philip Foner, *Business and Slavery*, 164. In *The Invention of the White Race*, vol. 1, *Racial Oppression and Social Control* (London: Verso, 1994), Theodore W. Allen ignores the strategic political as well as economic links that existed between New York City Democratic Party political leaders and merchants, on one hand, and Southern politicians and plantation owners on the other. The active presence of such ties greatly aggravated racial tensions and helped transform many Irish immigrants into racists. Allen's few references to the role the Democratic Party played in "inventing the white race" are couched in general terms (see pp. 171–173, 179, 184–188, 190–191, 195, 196, 198–199). While there is ample discussion of the racist views of Archbishop Hughes, nothing is written about Mike Walsh, Ely Moore, or Fernando Wood's Mozart Hall. Walsh was arguably more influential than Hughes in the late 1840s and 1850s among the Irish working class. Also significant is Allen's omission of the role that the Democratic Party played in forging, through appeals to

race supremacy, a European-American identity that transcended the divisions of native versus immigrant. Because he does not integrate politics into his analysis, he does not appreciate how white labor, regardless of country of origin, was made to feel that blacks were the chief threat to their jobs, even though, as Allen correctly points out, in most job categories, foreign-born whites vastly outnumbered blacks (p. 193). He therefore perceives Irish-American hostility to black competition as having "no basis in actual fact." Yet the ideology of white supremacist democratic republicanism did color the facts and energized racists to new frenzies of hatred.

53. Emerson, "Man the Reformer," a lecture read before the Mechanics' Apprentices' Library Association, Boston, January 25, 1841, in *Essays and Lectures*, 136–137.

54. Hietala, *Manifest Design*, 75–83. Hietala found the belief widespread "among Democrats that the United States could monopolize vital raw materials and use them to leash rival empires into submission" (p. 93).

55. Daniel Feller, *The Public Lands in Jacksonian Politics* (Madison: University of Wisconsin Press, 1984), 76, 81, 122, 159.

56. "New Territory Versus No Territory," *United States Magazine and Democratic Review*, October 1847, 291. Williamson, "American Prices and Urban Inequality Since 1820," 314.

57. *Subterranean*, March 23, 1844.

58. *Daily Plebeian*, August 13, September 20, 1844.

59. Harlow, *Old Bowery Days*, 52, 66, 106–109, 113–114, 149–150. See also Cornelius Mathews, *Big Abel and the Little Manhattan* (New York: Wiley & Putnam, 1845), 6; and the same author's *A Pen-and-Ink Panorama of New York City* (New York: John S. Taylor, 1853), 124–136, for a colorful evocation of the Bowery, "the greatest street on the Continent, the most characteristic, the most American, the most peculiar . . ." (p. 124). With more than 240 trades being conducted, Mathews added, the Bowery was "the great democratic, as Broadway is the great aristocratic, thoroughfare" (p. 126). Charles Astor Bristed, *The Upper Ten Thousand: Sketches of American Society* (New York: Stringer & Townsend, 1852), 23.

60. Herbert Asbury, *The Gangs of New York: An Informal History of the Underworld* (New York: Knopf, 1928), 115. The suffering of Five Points, a crime-plagued Irish slum just north of city hall, was alleviated by tearing it down to make way for federal and state office buildings.

61. Harlow, *Old Bowery Days*, 299. Gilfoyle, *City of Eros*, 88. *Daily Plebeian*, September 11, October 18, 1844. *New York Times*, October 22, November

15, 1884. See Rynders's obituary in the *New York Daily Herald,* January 14, 1885.

62. Robert Ernst found Mike Walsh puzzling because Ernst did not grasp the essential nature of democratic republicanism. Thus, he wrote, "We can only guess why Mike Walsh, the professed leader of the common people, admired and supported the best known defender of the slave system in the South." Robert Ernst, "The One and Only Mike Walsh," *New-York Historical Quarterly* 36 (January 1952): 58 n. 55. *Sketches of the Speeches and Writings of Michael Walsh* (New York: Thomas McSpedon, 1843), 20. Walsh made this unequivocal statement about third parties at a "Great Mass Meeting of the New York Democracy at Castle Garden." He continued, "The idea is the production of a weak and silly brain. Such things may be produced by local grievances, but they can exist but for a moment, and can never extend far."

63. See Hone's *Diary* of April 25, 1844, for an account of a characteristically bellicose display by Walsh and his followers; and earlier, Strong, *Diary,* April 13, 1842. *Subterranean,* December 9, December 2, August 19, 1843.

64. *Subterranean,* September 2, 1843. Levine, *The Spirit of 1848,* 113.

65. Bernstein, "Northern Labor Finds a Southern Champion," passim. See also J. William Harris, "Last of the Classical Republicans: An Interpretation of John C. Calhoun," *Civil War History* 30, no. 3 (September 1984): 255–267.

66. *Subterranean,* October 5, 1844.

67. *Subterranean,* September 23, October 14, October 21, October 28, November 11, November 25, 1843. The quote is from Henry David Thoreau, "Walden" (1854; reprint, New York: Penguin, 1983), 343.

68. *Daily Plebeian,* June 20, September 30, August 12, 1844; July 30, 1844; March 23, 1844.

69. "We are the nation of human progress, and who will set limits to our onward march," free-soil editor John O'Sullivan boasted, especially since "All history is to be rewritten . . . the whole scope of moral truth . . . reconsidered in the light of the democratic principle." John L. O'Sullivan, "The Great Nation of Futurity," *United States Magazine and Democratic Review,* November 1839; October 1837.

Often one such organization would serve as official sponsor for a rally, at which time a ranking of each organization might be furnished by its processional placement. *Daily Plebeian,* June 20, 1844.

70. *Daily Plebeian,* September 17, 1844. For a discussion of the social significance of the term *coon,* see David R. Roediger, *The Wages of Whiteness,* 97–100.

71. *Daily Plebeian,* September 21, 1844.

72. *Daily Plebeian,* October 23, 1844. Real estate speculator Moore embodied the identification of early United States labor leaders with capitalist values.

73. "Glances at Congress," *United States Magazine and Democratic Review,* 74–75. Hugins, *Jacksonian Democracy and the Working Class,* 63–67. Roediger, *The Wages of Whiteness,* 75.

74. *Daily Plebeian,* October 7, 1844. A year earlier, during the Democratic primary meeting attended by a few thousand Democrats, "gangs of ruffians" numbering upwards of two hundred Tyler supporters threatened the participants for favoring Van Buren. *Evening Post,* September 14, 1843. The first contemporary mention I found of the Butt-End Coon Hunters was in 1839, when they led a colorful political procession of banners, barouches, bands, and a "temple of liberty" through the eighth ward. *Evening Post,* October 30, 1839.

75. *Daily Plebeian,* October 29, 1844.

76. Richard Moody, *The Astor Place Riot* (Bloomington: Indiana University Press, 1958), 11, 99, 109, 126.

77. *Herald,* April 26, 1849. Moody, *The Astor Place Riot,* 1–12, 88–199; Headley, *The Great Riots of New York,* 112–128; Hone, *Diary,* May 8, May 10, 1849; Tailer, *Diary,* May 9–11, 1849. See also Peter G. Buckley, "The Case Against Ned Buntline: The 'Words, Signs, and Gestures' of Popular Authorship," *Prospects* 13 (1988): 252. For an account of earlier riots against British actors, see Gilje, *The Road to Mobocracy,* 248–249.

78. *Herald,* May 12, 1849; *Tribune,* May 12, 1849.

79. Jay Monaghan, *The Great Rascal, the Life and Adventures of Ned Buntline* (Boston: Little, Brown, 1952), 83, 104, 162. The quote is from E. C. Z. Judson [Ned Buntline], *Three Years After* (New York: Dick and Fitzgerald, 1850), 123.

80. Reynolds, *Beneath the American Renaissance,* 172, 451.

81. *Daily Plebeian,* November 2, 1844. Contrast the *Plebeian* reportage with Hone's cataloguing of banner slogans that read " 'Destruction to Clay!' 'Down with the Coons!' 'Polk and Texas!' 'No $50,000,000 Bank!' '*Americans shan't* rule us.' " Hone, *Diary,* November 1, 1844. Sheldon H. Harris, "John Louis O'Sullivan and the Election of 1844 in New York," *New York History* 41 (July 1960): 295.

82. Hone, *Diary,* November 8, 1844.

83. Stott, *Workers in the Metropolis,* 36, 47, 63–65.

84. Hone observed, "The Constitution is a dead letter, the ark of safety is

wrecked, the wall of separation which has hitherto restrained the violence of popular rage is broken down. . . ." Hone, *Diary*, March 1, 1845.

85. Whitman, in the *Brooklyn Eagle*, May 7, 1846, in Rogers and Black, *The Gathering of the Forces*, 1:247. Ralph Waldo Emerson, "Ode, Inscribed to W. H. Channing," *Poems* (Boston: Riverside Press of Houghton, Mifflin and Company, 1886), 72.

86. Bruce Levine notes how quickly Kriege forsook the ideology of communism for Evans's "democracy of the land." Levine, *The Spirit of 1848*, 104–106. Hugins, *Jacksonian Democracy and the Working Class*, 87. *Working Man's Advocate*, April 6, 1844; January 1849.

87. Fogel, *Without Consent or Contract*, 350. See also Levine, *The Spirit of 1848*, 151.

88. An awareness of the common interests of planter and artisan was conveyed in the *Evening Post*, June 5, 1841.

89. "The Repeal Question," *United States Magazine and Democratic Review*, August 1841, 116.

90. Stott, *Workers in the Metropolis*, 30 n. 33, 42–46. Fogel estimated that in 1850 the typical Northeast cotton mill employed 150 workers, with the top 10 percent having 500 employees. Fogel, *Without Consent or Contract*, 102.

91. See Samuel P. Hays for an analysis of how the Progressive phenomena were played out in the local urban arena. "The Politics of Reform in Municipal Government in the Progressive Era," *Pacific Northwest Quarterly* 55 (October 1964): 157–169. For a sketch of the sea change in labor politics and organization that occurred during the nineteenth century, see Gronowicz, "Labor's Decline Within New York City's Democratic Party, in *Immigration to New York*."

92. Hugins, *Jacksonian Democracy and the Working Class*, 216. For a discussion of New York State party breakdown on this issue, see John L. Stanley, "Majority Tyranny in Toqueville's America: The Failure of Negro Suffrage in 1846," *Political Science Quarterly* 84, no. 3 (1969): 412–435; and Field, *The Politics of Class and Race in New York*, 51–57, 91.

93. Ibid., 97. *Tribune*, November 5, 1845.

94. Myers, *The History of Tammany Hall*, 139. Hone, *Diary*, October 27, 1846.

95. Tailer, *Diary*, November 8, 1848. *Proceedings of the Herkimer Mass Convention of October 26, 1847* (Albany, 1847), 5. Kilroe Collection.

96. The 1842 congressional elections served as the political harbinger for a radical shift on the slave question from elections held two years earlier, with abolitionists more than quintupling their electoral share in ten states. *Evening Post*, December 21, 1842.

CHAPTER 7

1. Cooper to William Branford Shubrick, December 25, 1850, *The Letters and Journals*, 6:244–246.

2. Merle Curti, "Young America," *American Historical Review* 32 (October 1926): 34–35.

3. A term employed by Melville and cited by Reynolds, *Beneath the American Renaissance*, 278.

4. *The Radical in Continuation of The Working Man's Advocate*, 1:9 (September 1841): 129. John Ashworth, "The Democratic-Republicans Before the Civil War: Political Ideology and Economic Change," *Journal of American Studies* 20 (December 1986): 377. I have not found evidence to support Ashworth's contention that anti-bank Democrats became free-soilers (379). More likely than not, anti-bank Democrats were pro-slavery, as pointed out in Chapter 4. Bank supporters, especially if they were Whig, tended to oppose slavery's expansion. John Brooke has found this to be the case in Worcester County, the center of abolitionism in Massachusetts. *The Heart of the Commonwealth*, 337.

5. Levine, *The Spirit of 1848*, 160. German Americans divided over the slave question, with the majority continuing to back the Democratic Party in New York City, if not in the mid-west (161–169). *Tribune*, February 14, August 23, 1854. Jean Baker, "From Belief to Culture: Republicanism in the Antebellum North," *American Quarterly* 37, no. 4 (Fall 1985): 534. William Henry Seward, *Works*, ed. George E. Baker (Boston: Houghton, Mifflin & Co., 1884), 4:258.

6. *Tribune*, July 26, 1850. Arthur Brisbane, *United States Magazine and Democratic Review*, April 1842, 331–332. Stott, *Workers in the Metropolis*, 145. See table 2, 93. The quotation is from *The United States Magazine and Democratic Review*, July 1850. See Foner, *Free Soil, Free Labor, Free Men*, 60–61.

7. Irving to John P. Kennedy, April 27, 1851, vol. 4 of *Letters*, ed. Ralph M. Aderman, Herbert L. Kleinfeld, and Jennifer S. Banks (Boston: Twayne, 1982).

8. As quoted in Peter Ackroyd, *Dickens* (New York: HarperCollins, 1990), 544.

9. *Iron Platform Extra*, December 1856, Bourne Papers, New-York Historical Society.

10. "Address to the Working-Men of the United States." Bourne Papers.

11. *Iron Platform*, May 1, 1856. Bourne Papers.

12. Charles Mackay, *Life and Liberty in America: or, Sketches of a Tour in the*

United States and Canada, in 1857–8, 2 vols. (London: Smith, Elder & Co., 1859), 2:46–47. See also Burns, *The "Beggar Boy,"* 311.

13. Glickstein, *Concepts of Free Labor in Antebellum America,* 15, 326 n. 56.

14. Ibid., 208–209.

15. Stephanie McCurry, *Masters of Small Worlds; Yeomen Households, Gender Relations, and the Political Culture of the Antebellum South Carolina Low Country* (New York: Oxford University Press, 1995), 210. See also Issac, *The Transformation of Virginia,* for an account of how the Founding Fathers exploited the structural weaknesses of yeomen and plebeian society through joint appeal to racism and masculine privilege.

16. McCurry, *Masters of Small Worlds,* 208–234. See Mitchell Snay, "American Thought and Southern Distinctiveness: The Southern Clergy and the Sanctification of Slavery," *Civil War History* 35, no. 4 (December 1989): 311–328. A contemporary account of Albany farmers and their slaves concludes, "They sought their code of humanity in the Bible, and there, imagined they found this hapless race condemned to perpetual slavery." Freeman Hunt, *Letters About the Hudson River. And its Vicinity. Written in 1835 & 1837* (New York: Freeman Hunt & Co., 1836), 126, Kilroe Collection. Levine, *The Spirit of 1848,* 238–239.

17. Nash, *Forging Freedom,* 17, 24, 26. Bertram Wallace Korn, *Jews and Negro Slavery in the Old South, 1789–1865* (Elkins Park, Pa.: Reform Congregation Keneseth Israel, 1961), 26. McCurry, "The Two Faces of Republicanism: Gender and Proslavery Politics in Antebellum South Carolina," *Journal of American History* 78, no. 4 (March 1992): 1249.

18. David Brion Davis, *Slavery and Human Progress* (New York: Oxford University Press, 1984; reprint), xvii. Davis, *The Problem of Slavery in Western Culture,* 184; see especially chap. 7, which deals with "the failure of Christianization" to tackle the slavery issue.

In practice, belief in God coupled with democratic republican values provided a powerful rationalization for imperialism. For example, in 1846, Congressman Timothy Pillsbury of Texas justified the conquest of northern Mexico on the following grounds: "A country kept vacant by the policy of a nation which claims the right of ownership over it, is common property, and reverts to the situation in which all land was before it became property, and is open to be occupied, subdued and cultivated by man—by those who will do so—as the Creator designed it should be." *Congressional Globe,* 29th Cong., 1st sess., June 16, 1846, 980, as quoted in Hietala, *Manifest Design,* 194. Democracy and empire were compatible in this American vision.

19. Freeman, *The Free Negro in New York City*, 46.

20. Gilbert Osofsky, "Abolitionists, Irish Immigrants, and the Dilemmas of Romantic Nationalism," *American Historical Review* 80, no. 4 (October 1975): 911. Eric Foner, "Racial Attitudes of the New York Free Soilers," in *Politics and Ideology in the Age of the Civil War* (New York: Oxford University Press, 1980), 93.

21. Strong, *Diary*, August 4, 1856. Equal rights rhetoric was also construed to mean the right of states to have slavery and to expand the rights of slaveholders into new states. During the Civil War, "Peace" Democrats voiced such views. *Herald*, July 4, 1863.

22. Way, "Evil Humors and Ardent Spirits," 1417–1418. The collusion of religious figures with capitalists was widespread. Edward J. Davies III has found that "priests and ministers often received their salaries from coal operators through deductions from the pay of miners and laborers." "Class and Power in the Anthracite Region, the Control of Political Leadership in Wilkes-Barre, Pennsylvania, 1815–1885," *Journal of Urban History* 9, no. 3 (May 1983): 323. Gienapp, *The Origins of the Republican Party*, 445. See also Horace Greeley's rejoinder to a Catholic Democratic physical attack on an abolitionist meeting in the *Tribune*, May 11, 1850. Frederik Rinehart Anspach, *The Sons of the Sires; A History of the Rise, Progress, and Destiny of the American Party and its Probable Influence on the Next Presidential Election* (Philadelphia: Lippincott, Grambo & Co., 1855), 57, 123, 125. Edward L. Pierce to Salmon P. Chase, November 9, 1850, Chase Papers, as quoted in Gienapp, *The Origins of the Republican Party*, 223. *Evening Post*, April 27, 1807; *Public Advertiser*, August 19, 1811. Of a total New York City population of 516,000 in 1850, 96,580 men and 117,120 women had been born in Ireland. Stott, "The Worker in the Metropolis," 126.

23. Lindstrom, "Economic Structure, Demographic Change, and Income Inequality," 11; table 1.4, 12–13. Williamson, "American Prices and Urban Inequality Since 1820," 317. Stott, *Workers in the Metropolis*, 201, 204, 86.

24. Curti, "Young America," 35. Strong described the 1848 revolutions as a "Democratic influenza," a characterization consistent with his patrician Whig principles. *Diary*, April 9, 1848.

25. Davis, *The Problem of Slavery in the Age of Revolution*, 350, and more generally, 347–361. The two classic accounts to argue that Protestantism provided an ideal spiritual climate for capitalism are Max Weber, *The Protestant Ethic and the Spirit of Capitalism* (1930; reprint, New York: Scribner, 1958); and R. H. Tawney, *Religion and the Rise of Capitalism, a*

Historical Study (1926; reprint, Gloucester, Mass.: P. Smith, 1962). Dickens, *Martin Chuzzlewit,* 258.

26. Monaghan, *The Great Rascal,* 208–209.

27. Gienapp, *The Origins of the Republican Party,* 92, 227, 372.

28. *Public Advertiser,* April 24, 1810. See Patrick Carey, "Republicanism Within American Catholicism, 1785–1860," *Journal of the Early Republic* 3 (Winter 1983): 413–437. E. P. Thompson argues that the Catholic Church acted as a damper on Irish radicals; see his *The Making of the English Working Class,* 442–443. The same appeared to be true of German radicals; see Levine, *The Spirit of 1848,* 98.

29. Joel H. Silbey, "The Surge of Republican Power: Partisan Antipathy, American Social Conflict, and the Coming of the Civil War," in *The Partisan Imperative, the Dynamics of American Politics Before the Civil War* (New York: Oxford University Press, 1985), 168. Levine, *The Spirit of 1848,* 15, 17. Gorn, " 'Good-bye Boys, I Die a True American,' " 390. *Tribune,* September 27, 29, October 2, 4, 21, 1856.

30. *New York Herald,* January 14, 1885. Anspach, *The Sons of the Sires,* 31.

31. Foner, *Business and Slavery,* 164–168. *London Times* in *Tribune,* September 29, 1860, as quoted in Foner, *Business and Slavery,* 164. Karl Obermann, *Joseph Weydemeyer, Pioneer of American Socialism* (New York: International, 1947), 83–84. The German socialist organizer Herman Kriege warned that abolition of slavery would free blacks to compete with whites; see Levine, *The Spirit of 1848,* 152; Herman Schluter, *Lincoln, Labor and Slavery, A Chapter from the Social History of America* (New York: Socialist Literature Co., 1913), 75–77. It is clear from his focus on German workers that Weydemeyer organized along ethnic and not class lines. After recruiting some German workers, Weydemeyer failed to unite them with English-speaking unions; see Nadel, *Little Germany,* 128–130. Douglass is as quoted in Levine, *The Spirit of 1848,* 9, 150.

32. *The Liberator,* October 1, 1847.

33. The clear link between Christian zeal and Union loyalty is examined in George M. Fredrickson, *The Inner Civil War: Northern Intellectuals and the Crisis of the Union* (New York: Harper & Row, 1965).

34. Gates, *The Farmer's Age,* 420.

35. Silbey, " 'The Undisguised Connection': Know Nothings into Republicans: New York as a Test Case," in *The Partisan Imperative,* 133. Gienapp, *The Origins of the Republican Party,* 231, 375.

36. Stott, "The Worker in the Metropolis," 95, 96, 180. Fogel, *Without Consent or Contract,* 356–359.

37. The *Tribune* reporter took note of the priority of land reform when he titled his story, "Land Reform and Labor Association," *Tribune*, July 24, 1860. See also July 20, 1850. The *Tribune* introduced a daily column, "Labor Movements," which assisted Republican Party ideologues in formulating a more effective pro-labor public stance. See also Levine, *The Spirit of 1848*, 136. Wilentz ahistorically treats land reform as a radical issue, so that he can then tag New York City labor organizations as radical; see his *Chants Democratic*, 335–337, 340–342. Needless to say, relying on the same sources as Wilentz, and given the evidence, I cannot see how he could characterize the New York Industrial Congress as a radical movement (as he does on pp. 364–372); reactionary is more apt. Iver Bernstein concludes that "with their plan to use government to supervise economic growth, the leaders of the 1850 Industrial Congress had conceived a radical alternative to the topsy-turvy course of development New York had taken at mid-century"; this assessment does not take into account that Federalists and Whigs had historically taken the same position; and, of course, there is little that is radical about their ideology. Bernstein, *New York City Draft Riots*, 124.

38. Gates, *The Farmer's Age*, 77. From 1847 until 1862, and especially after 1854, an increasing proportion of land was being sold to speculators. Ibid., 78, 80–89, and passim. Homestead Act, May 20, 1862. Foner, *Free Soil, Free Labor, Free Men*, 27–29.

39. Walt Whitman, *Democratic Vistas* (1870), in Kaplan, *Complete Poetry and Collected Prose*, 981. Monaghan, *The Great Rascal*, 194.

40. Wilentz, *Chants Democratic*, 384. Democratic involvement in land reform began for Wilentz "in the early 1840s, [when] different factions within the national parties and shifting sectional alliances focused on land as never before. . . ." (p. 335).

41. *Tribune*, July 3, 1850.

42. As cited in Iver Bernstein, *The New York City Draft Riots*, 100.

43. *Tribune*, July 7, September 23, 1850.

44. *Tribune*, July 24, 1850.

45. *Tribune*, June 11, 1850.

46. *Tribune*, May 1, 8, 1850.

47. Frederick Douglass, *Life and Times of Frederick Douglass* (Hartford: Park Publishing Co., 1882), 284.

48. *Tribune*, May 8, 1850. The only biographical treatment of Ward is Ronald K. Burke, "Samuel Ringgold Ward: Christian Abolitionist" (Ph.D. diss., Syracuse University, 1975). Other than his autobiography, a key source for Ward's thought is the *Impartial Citizen*, the newspaper he edited. When

the Fugitive Slave Law was enacted, Ward was forced to flee the United States.

"Boanerges" refers to the name Christ gave to James and John in recognition of the dynamic quality of their preaching.

49. *Tribune,* May 9, 10, 1850.

50. *Tribune,* September 28, 30, October 1, 7, December 24, 1850. Johnson, *Black Manhattan,* 18–19. Freeman, *The Free Negro in New York City,* 85–89.

51. *Tribune,* September 9, 1855; September 24, 1856.

52. *The Softs, the True Democracy of New York,* 13, 7, 16–34, 70.

53. *Evening Post,* September 5, 1854.

54. *Herald,* July 21, 1855.

55. Jerome Mushkat, *Fernando Wood, a Political Biography* (Kent, Ohio: Kent State University Press, 1990), vii. Mushkat pictures Loco Focos as stressing "equal rights for all, special privileges to none" (p. viii). He ignores their exclusion of Africans, Native Americans, and women and does not recognize how democratic republican precepts allowed Loco Focos to be pro-South and anti-bank at the same time. Thus Mushkat is puzzled: "Why this affinity existed was never clear" (p. 83).

56. *Herald,* November 24, 1857.

57. *Proceedings of the Board of Aldermen* (1855), 57:16–17.

58. Spann, *The New Metropolis,* 371. There were those who disagreed. *A History of the Private, Political, and Official Villanies of Fernando Wood* (New York, 1856). Kilroe Collection. *Tribune,* June 7, July 2, 3, 4, 6, 1855. Mushkat, *Fernando Wood,* 11–12.

59. Jerome Mushkat, *The Reconstruction of the New York Democracy, 1861–1874* (Rutherford, N.J.: Fairleigh Dickinson University Press, 1981), 17. The quotation is from Peter Dobkin Hall, *The Organization of American Culture, 1700–1900: Private Institutions, Elites, and the Origins of American Nationality* (New York: New York University Press, 1982), 213. Spann, *The New Metropolis,* 377. Championing Central Park brought Wood economic as well as political capital because he had bought lots fronting the park for a few hundred dollars and they were worth ten thousand each by 1860. Rosenzweig and Blackmar, *The Park and the People,* 56.

60. Mushkat, *Tammany,* 297.

61. Mushkat, *Fernando Wood,* 63–64.

62. *New York Times,* May 7, 1857.

63. Strong, *Diary,* June 17, 1857.

64. The methodological difficulties of analyzing the social composition of these gangs is discussed in Joshua Brown, "The 'Dead Rabbit'—Bowery Boy

Riot: An Analysis of the Antebellum Gang" (M.A. thesis, Columbia University, 1976), 52–67. Tailer, *Diary*, July 4, 1857.

65. Strong, *Diary*, July 14, 1857. *New York Times*, July 6, 1857. *Tribune*, July 7, 1857.

66. Charles W. Calomiris and Larry Schweikart, "The Panic of 1857: Origins, Transmission, and Containment," in *Journal of Economic History* 51, no. 4 (December 1991): 809, 810, 816. Headley, *The Great Riots*, 130–135. Rosenzweig and Blackmar, *The Parks and the People*, 152–158.

67. Gilfoyle, *City of Eros*, 125, 124.

68. Nonetheless, Strong maintained, "Certainly the destitute are a thankless set and deserve little sympathy in their complaints." On the other hand, unlike his Democratic opposition, Strong believed that "civilization at the South is retrograde and that the Carolinas are decaying into barbarism." Strong characterized "Southern gentlemen" as "a race of lazy, ignorant, coarse, sensual, swaggering, sordid, beggarly barbarians, bullying white men and breeding little niggers for sale. . . . The South has all the culture, civilization, intelligence, and progress of the nineteenth century against it, unanimous in declaring that it lives on oppression and robbery." True to his patrician beliefs, he asserted, "I still firmly believe that the relation of master and slave violates no moral law." Strong then ventured a historical explanation for this all-important belief of his social set: "There was the Hebrew form, with all the privileges and safeguards with which the Gentile servant was surrounded; and the medieval form of serfdom which gave Gurth and first Wamba their home in the forests of Rotheswood. . . . There was classical servitude, under which the slave might be a scholar or an artist and was expressly debarred from no kind of culture or development. . . ." But "slavery as it exists at the South—is the greatest crime on the largest scale known in history. . . . It is deliberate legislation intended to extinguish and annihilate the moral being of men for profit. . . ." *Diary*, October 22, 1857; January 21, 1855; May 28, 29, June 8, October 19, 1856. As for Tailer, he was vacationing in England during the panic.

69. *New York Times*, October 9, 21, 23, 27, 1857. *Tribune*, November 16, 1857.

70. Tailer favored Tiemann over Wood because he was "opposed to a man who would cheat and defraud his own partner." Tailer, *Diary*, November 27, 1857.

71. *New York Times*, January 8, 1858.

72. Strong, *Diary*, August 10, 24, 1858. W. J. Rorabaugh, "Rising Democratic Spirits: Immigrants, Temperance and Tammany Hall, 1854–1860," *Civil War History* 22 (June 1976): 138–157. Gienapp, *The Origins of the Republi-*

can *Party,* 230. Degler, "Labor in the Economy and Politics of New York City," 333.

73. Danforth, "Merchants and Politics," 163, 164, 191.

74. My reading of this work has been greatly aided by Helen P. Trimpi, *Melville's Confidence Men and American Politics in the 1850s* (Hamden, Conn.: Academy of Archon Books, 1987).

CHAPTER 8

1. Strong's term. *Diary,* December 16, 1858.

2. In the cultural sphere, incipient Republicans practiced a pyramiding of power. The 1853 five-man board to oversee the acquisition of land for Central Park consisted of "retired judges, large landowners and civic leaders" who appreciated the value of real estate above all else. Rosenzweig and Blackmar, *The Park and the People,* 78. Four years later, an eleven-man Board of Commissioners of the Central Park was established, weighted with Republicans who would supervise design and construction. All but one could be classified as rich. Ibid., 97–99, 259.

3. Mushkat, *The Reconstruction of the New York Democracy,* 17.

4. Robert Goldstein, *Political Repression in 19th Century Europe* (Totowa, N.J.: Barnes & Noble, 1983), 4.

5. Alan Dawley, *Class and Community: The Industrial Revolution in Lynn* (Cambridge, Mass.: Harvard University Press, 1976), 70.

6. Saxton, *The Rise and Fall of the White Republic,* 174–175.

7. Strong, *Diary,* December 27, 1862.

8. *Daily News,* October 6, 1859.

9. Myers, *The History of Tammany Hall,* 194. Tailer, *Diary,* December 3, 6, 22, 1859.

10. Tailer, *Diary,* December 6, 7, 1859. Nadel, *Little Germany,* 136. Degler's straight coefficient of correlation between one's vote and poverty was highest for any candidate at .80 for Wood in the 1857 election, which he lost. "Labor in the Economy and Politics of New York City," 315.

11. Myers, *The History of Tammany Hall,* 197, 198.

12. Ibid., 195. *Herald,* March 3, 6, 1863.

13. *Herald,* November 9, 1860.

14. *Herald,* October 9, 1860.

15. Degler, "Labor in the Economy and Politics of New York City," 317. *Tribune,* November 25, 1846; November 26, 30, 1859. *Herald,* October 24,

1860; *Times,* October 24, 1860. *Sun,* October 24, 1860. Strong, *Diary,* December 17, 1860. Tailer, *Diary,* November 6, 1860.

16. Strong, *Diary,* December 15, 1860.

17. Hammond, *Banks and Politics in America,* 718.

18. For the *Atlantic Monthly*'s editors, the question became "whether a certain exceptional kind of property always privileged beyond all others, shall be entitled to still further privileges at the expense of every other kind. The extension of slavery over new territory means just this—that this one kind of property, not recognized as such by the Constitution, or it would never have been allowed to enter into the basis of representation, shall control the foreign and domestic policy of the Republic." "The Election in November," *Atlantic Monthly,* October 1860, 496.

19. Mushkat, *Fernando Wood,* 111.

20. Nadel, *Little Germany,* 148, 136, 132.

21. Strong, *Diary,* January 13, March 12, 1861.

22. Albon P. Man, Jr., "Labor Competition and the New York City Draft Riots of 1863," *Journal of Negro History* 36 (October 1951): 390–398, 404.

23. Strong, *Diary,* July 12, 1863.

24. Ultimately, 38,000 African Americans lost their lives in battle during the Civil War, a rate 40 percent higher than that experienced by European Americans. Franklin, *From Slavery to Freedom,* 224.

25. Strong, *Diary,* April 22, 1863.

26. *Herald,* March 3, June 1, 1863.

27. *Herald,* January 10, 1863. Myers, *The History of Tammany Hall,* 199–200. Strong, *Diary,* May 15, 1861.

28. As quoted in Michael O'Malley, "Specie and Species: Race and the Money Question in Nineteenth Century America," *American Historical Review* 99, no. 2 (April 1994): 378.

29. Levine, *The Spirit of 1848,* 254–262. Bernstein, *The New York City Draft Riots,* 23–30, 36.

30. Harlow, *Old Bowery Days,* 340–349. *Herald,* February 3, 1863.

31. Strong, *Diary,* March 20, 1863.

32. *Irish American,* May 24, 1862. *Leader,* May 24, 1862. Myers, *The History of Tammany Hall,* 196. *New York World,* February 24, March 17, April 8, 1865. Strong, *Diary,* February 17, 1863.

33. Headley, *The Great Riots of New York,* 168.

34. "The Election in November," *Atlantic Monthly,* October 1860, 497.

35. *Herald,* June 4, 5, 1863.

36. Bernstein, *The New York City Draft Riots,* 264.

37. Eric Foner's summation of the draft riots accurately captures the horrible flavor of this despicable episode in working-class history; see his *Reconstruction: America's Unfinished Revolution, 1863–1877* (New York: Harper and Row, 1988), 32–33. See also Headley, *The Great Riots of New York,* 140–359.

38. Iver Bernstein, "What Did New York City Draft Rioters Think They Were Doing?" William H. Sewell, Jr., *Work and Revolution in France: The Language of Labor from the Old Regime to 1848* (New York: Cambridge University Press, 1980).

39. Headley, *The Great Riots of New York,* 18–19.

40. James M. McPherson, review of *The New York City Draft Riots,* by Iver Bernstein, in *The New York Review of Books,* April 12, 1990, 34. *Tribune,* July 15, 1863. Headley, *The Great Riots of New York,* 169–171, 181, 206–207, 213, 226, 231, 233, 236, 242, 271–277. Bernstein, *The New York City Draft Riots,* 44. Belmont represented Rothschild interests in the United States while at the same time enthusiastically backing Southern fire-eaters. Levine, *The Spirit of 1848,* 157. Headley, *The Great Riots of New York,* 223, 256. Bernstein, *The New York City Draft Riots,* 197. Similar anti-draft, anti-black riots occurred, although on a smaller scale, in Boston, Hartford, Albany, Troy, and Yonkers.

41. Herman Melville, "The House-top. A Night Piece," from *Battle-Pieces* (1866; reprint, New York: Harper & Bros., 1963), 89–90.

42. Bernstein, *The New York City Draft Riots,* 71–72.

43. Ibid., 41.

44. Ibid., 123.

45. Ibid., 119. Strong, *Diary,* July 16, 1863.

46. *Abraham Lincoln: His Speeches and Writings,* ed. Roy P. Basler (Cleveland and New York: The World Publishing Co., 1946), 634. Gates, *The Farmer's Age,* 86.

47. Emerson, "The American Scholar," an Oration delivered before the Phi Beta Kappa Society, Cambridge, August 31, 1837, in *Essays and Lectures,* 54.

48. Melville's sense of irony had no echo in the "city-mystery" novels of the 1840s that sensationalized the bleak poor and depraved rich. David S. Reynolds, *Beneath the American Renaissance,* 82. The richest and poorest people in the nation could now be found in New York City.

49. Alfred Kazin, *On Native Grounds: An Interpretation of Modern American Prose Literature* (New York: Harcourt, Brace & World, 1942), ix.

50. Henry David Thoreau, "Civil Disobedience" (1849; reprint, New York: Penguin, 1983), 387–389, and "Walden," 48, 69, 80, 239–240.

51. Thoreau, "Walden," 49.

52. "Report of the Committee of Merchants For the Relief of Colored People Suffering from the Late Riots in the City of New York," in James M. Mc-Pherson, ed., *Anti-Negro Riots in the North, 1863* (New York: Arno, 1969), 24–25. Strong, *Diary,* July 19, 1863.

53. As quoted in Lloyd Gardner, Walter LaFeber, and Thomas McCormick, *The Creation of the American Empire, U.S. Diplomatic History* (Chicago: Rand McNally, 1973), 194.

54. William A. Williams assigns the American farmer considerable responsibility for the imperialist expansion of the United States in the last third of the nineteenth century. The farmers' need for markets dovetailed neatly with the aims of American industrial and banking corporations. Williams expounds on this thesis in *The Roots of the Modern American Empire, a Study of the Growth and Shaping of Social Consciousness in a Marketplace Society* (New York: Random House, 1969).

55. Thoreau, "Civil Disobedience," 385, 389. For examples of Hawthorne's and Melville's profound pessimism, see Hawthorne's novels, *The House of the Seven Gables* and the *Blithesdale Romance,* and his short stories, "The Celestial Railroad" and "Earth's Holocaust"; and Melville's novels, *Moby-Dick, Pierre,* and *The Confidence-Man,* and his short stories, "The Tartarus of the Maids," and of course, "Bartleby, The Scrivener: A Story of Wall-Street."

56. One example is *The New Democratic Doctrine, Slavery Not to Be Confined to the Negro Race, But to be Made the Universal Condition of the Laboring Classes of Society* (New York, 1856). Bernstein, *The New York City Draft Riots,* 64.

57. Ibid., 92.

58. Strong, *Diary,* July 19, 1863.

59. Bernstein, *The New York City Draft Riots,* 57. Just as skewed is Bernstein's equation of African-American passivity during the draft riots with deference. But surely, given the lynch-mob atmosphere of the city in July 1863, the instinct for self-preservation was a more vital reason.

60. In the 1960s, influenced by the civil rights movement and the New Left, several young American historians began to examine in rich detail the correspondence between labor and wider nineteenth-century culture. Their literary model was E. P. Thompson's *The Making of the English Working Class,* published in 1963. Thompson's study of labor, drawn from his read-

ings of contemporary sources, disclosed the evolution of a political identity for artisans made to exemplify a heroic English working-class experience from the 1789 French Revolution to the rise of Chartism in the 1830s. He contended that artisans threatened by industrialization and political repression were compressed into conceiving of themselves in class terms.

The book's appearance almost single-handedly revived the flagging field of social history. It introduced cultural evidence not found in traditional accounts, which treated labor either as an economic or political category that made men into objects rather than the subjects of their own history.

European-American social historians, some with the assistance of cultural anthropologists like Clifford Geertz, have tried to replicate Thompson's panoramic tour de force for the comparable stage of structural evolution for the United States. Geertz presented "descriptions" of cultural groups "cast in terms of the constructions we imagine [those cultures] . . . place upon what they live through." Geertz asserted that, "They must be cast in terms of the interpretations to which persons of a particular denomination subject their experience, because that is what they profess to be descriptions of. . . ." However, studies that subscribe to this approach become *explications de texte,* and ignore the social formation. They obviate the need for historical analysis through acceptance of the cultural group on its own terms. See Clifford Geertz, *The Interpretation of Cultures: Selected Essays* (New York: Basic Books, 1973), 15.

For example, Wilentz's *Chants Democratic* makes the case for the emergence of a working-class consciousness in New York City during the first half of the nineteenth century, ending his upbeat interpretation in 1850. Wilentz minimizes the issue of race and the unskilled worker in much the same manner as Thompson skirted the Irish question. The chants democratic that Wilentz heard can more convincingly be interpreted as a lynch mob hell-bent on violence, whether against an English actor in 1849 or against African-American orphans in 1863.

Methodologically, Thompson tacks the Irish onto his ebullient romantic depiction of the English working class. One could perhaps object, given the title of his work, that this was not Thompson's concern. Including the Irish would have markedly diminished his case because he would have been forced to reveal how English labor acquiesced to the imperial racism of the empire. Thompson does admit that "one ingredient in the new working-class community has necessarily evaded this analysis: the Irish immigration." He does note that "the disasters which afflicted Ireland came less from the potato-blight than from the after-effects of a counter-revolution following upon the merciless repression of the United Irishmen's rebellion (1798) far more savage than anything enacted in England; and from the political, economic and social consequences of the Act of Union (1800)." (p. 429) Yet he does not consider the English workers' reaction or their active participation in this effort.

Craig Calhoun has skillfully challenged Thompson's assumptions concerning the alleged radicalism of the English working class in his *The Question of Class Struggle.*

61. Bernstein, *The New York City Draft Riots,* 56–57.

62. Thus Whitman's frustration: "I say it were a standing disgrace to these States . . . not to . . . soar above others also in its original styles in literature and art. . . . What has America? . . . so far wanting." *Democratic Vistas,* 981.

⊰ INDEX ⊱